A
MIGHTY
CHANGE

A MIGHTY CHANGE

**An Anthology of
Deaf American Writing,
1816–1864**

Christopher Krentz, Editor

Gallaudet University Press
Washington, D.C.

Gallaudet Classics in Deaf Studies
A Series Edited by John Vickrey Van Cleve

Gallaudet University Press
Washington, DC 20002

Library of Congress Cataloging-in-Publication Data
A mighty change : an anthology of deaf American writing, 1816–1864 /
Christopher Krentz, editor.
    p.   cm.—(Gallaudet classics in deaf studies)
Includes index.
ISBN 1-56368-098-X (alk. paper)—ISBN 1-56368-101-3 (pbk. : alk. paper)
1. Deaf, Writings of the, American.   2. Deaf—United States—History—19th
century—Sources.   3. American literature—19th century.   4. Deaf—Literary
collections.   I. Krentz, Christopher.   II. Series.
PS508.D43 M54   2000
810.8'09208162—dc21   00-060976

The cover photograph is from a letter that Laurent Clerc wrote to the Rhode
Island State Legislature on May 28, 1818.

The photographs in chapter 3 are reprinted from *Tales of the Deaf and Dumb,
With Miscellaneous Poems* by John Burnet (Newark, N.J.: Benjamin Olds,
1835), with the permission of the Clifton Waller Barrett Library of
American Literature, Special Collections Department, University of Virginia
Library. The photograph in chapter 1 of Charles Wilson Peale's 1822
portrait of Laurent Clerc is reprinted with the permission of the American
School for the Deaf. John Carlin's self-portrait in chapter 4 is reprinted with
the permission of Patricia Carlin Friese. All other photographs appear
courtesy of Gallaudet University Archives.

CONTENTS

Preface   vii

Introduction   xi

PART ONE: INDIVIDUAL AUTHORS

1 Laurent Clerc   1

2 James Nack   32

3 John Burnet   38

4 John Carlin   89

5 Edmund Booth   107

6 Adele M. Jewel   118

7 Laura Redden Searing   129

PART TWO: EVENTS AND ISSUES

8 1850 Grand Reunion   139

9 Dedication of the Gallaudet Monument   153

10 Debate over a Deaf Commonwealth   161

11 Inauguration of the National
       Deaf-Mute College   212

Sources   225

Index   229

PREFACE

A Mighty Change celebrates writing by deaf people in the United States between 1816 and 1864. While histories of the American deaf community often quote deaf people, I believe this anthology is the first to foreground deaf Americans' words during this transformative period, to let them share their stories, experiences, and opinions themselves. In selecting the works for this collection, I followed two basic criteria. First, I looked for quality writing that merits preservation and provokes interest. Second, I limited potential authors to those who lost their hearing before age eleven and who identified primarily with the signing deaf community. This latter criterion excluded figures like Frederick A. P. Barnard and George Catlin, who became deaf as adults. The selections cut across genres, running from essays, lectures, and letters to poetry and fiction. I hope these texts will introduce readers to deaf leaders and issues during this remarkable period, and invite more in-depth study. While documents have been edited to fit space constraints, I have made every effort to preserve the integrity of the authors' intentions.

Perhaps not surprisingly, several of the first deaf authors to achieve prominence in the United States actually became deaf after they had learned some English. Of the seven writers who have individual sections in this volume, four—James Nack, John

Burnet, Edmund Booth, and Laura Redden Searing—fall into this category. They became deaf between the ages of four and ten. Their situation was not unusual; in nineteenth-century America, meningitis, high fever, and other illnesses deafened more children and adults than today. Such individuals were profoundly deaf, but they were sometimes called "semi-mutes" or "semi-deaf" to acknowledge their difference from congenitally deaf people. In contrast, Laurent Clerc, John Carlin, and Adele Jewel were born deaf or lost their hearing as infants, making their accomplishments with the written word that much more impressive.

The writers in this volume are, with the exception of Searing and Jewel, all white males. Despite searching for writing by deaf people of color and women from this period, I regrettably did not have much success. Oppression probably explains much of this lack. In every southern state except Maryland and Kentucky, it remained illegal to teach a slave—hearing or deaf—to read and write until after the Civil War. Information on education of African American deaf people in the North during this period is exceedingly difficult to locate. In 1834, the *American Annals of Education* reported that "in the Northern institutions, colored pupils are received as well as white; but . . . a very small number are yet under instruction."[1] Most black deaf people presumably went without education or attended segregated schools. Given such dire circumstances, we perhaps should not be surprised that we do not have much black deaf writing from this time. Jewel mentions a private school for deaf African Americans near Niagara Falls, indicating that such institutions did exist. Moreover, in the chapter on the proposal for a deaf commonwealth, Booth and John J. Flournoy touch on the subject of slavery (Flournoy was a slaveowner who apparently wanted to ship all black people to Africa). For

---

1. Reprinted in *The Deaf and Dumb, or, a Collection of Articles Relating to the Condition of Deaf Mutes,* ed. Edwin Mann (Boston: D. K. Hitchcock, 1836): 15.

the most part, however, African Americans, let alone deaf African Americans, are lamentably absent from the following documents.

Deaf women also have a disappointingly small presence in these pages. They did attend residential schools, and many, such as Booth's wife Mary, were literate. Yet most deaf women seem to have stayed out of the public eye. Almost all published deaf writing from this period is by men. The first issue of *The Deaf-Mutes' Friend* contains "An Appeal to the Ladies" asking deaf women to contribute to the new periodical. "Let us not be afraid to send articles to the Editor," a woman identified only as Stella writes. "No one but himself will know who writes articles so there is no need to be afraid."[2] The references to fear suggest that writing for publication was an unfamiliar activity for deaf women. Jewel confirms such a view, saying that when it came to writing her autobiography, "I shrunk from it, and could never have done so, had it not been really necessary for me to do something for my own maintenance."[3] Only Jewel's poverty and extreme situation caused her to write the valuable memoir we have today. Women also seem not to have played an active role at deaf events. During the 1869 meeting of the Empire State Association of Deaf-Mutes, a Mr. Fitzgerald moved to repeal the right of women to vote in elections, since "the ladies never availed themselves of the privilege."[4] In antebellum America, deaf women appear to have remained largely in the domestic sphere.

This anthology represents only a beginning. We need additional research to uncover letters, journals, notes, published arti-

---

2. Stella, "An Appeal to the Ladies," *The Deaf-Mutes' Friend* 1 (Sept. 1869): 30.

3. Adele M. Jewel, *A Brief Narrative of the Life of Mrs. Adele M. Jewel (Being Deaf and Dumb)* (Jackson, Mich.: Daily Citizen Steam Printing House, circa 1860), 17.

4. "Empire State Association of Deaf-Mutes: Proceedings of the Third Biennial Convention," *The Deaf-Mutes' Friend* 1 (Sept. 1869): 269.

cles, and other writing by deaf people of color and women during the first part of the nineteenth century. Certainly more such writing exists. With continued scholarship, we can likely recover more of these voices and obtain a better and more complete understanding of this important period.

I am indebted to many people who helped with this project. I would like to thank John Vickrey Van Cleve, Ivey Pittle Wallace, and Christina Findlay at Gallaudet University Press for their patience and enthusiasm. David Halberg, Winfield McChord, Jr., and Chris Thorkelson at the American School for the Deaf in Hartford gave me useful tips and free access to the school's valuable museum. The library staffs at Gallaudet, Yale, Harvard, the University of Virginia, and the University of Chicago provided much assistance in locating archival materials. Stephen Railton, Eric Lott, Lisa J. Berke, Ellen Contini-Morava, Douglas Baynton, Lakshmi Fjord, and Margaret Croskery, among many others, challenged my ideas and offered helpful suggestions. Finally, I wish to thank my parents and siblings for all of their encouragement, love, and support.

Christopher Krentz
Charlottesville, Virginia
January 12, 2000

INTRODUCTION

"I need not tell you that a mighty change has taken place within the last half century, a change for the better," Alphonso Johnson, the president of the Empire State Association of Deaf-Mutes, signed to hundreds of assembled deaf people in 1869.[1] Johnson pointed to an important truth: the first half of the nineteenth century was a period of transformation for deaf Americans, a time that saw the rise of deaf education and the coalescence of the nation's deaf community. In 1816, no schools for deaf students existed in the United States, and people commonly perceived "the deaf and dumb" as ineducable. Many deaf individuals lived scattered, largely isolated from each other, and illiterate. Fifty years later, the nation had more than twenty-five schools for the deaf. These schools enabled deaf people to come together, gain an education, develop American Sign Language (ASL), and find their own collective identity: after their establishment, deaf organizations and publications gradually began to appear. Deaf people also became more visible in society, making an impression upon the nation's consciousness and challenging traditional stereotypes. When, in 1850, over four hundred deaf people assembled in Hartford, Connecticut, the event showed just how strong the deaf communal identity had become. And when, in 1864, Congress authorized the National Deaf-Mute College, the act affirmed just how much society's views of deaf people had evolved. Now, many Americans recognized deaf people as full human beings with talent and intellectual potential.

This volume contains original writing by deaf people that both directed and reflected this remarkable period of change. It begins with works by Laurent Clerc, a deaf Frenchman who came to the United States in 1816 to help found the first permanent school for deaf students in the nation. Through his writing, Clerc impressed hearing Americans—most of whom had never met an educated deaf person before—with his intelligence and humanity. Other deaf writers soon followed, sharing their views with society through the democratic power of print. Included here are selections by James Nack, a deaf poet who surprised readers with his mellifluous verse; John Burnet, who published a book of original essays, fiction, and poetry; Edmund Booth, a frontiersman and journalist; John Carlin, who galvanized the drive for a national college for deaf people; Adele Jewel, a homeless deaf woman living in Michigan; and Laura Redden Searing, a high-achieving student who would go on to become an accomplished reporter. The final sections contain documents related to deaf events and issues at mid-century: the grand reunion of alumni of the American Asylum for the Deaf in 1850; the dedication of the Gallaudet monument; the debate over the idea of a deaf state; and the triumphant inauguration of the National Deaf-Mute College (now Gallaudet University) in 1864, which in many ways climaxed this period of change. Taken together, these disparate texts provide a record of cultural transformation. They give us a direct glimpse of the experiences, attitudes, and rhetoric of deaf Americans during this time.

The selections also demonstrate the complicated role that the written word played in the emergence of the American deaf community. Writing served as a bridge between deaf and hearing people, giving deaf Americans a means to demonstrate their reason and humanity to the hearing majority. It also enabled deaf Americans separated by distance or time to communicate, and aided collective memory by preserving deaf experience in print. Yet writing also had limitations. Since English cannot truly convey ASL, which was often referred to as the "natural language" of deaf Americans, in a sense it misses one of the most essential components of the deaf community. Deaf writers sought to express their views in the language of hearing people. To say they did so despite great challenges does not begin to convey the heroic proportions of their accomplishment.

The Deaf American Creation Story

Most deaf Americans know the tale of the beginning of deaf education in the United States. The story has been (literally) handed down from generation to generation; it is also well-documented in written records. The narrative tells how Thomas Hopkins Gallaudet, a hearing minister from Connecticut, and Laurent Clerc, a deaf teacher from France, came together to establish the first permanent school for deaf students in the country.[2] It goes like this:

> In the spring of 1814, a young minister named Thomas Hopkins Gallaudet was home in Hartford, Connecticut, recuperating from an illness. One day, he observed his younger brother playing with the neighbor's children, including the eight-year-old Alice Cogswell. She had become deaf at age two due to German measles, and had not heard or spoken since then. Gallaudet went over to her. He showed her his hat and wrote the letters H–A–T on the ground. He pointed from the hat to the written word. Alice responded eagerly, seeming to understand that the letters represented the hat.[3]

The young Alice could represent many deaf Americans before the advent of deaf education. Although full of life and curiosity, she is uneducated and in some ways cut off from the people around her. Since she does not hear or speak, she cannot readily communicate with hearing people. We might also note that she lives apart from deaf people and does not know sign language. Through writing, Gallaudet attempts to bridge the deaf–hearing chasm. He realizes that speech will be of little use, but writing, which is silent and visual, offers a way for the two to interact. The letters on the ground reveal the possibility of deaf intellectual potential; through them, Alice shows that she can learn and understand.

Alice's first brush with literacy epitomizes a common theme in nineteenth-century literature. It has all the drama and potential of the young slave Frederick Douglass learning to read, or even the wild boy Tarzan crouching over a book, puzzling over its contents. Through literacy, Alice, like Douglass and Tarzan, begins to move from ignorance to knowledge, from isolation to social engagement, and from dependency to self-empowerment. She can become less of an Other and more a part of mainstream society.

Alice's intellectual promise provokes a sequence of events that will eventually lead to the rise of American deaf education. The story continues:

> Over time, Gallaudet taught Alice other words and simple sentences. Alice's father, Mason Cogswell, was thrilled at Gallaudet's success. He assembled a group to establish a school for deaf children. They chose Gallaudet to go to England to learn the methods of deaf education used there. In 1815, Gallaudet sailed across the ocean. In England, he visited the Braidwoods, who had pioneered a technique of teaching deaf children orally. However, they were reluctant to share their highly profitable methods. Frustrated, Gallaudet went to a London exhibition by the famed Abbé Sicard, director of the National Institute for the Deaf in Paris, and two of his former students, Jean Massieu and Laurent Clerc. Sicard invited the audience

to ask questions of Massieu and Clerc. He translated the que-
ries into sign language, and Massieu and Clerc wrote answers
in French on a blackboard. Gallaudet was impressed. In 1816,
at Sicard's invitation, Gallaudet visited the school in Paris,
where he spent several months attending classes.

Once again, through writing, deaf people demonstrate their intellectual potential. While Alice was a new reader, getting her initial
glimmer of literacy as she gazed from Gallaudet's hat to the letters
scratched on the ground, Massieu and Clerc are polished writers,
confidently responding to the questions from the audience. Their
written answers show their acumen and help to spur Gallaudet's
interest in the manual approach to deaf education. The oralists
come off as greedy and selfish; they appear more concerned with
their own profit line than with deaf people's welfare. The manual-
ists, however, are generous and warm; they welcome Gallaudet
and share their sign language and teaching methods with him.
That turn of events helps to determine the future of American
deaf education, fostering the rise of sign language and deaf culture
in America. The tale concludes:

> Running low on funds and impatient to return home, Gal-
> laudet invited Clerc to accompany him back to America.
> Clerc agreed. Their voyage across the ocean took fifty-two
> days. During the trip, Clerc taught Gallaudet French Sign
> Language, while Gallaudet taught Clerc written English. Once
> they arrived in the United States, Gallaudet and Clerc traveled
> around New England to raise funds. They collected $5,000,
> which was matched by the Connecticut Legislature. In April
> 1817, the new school opened in Hartford. The first class had
> seven students, including Alice Cogswell. That number rap-
> idly increased. Thanks to Gallaudet and Clerc for bringing deaf
> education to America!

The new school is established through a unique deaf–hearing partnership. Gallaudet and Clerc work together as equals, each with something crucial to contribute to the enterprise. Without Clerc, Gallaudet not only would have had difficulty learning sign language and how to teach deaf students, but he also would have had trouble convincing the public that deaf people could be educated. And without Gallaudet, Clerc may never have come to the United States at all, or navigated American society and the English language so effectively. The tale concludes with their joint efforts allowing Alice and other deaf people to begin to realize their potential.

The narrative became a creation story for the signing deaf community, taking on a mythic aura. Embedded in the tale, we can discern values that many deaf Americans share: sign language over oralism, community over isolation, education over ignorance, generosity over selfishness, mutual respect and collaboration between deaf and hearing people, and so forth. The heroes of the story are Gallaudet and Clerc. Even during their own lifetimes, they were revered as benefactors who brought sign language, education, and community to the American deaf population. They became something like founding fathers, the George Washington and Thomas Jefferson of the deaf community. In 1850, hundreds of deaf people gathered in Hartford to honor and thank the pair. Fisher Ames Spofford, a former student and teacher at the American Asylum, gave an eloquent address in sign language. "We all feel the most ardent love to these gentlemen who founded this Asylum," he signed. "This gratitude will be a chain to bind all future pupils together."[4] The gratitude and respect have continued unabated through the years, helping to unite deaf Americans. Today, students at schools for the deaf often perform the story of Gallaudet and Clerc each December on Gallaudet's birthday.[5]

Impact of the Schools

The opening of the new American Asylum for the Deaf in 1817 soon stimulated the establishment of other schools for deaf students: the New York school in 1818, the Pennsylvania school in 1820, the Kentucky school in 1823, and so on.[6] These residential institutions quickly made an impact. First, they helped deaf people to come together. Because the United States was primarily an agrarian nation in the early nineteenth century, and because the majority of deaf children were born to hearing families, deaf individuals often lived far apart. The schools enabled them to come into contact. In 1818, Clerc wrote that of forty-two students at the American Asylum, only "four or six" had met other deaf people before coming to Hartford.[7] Prior to attending school, such children sometimes did not even realize that there were others like themselves. As a student wrote in 1847, "When at home, I thought that I was the only deaf and dumb girl in the world, before I had seen any other one."[8] The schools helped deaf young people to learn that they were not strange or alone, but members of a larger community of similar individuals.

The schools not only brought deaf people together, but also enabled them to develop their own language. Before 1817, some signed languages existed in the United States. On Martha's Vineyard, a high rate of hereditary deafness led to a vibrant community in which both deaf and hearing people used a sign language.[9] Other deaf people, especially those from deaf families, also signed. When the American Asylum opened, some students brought their sign languages to the school. There, they encountered Clerc's elegant French Sign Language, which he had learned in Paris, a city with a large deaf community and an established deaf school. American Sign Language evolved out of this mixture of French and indigenous sign languages.[10] Students graduated from the American Asylum and became teachers at other schools, spreading the language to states across the nation. In the process, ASL became a force that united deaf Americans, making them akin to a linguistic minority.

As deaf students spent years living together, they frequently developed a strong communal bond. They shared not only their own language, but also social rules, group norms, values, and ASL poetry and storytelling traditions—in other words, the components of a distinct culture. Edwin Mann, a graduate of the American Asylum, wrote, "To the teachers and pupils . . . I was bound by the strongest ties of affection, ties ever dear, but doubly so to the lonely mute, who first learns, in their society and by their aid, to communicate all his thoughts and feelings."[11] Not surprisingly, deaf people began to seek ways to come together after they had graduated, forming deaf associations, churches, and clubs. In 1869, Alphonso Johnson welcomed hundreds of deaf people to a convention by pointing out the ties they shared: "Most of us were educated in the same Institution, where we spent from five to fifteen years," he signed. "Like members of the same family, which have been scattered abroad, we have a desire to see each other again. . . . here we meet and our language of signs is brought into full play. . . . we feel elated, so much so, indeed, as to forget our misfortune."[12] As Johnson indicates, for many deaf people the deaf community functioned as a second family, a group where one was understood and accepted, where one felt happy, normal, and at home. Most deaf people chose to marry other deaf individuals who shared the same language and cultural identity. In the 1850s, such feelings of solidarity even prompted one activist to propose establishing a separate state where deaf people could live apart from the hearing world. Although the idea was ultimately rejected, the seriousness with which deaf people discussed it shows how much they came to view themselves as a distinct group.

As we can see, one great change effected by the schools was to nourish the development of ASL and a deaf communal identity. A second transformation wrought by the schools was to make deaf Americans more visible. Hearing citizens began to *see* deaf people signing for the first time, and what they saw often challenged their assumptions about deafness. For example, instead of encountering lonely, isolated individuals, they sometimes found a flourishing community. When the American Asylum had its first alumni reunion in 1850, one teacher noted: "A more happy assemblage it was never our good fortune to behold. It was most pleasant to see the joy that beamed from all their faces, and gave new vigor and animation to their expressive language of signs."[13] Such deaf people did not fit the public's construction of deafness. They did not look like victims of social isolation, and their cheerfulness probably caught many hearing observers off guard.

For hearing Americans, the sight of deaf people interacting frequently upended another traditional meaning of deafness: the absence of language. Hearing observers often reacted with fascination, even awe, when they saw deaf signers eloquently communicating with each other. After watching a deaf minister preach in ASL, a hearing correspondent wrote: "He is so expert, so facile, so swift, so fleet, he fills us with ever increasing wonder; and forces us to think it is we who are imperfect, and not he, who leaves us so deeply impressed."[14] Through their sign language, deaf Americans came to be seen (and to see themselves) as possessing something unique and beautiful that most others did not have. Thomas Hopkins Gallaudet articulated this view in 1847, when he wrote: "[This] novel, highly poetical, and singular descriptive language, adapted as well to spiritual as to material objects, and bringing kindred souls into a much more close and conscious communion than that of speech can possibly do—is to be regarded rather in the light of a blessing than of a misfortune."[15] In this way, ASL complicated the traditional formulation of deaf people as lacking and inferior; through their language and close-knit culture, they subtly began to challenge the whole notion of what constitutes a disability.

Deaf people's sign language also provided tangible proof of their intelligence. Since the time of Aristotle, who was credited with saying that people born deaf were incapable of reason, hearing individuals had linked deafness with ignorance, confusion, and even insanity.[16] But the sight of deaf people signing contradicted such assumptions. F. A. P. Barnard, who lost his hearing while an undergraduate at Yale and became a teacher at the New York Institution, wrote that "this beautiful language is [deaf people's] own creation, and is a visible testimony to the activity of their intellect."[17] In 1834, the *American Annals of Education* agreed, noting the change in how deaf Americans were perceived:

> The instruction of deaf mutes has now become so general, that it has almost ceased to excite the amazement which was at first felt, on seeing those who were deemed beyond the pale of intellectual beings, addressing themselves to others, in intelligible language, often in signs and gestures far more expressive than words. The prejudice . . . is vanishing before the demonstrative evidence . . . that they possess minds not less susceptible of cultivation than those of other men, and often far above the ordinary level.[18]

By allowing deaf Americans to emerge in society, the schools enabled them to contest traditional, patronizing stereotypes hearing people had about them.

A final way that deaf people challenged conventional thinking was through their ability to read and write. While the schools began to change deaf Americans' lives by nurturing deaf culture and making deaf people more visible, the schools also made large numbers of deaf citizens literate for the first time. Writing became the synapse through which deaf people communicated directly with hearing people who did not know sign language. Thus when Clerc visited the White House, he and President James Monroe conversed by writing back and forth; when a deaf man named Mestapher Chase was robbed in the 1830s, he gave testimony in court by writing; and at her wedding, a deaf woman named Mary Rose made her vow by reading the marriage covenant and signing her name on it. The written text gave deaf and hearing people a place where they could interact; after all, one does not need to hear to read and write. Such writing, together with deaf people's signing, exploded the notion that deaf people existed outside the realm of language. It helped deaf Americans to show that they thought and felt much as hearing people did. When, in 1816, Clerc was asked how he knew he had the same mental capacities as hearing people, he wrote, "I can express my own ideas by writing, and as what I write is what you speak, I can judge that I possess the same faculties of mind as you do."[19] Writing proved that deaf people could reason, helping to humanize them in society's eyes.

Writing not only allowed deaf people to prove themselves to mainstream society, but also helped to link deaf Americans separated by space or time. Deaf people such as Edmund Booth and his wife commonly wrote letters to each other when they were living in different states. In the 1830s, Levi Backus, a graduate of the American Asylum, wrote a column in his weekly newspaper that often addressed the interests of deaf readers. In 1849, the North Carolina Institution began publishing *The Deaf Mute,* the first of many periodicals put out by schools for the deaf. Such publications helped deaf people to share news and keep in contact with other members of the community. Even though it was not the native language of deaf Americans, written English played an important role in the maintenance of a national deaf community.

During the first half of the nineteenth century, then, the schools empowered deaf Americans in a variety of ways. They fostered a deaf cultural identity, made deaf people more visible in society, and enabled many more deaf citizens to become literate. These shifts led to an interesting paradox: while in some respects the schools separated deaf people from their hearing counterparts, nurturing a distinct language and culture, they also broke down barriers by enabling more deaf Americans to read and write. In effect, the schools simultaneously made deaf students more and less of an Other. During public exhibitions, instructors usually displayed both students' differences from and similarities to the hearing majority. For example, at an examination at the New York

Institution, there were "1st, exhibitions of the graphic power and eloquence of the language of pantomime, which excited great interest, and elicited much laughter and applause, and 2d, written exercises by some selected pupils, to show to what elevation of thought and correctness, even eloquence of language, deaf-mutes are capable of attaining."[20] The students' visual performance provoked wonder and fascination; they were seen as possessing a beautiful language and skills that most hearing people did not have. Through the written demonstration, the students showed their mastery of logocentric forms, proving that, despite their ostensible difference, they were also sensible, intelligent human beings. By moving back and forth between the two languages, deaf people displayed what W. E. B. Du Bois termed "double-consciousness," that sense of experiencing "two-ness . . . two souls, two thoughts, two unreconciled strivings."[21] Like other American minorities, deaf people had to learn the precarious art of navigating between their own culture and the culture of the majority among whom they lived.

Writing Deafness

Although we unfortunately cannot see nineteenth-century deaf Americans sign, we can read their writing in English. Yet for modern readers to appreciate such texts fairly and accurately, we must remember the obstacles deaf Americans faced when they sought to express themselves in the written form of a spoken language. Especially for those who were congenitally deaf, learning English was often a daunting task. The process could be compared to a hearing American trying to master Chinese without ever hearing it spoken. Since deaf students in antebellum America typically did not go to school until they were eight, nine, or even older, they often did not begin to study English until well after the critical peak years for language acquisition had passed. In 1854, Collins Stone, the superintendent of the Ohio Institution, lamented that "the results of education which are attained in our Institutions, are to so great an extent incomplete and partial; that the grand end at which we aim, the free and accurate use of language, is so seldom reached."[22] The schools did give masses of deaf people the ability to use written English, but we should be careful not to overstate their ease with the language. ASL remained the surest and most comfortable language for deaf Americans, as Searing noted in 1858:

> Signs are the natural language of the mute. Writing may be used in his intercourse with others, but when conversing with those who are, like himself, deprived of hearing and speech, you will always find that he prefers signs to every other mode of intercourse; and every other established means of communicating his thoughts, no matter what facility he may have acquired in it, is no more nor less than what a foreign language is to those who hear and speak.[23]

English, for all its value, resembled a foreign language to congenitally deaf people, one that came only through years of sustained study.

Deaf authors also had to grapple with the fact that written English cannot truly represent their cherished language of signs. As Burnet pointed out in 1835, "To attempt to describe a language of signs by words, or to learn such a language from books, is alike to attempt impossibilities."[24] Since American Sign Language was often such an integral part of deaf identity, and the wellspring of positive constructions of deafness, its absence in written materials leaves a conspicuous gap. At times we can obtain a glimmer of the beauty of ASL through written accounts, such as when Burnet describes the conversation of two educated deaf signers as a "thousand changing motions through which every thought of the mind flashes and disappears."[25] More often, though, the original nature of the signing is lost. We cannot directly experience the awe that hearing observers felt on seeing deaf people animatedly signing. We can read the lectures that Clerc and Carlin wrote in English, but their actual delivery of these presentations in ASL, their signs and the flavor of their interaction with the audience, are forever gone.[26] We are left with the somewhat odd sense that we cannot now experience the natural language of most of these writers, the language they used when they interacted with each other in person. The culture that such deaf writers experienced remains elusive, peeking out from behind English words, existing in a mood, a spirit that is hinted at, even described, but never quite directly conveyed.

Along the same lines, deaf writers had to struggle to preserve their identity in a language freighted with negative assumptions about deafness. In English, *deaf* not only means "does not hear," but also has been associated with callousness, insensitivity, evil, insanity, isolation, difference, inferiority, impairment, and so forth. Even the word "deaf" contains negative connotations; it has its roots in the Indo-European base *dheubh,* which denotes confusion, stupefaction, and dizziness. If we subscribe to the Sapir–Whorf hypothesis, which contends that the categories of language one uses shape the lens through which one sees the world, it follows that deaf people writing in English must almost necessarily recycle some negative interpretations of deafness.[27] Such meanings are inscribed in the language, in its idioms (from "turn a deaf ear" to "dialogue of the deaf"), its metaphors, and its very etymology.

We can discern adverse views of deafness throughout the selections in this volume. The writers here routinely refer to themselves as "unfortunates" and look forward to going to heaven, where, in Searing's words, "the deaf ear will be unsealed, and the mute voice gush out in glorious melody."[28] Such depictions are perhaps not surprising in a society that gave relatively few opportunities to deaf people. Searing, Jewel, and many of the other writers here undoubtedly had harder lives because they were deaf. No surprise, then, that they anticipate having such obstacles removed. As Jewel says, "What a comfort it is for me to believe thus!"[29] Yet deaf writers probably produced these statements partially because existing models in written English, such as the Bible, sermons, and prayer books, frequently make use of such rhetoric. Students at the schools attended chapel quite often; at the American Asylum, they went to both morning and evening devotion, as well as to worship on Sunday.[30] They must have frequently encountered biblical language that equated deafness with humanity's fallen condition.

In the same way, the authors follow hearing precedents in the exaggerated manner that they often describe deaf people before education. For example, in 1816, Clerc wrote to an audience in Boston that "Mr. Gallaudet and I are in the design of raising those unfortunates from their nothingness."[31] Clerc may have shrewdly used such language to add drama to his appeal for funds to open a new school. Yet even so, he was imitating his hearing teacher in Paris, the Abbé Sicard, who in public lectures often compared uneducated deaf people to blocks of unchiseled marble or statues not yet animated with life.[32] Such rhetoric added to the processing of history into myth; it made deaf people before education seem lifeless and inhuman. Similarly, when Nack, Burnet, and John Carlin call uneducated deaf people "heathens," they echo Thomas Hopkins Gallaudet, who in a well-known 1824 sermon called uneducated deaf people "long-neglected heathen" because they could not read or understand the Gospel.[33] Their language encouraged a view of uneducated deaf people as uncivilized barbarians. F. A. P. Barnard, one of the few people to protest such discourse, pointed out in 1834 that "To be deaf from birth . . . is to be ignorant, not weak, stupid, or savage."[34] Yet the theatrical rhetoric persisted for most of the nineteenth century. Although deaf people produced the writing in this collection, we can nevertheless detect hearing people's influence and voices.

Perhaps Carlin's 1847 poem, "The Mute's Lament," best epitomizes such negative attitudes. It begins:

I move—a silent exile on this earth;
As in his dreary cell one doomed for life,
My tongue is mute, and closed ear heedeth not;
No gleam of hope this darken'd mind assures
That the blest power of speech shall e'er be known.[35]

The poem is graceful, harmonious, an impressive achievement for a person born deaf. Part of its power lies in the fact that a "mute," someone who cannot speak and who was usually seen as outside of language, can produce English verse of such merit. However, Carlin appears to have internalized traditional negative attitudes so completely that his work overflows with sentimental self-pity and woe. Again, such dejection is perhaps understandable, given the barriers that Carlin, a gifted deaf man, must have encountered in antebellum America. At any rate, by reinforcing negative assumptions that deaf people are lonely and miserable, Carlin buttresses the view that hearing people are superior. He assigns primary value to speech and hearing, while sign language and the deaf community are nowhere to be found.

Yet while deaf writers sometimes reify traditional constructions of deafness, they also challenge such interpretations. In the following pages, they regularly bring their own culture and worldviews to English, imbuing established words with new meanings. To begin with a seemingly trivial example: when Clerc writes, "Why are we Deaf and Dumb," he subtly alters the traditional English meaning of "deaf" as other, different.[36] Instead, he equates "deaf" with "we," converting the word into a signifier of group identity. Subsequent authors also write about deafness in the first person, making it appear more of a normal human variation than a mark of almost unfathomable deviance. When Clerc also suggests that being deaf could actually be an advantage, he implicitly questions centuries of received wisdom that routinely assumed deaf people were inferior, lesser beings. Similarly, when Burnet insists that isolated deaf children are neglected, not obtuse, and when Carlin urges that a college be established for deaf Americans, they associate "deaf" with capability and potential.

Perhaps we can see this positive treatment of deafness most clearly in the writing about deaf people interacting with each other. In his 1835 poem "Emma," about a deaf girl, Burnet offers an almost jubilant account of deaf signers at school:

> *Here,* from the speaking limbs, and face divine,
> At nature's bidding, thoughts and feelings shine,
> That in thin air no more her sense elude—
> Each understands—by each is understood.
> Here can each feeling gush forth, unrepressed,
> To mix with feelings of a kindred breast.[37]

Burnet skillfully evokes the headiness of ASL and deaf culture. Along the same lines, in writing from the 1850 tribute to Gallaudet and Clerc, we can sense some of the pride and "elation," as Alphonso Johnson put it, of being among deaf peers. By insisting on giving their own tribute to Gallaudet and Clerc, and, later, on raising their own monument to Gallaudet, deaf Americans showed just how self-respecting and independent they were. In texts like these, the confident deaf "we" is apparent, whereas in poetry by Nack and Carlin, readers encounter a lonely, cut-off deaf "I." Such affirmative treatments of deafness almost invariably stem from a strong sense of community, of belonging to a group of vibrant, talented people.

Positive depictions of deafness also stem from American Sign Language. By using "deaf" in an affirmative manner, authors assign the word a meaning that more closely resembles the sign DEAF than traditional English. In American Sign Language, DEAF not only means "does not hear," but also connotes us, uses sign language, behaves in expected ways, shares deaf values, and so on.[38] The sign DEAF has more positive colorings than the traditional English "deaf." While ASL cannot be directly written, it still shapes some of the meanings and messages that deaf authors produce in these texts. We can perceive what Mikhail Bakhtin calls double-voiced words, that is, English words that are appropriated for deaf purposes "by inserting a new semantic orientation into a word which already has—and retains—its own orientation."[39] Double-voiced is not the best term for the dynamic here, since of course ASL is not voiced at all; but nonetheless, double-voiced helps to elucidate how deaf writing in English is influenced by ASL discourse.

As we can see, the authors in this volume are immersed in two separate languages and ways of living. They move back and forth between seemingly contradictory views of deafness and themselves. Clerc assures a hearing shipmate on the way to America that he would never marry a deaf woman; yet just two years later, he did exactly that. Carlin advocates using fingerspelling in schools and states he prefers the company of hearing people, but he gave eloquent speeches in ASL, married a deaf woman, and associated with the deaf community throughout his life. The whole debate over the idea of a separate deaf state can be seen as a confrontation of these issues; in a sense, John J. Flournoy's radical proposal was an attempt to escape from feelings of two-ness, to escape to a place where sign language and deaf culture would be the dominant modes of being.

Such double-consciousness is never quite resolved in these pages. The writers here sometimes struggle to express their experience accurately, searching for ways to free English from its traditional negative associations with deafness. By adding to the meaning of words such as "deaf," the authors helped to enrich the English language, making it more elastic and democratic, and more of their own. Although the writing here is exclusively by deaf authors, the texts are profoundly hybrid, shaped by traditional meanings of deafness in English, by influential hearing authors such as Gallaudet and Sicard, by religious rhetoric, by American Sign Language, by the emerging community of deaf Americans, and other factors. The result is a fascinating, contradictory, valiant effort to explore what it meant to be deaf in antebellum America.

Notes

1. "Empire State Association of Deaf-Mutes: Proceedings of the Third Biennial Convention," *The Deaf-Mutes' Friend* 1 (Sept. 1869): 258.

2. There was at least one attempt at a school for deaf students before Gallaudet and Clerc opened the American Asylum. In March of 1815, John Braidwood, the grandson of the founder of the Braidwood Academy in Scotland, opened a school on a Virginia plantation owned by William Bolling, the father of two deaf children. Braidwood took on at least five students, and taught using the oral method. However, the school closed after only a year and a half when Braidwood, a habitual drinker and gambler, disappeared. See John Vickrey Van Cleve and Barry A. Crouch, *A Place of Their Own: Creating the Deaf Community in America* (Washington, D.C.: Gallaudet University Press, 1989), 26–27.

3. I have culled this version of the Alice–Gallaudet–Clerc story from many sources: the various renditions I have seen by deaf people in American Sign Language (see note 5); a display in the museum of American School for the Deaf in Hartford; the written testimonials in this anthology; and the accounts in Jack R. Gannon's *Deaf Heritage: A Narrative History of Deaf America* and the other reference sources listed in the selected bibliography (see pp. xxxii–xxxiii).

4. Spofford's speech was included in Luzerne Rae, "Testimonial of the Deaf Mutes of New England to Messrs. Gallaudet and Clerc," reprinted in *Tribute to Gallaudet: A Discourse in Commemoration of the Life, Character, and Services, of the Rev. Thomas H. Gallaudet, with an Appendix,* 2nd ed. (Hartford, Conn.: Hutchinson and Bullard, 1859), 194.

5. In the early 1990s, I saw the Gallaudet–Clerc story performed during assemblies at three schools for deaf students. At the Texas School for the Deaf, a high school senior gave a one-man show in which he played all the parts. At the Florida School for the Deaf and the Blind, students presented a full enactment, complete with period costumes. And at the Virginia School for the Deaf and the Blind in Staunton, a teacher signed the story.

6. Initially called the Connecticut Asylum for the Education and

Instruction of Deaf and Dumb Persons, the school was soon renamed as the American Asylum in recognition of its national character. It took on its current name, the American School for the Deaf, in the 1890s. For a history of deaf schools in the United States and the chronology in which they were founded, see Jack Gannon, *Deaf Heritage: A Narrative History of Deaf America* (Silver Spring, Md.: The National Association of the Deaf, 1981), 16–58.

7. Laurent Clerc, *An Address Written by Mr. Clerc: And Read by His Request at a Public Examination of the Pupils in the Connecticut Asylum, before the Governour and Both Houses of the Legislature, 28th May, 1818* (Hartford, Conn.: Hudson and Co., printers, 1818), 12.

8. H. K., "My Thoughts Before I Was Educated," in *The Thirty-First Annual Report of the Directors of the American Asylum, at Hartford, for the Education and Instruction of the Deaf and Dumb* (Hartford, Conn.: Case, Tiffany, and Burnham, 1847), 29.

9. Nora Ellen Groce, *Everyone Here Spoke Sign Language: Hereditary Deafness on Martha's Vineyard* (Cambridge: Harvard University Press, 1985).

10. Although they have diverged considerably over the years, ASL still resembles French Sign Language more closely than any other signed language. See James Woodward, "Historical Bases of American Sign Language," in *Understanding Language through Sign Language Research,* ed. Patricia Siple (New York: Academic Press, 1978), 338–48; Clayton Valli and Ceil Lucas, *The Linguistics of American Sign Language* (Washington, D.C.: Gallaudet University Press, 1992), 15.

11. Edwin Mann, "Preface," *The Deaf and Dumb, or, a Collection of Articles Relating to the Condition of Deaf Mutes* (Boston: D. K. Hitchcock, 1836), viii.

12. "Empire State Association of Deaf-Mutes: Proceedings of the Third Biennial Convention," *The Deaf-Mutes' Friend* 1 (Sept. 1869): 258.

13. Rae, "Testimonial of the Deaf Mutes of New England," 201.

14. Anonymous, "The Sign Language: Graphic Description of a Church Service among the Deaf and Dumb," *The Deaf-Mutes' Friend* 1 (July 1869): 199.

15. Thomas Hopkins Gallaudet, "On the Natural Language of Signs; And Its Value and Uses in the Instruction of the Deaf and Dumb," *American Annals of the Deaf and Dumb* 1 (Oct. 1847): 56.

16. For a helpful examination of Aristotle's supposed comment on

deafness, see Harlan Lane, *When the Mind Hears: A History of the Deaf* (New York: Vintage, 1984), 427 n. 88.

17. F. A. P. Barnard, *Observations on the Education of the Deaf and Dumb* (Boston: J. H. Low, 1834), 19.

18. Anonymous, "Education of the Deaf and Dumb," *American Annals of Education* 4 (1834): 53–58, reprinted in Mann, ed., *The Deaf and Dumb* (Boston: D. K. Hitchcock, 1836), 2.

19. Laurent Clerc Papers no. 69, Manuscripts and Archives, Yale University Library.

20. John R. Burnet, "Annual Examination at the New York Institution," *The Deaf-Mutes' Friend* 1 (Aug. 1869): 233.

21. W. E. B. Du Bois, *The Souls of Black Folk* (Chicago: McClurg, 1903), 3.

22. Collins Stone, *On the Difficulties Encountered by the Deaf and Dumb in Learning Language* (Columbus: Statesman Steam Book and Job Press, 1854), 4. The persistent concern about teaching English to deaf students continues today, when an eighteen-year-old congenitally deaf person typically does not read above the fifth-grade level. See Ronnie Wilbur, "Reading and Writing," in *Gallaudet Encyclopedia of Deaf People and Deafness,* vol. 3, ed. John V. Van Cleve (New York: McGraw-Hill, 1987), 146.

23. Laura Redden, "A Few Words about the Deaf and Dumb," *American Annals of the Deaf and Dumb* 10 (1858): 178.

24. John R. Burnet, *Tales of the Deaf and Dumb, with Miscellaneous Poems* (Newark, N.J.: Benjamin Olds, 1835), 24. Despite the development of glosses and other systems for representing ASL through writing, Burnet's observation still holds largely true today.

25. Ibid, 18.

26. It was not until the advent of motion picture technology in the early twentieth century that ASL lectures and performances began to be recorded and preserved.

27. Benjamin Lee Whorf (1897–1941), a student of the linguistic anthropologist Edward Sapir, came up with the theory of "linguistic relativity," which is sometimes also called the "Sapir–Whorf hypothesis" or the "Whorf hypothesis." For an interesting selection of Whorf's work, see John B. Carroll, ed., *Language, Thought, and Reality: Selected Writings* (Cambridge: MIT Press, 1956). For a more recent assessment of the Sapir–Whorf hypothesis, see John J. Gumperz and Stephen C. Levinson, eds., *Rethinking Linguistic Relativity* (New York: Cambridge University Press, 1996).

28. Redden, "A Few Words about the Deaf and Dumb," 180.

29. Adele M. Jewel, *A Brief Narrative of the Life of Mrs. Adele M. Jewel (Being Deaf and Dumb)* (Jackson, Mich.: Daily Citizen Steam Printing House, circa 1860), 15.

30. As Douglas Baynton has shown, religion played an influential role in the rise of American deaf education; for the Reverend Thomas Hopkins Gallaudet and others, the desire to bring the Gospel to deaf Americans was a primary motivator for educating deaf people. See Douglas Baynton, *Forbidden Signs: American Culture and the Campaign Against Sign Language* (Chicago: University of Chicago Press, 1996), 15–22.

31. Laurent Clerc, "Laurent Clerc," in *Tribute to Gallaudet: A Discourse in Commemoration of the Life, Character, and Services, of the Rev. Thomas H. Gallaudet, with an Appendix,* 2nd ed. (New York: F. C. Brownell, 1859), 109.

32. Anonymous, "An Account of the Institution in Paris for the Education of the Deaf and Dumb," reprinted in Mann, ed., *The Deaf and Dumb* (Boston: D. K. Hitchcock, 1836), 234.

33. Thomas Hopkins Gallaudet, "The Duty and Advantages of Affording Instruction to the Deaf and Dumb," reprinted in Mann, ed., *The Deaf and Dumb* (Boston: D. K. Hitchcock, 1836), 217.

34. Barnard, *Observations,* 6.

35. John Carlin, "The Mute's Lament," *American Annals of the Deaf and Dumb* 1 (1847): 15–16.

36. Clerc, *An Address Written by Mr. Clerc,* 12.

37. Burnet, "Emma," in *Tales of the Deaf and Dumb* (Newark, N.J.: Benjamin Olds, 1835), 196.

38. For an insightful discussion of the meanings of DEAF, see Carol Padden and Tom Humphries, *Deaf in America: Voices from a Culture* (Cambridge: Harvard University Press, 1988): 13–17, 49–50.

39. Quoted in Henry Louis Gates, Jr., *The Signifying Monkey: A Theory of African-American Literary Criticism* (New York: Oxford University Press, 1988), 50.

SELECTED BIBLIOGRAPHY

Baynton, Douglas C. *Forbidden Signs: American Culture and the Campaign Against Sign Language.* Chicago: University of Chicago Press, 1996.

Booth, Edmund. *Edmund Booth, Forty-Niner: The Life Story of a Deaf Pioneer*. Stockton, Calif.: San Joaquin Pioneer and Historical Society, 1953.

Gannon, Jack R. *Deaf Heritage: A Narrative History of Deaf America*. Silver Spring, Md.: National Association of the Deaf, 1981.

Lane, Harlan. *When the Mind Hears: A History of the Deaf*. New York: Vintage, 1984.

Lang, Harry G., and Bonnie Meath-Lang. *Deaf Persons in the Arts and Sciences: A Biographical Dictionary*. Westport, Conn.: Greenwood Press, 1995.

Padden, Carol, and Tom Humphries. *Deaf in America: Voices from a Culture*. Cambridge, Mass.: Harvard University Press, 1988.

Van Cleve, John Vickrey, and Barry A. Crouch. *A Place of Their Own: Creating the Deaf Community in America*. Washington, D.C.: Gallaudet University Press, 1989.

Van Cleve, John Vickrey, ed. *Gallaudet Encyclopedia of Deaf People and Deafness*. 3 vols. New York: McGraw-Hill, 1987.

A
MIGHTY
CHANGE

PART ONE

INDIVIDUAL
AUTHORS

1

LAURENT CLERC

(1785–1869)

The most influential deaf person in America during the first half of the nineteenth century was Laurent Clerc. With his intelligence, gentlemanly demeanor, sign language skills, and ability to read and write, Clerc gave living proof to the public that deaf individuals could be educated, and educated well. He came from France in 1816 to help found the first permanent school for deaf students in the United States, and taught there for over four decades. An excellent instructor and role model, Clerc had tremendous impact on his pupils, some of whom went on to become teachers, community leaders, and heads of other deaf schools. Deaf Americans linked Clerc with Thomas Hopkins Gallaudet and revered them both as their benefactors.

Louis Laurent Marie Clerc was born December 26, 1785, in LaBalme, France. He came from a genteel family; his father was a notary public and the village mayor. As Clerc explains in his autobiographical sketch, when he was one year old, he fell into a fireplace and burned his right cheek, leaving a permanent scar. His parents attributed his deafness and loss of smell to the accident.

Clerc had no formal education until he was twelve, when he entered the National Institute for the Deaf in Paris. His first teacher was Jean Massieu, an accomplished deaf man who became his close friend. He was also taught by the school's director, Abbé Roch Ambroise Sicard. Clerc completed his studies in eight years and proved himself brilliant. He became a tutor at the school, and later began teaching the highest class.

In 1808, Clerc had the opportunity to go to St. Petersburg, Russia, to help run a new school for deaf students. The proposed director of the school, Jean-Baptiste Jauffret, knew little of deaf people or sign language, so Clerc urged Sicard to let him accompany Jauffret to Russia. To Clerc's elation, Sicard agreed. However, the Russians provided funds for only one person, and Clerc reluctantly gave up the idea. Little did he know that he would get another chance to spread deaf education to a different land.

During the political upheaval in 1815 due to Napoleon's return to France, Sicard took Massieu and Clerc to London, where they gave exhibitions to publicize the school's teaching methods. On July 10, 1815, one of the audience members was Thomas Hopkins Gallaudet, a hearing minister from Connecticut. Gallaudet had just arrived in England; a group of Hartford citizens had sent him to learn how to teach deaf students so he could establish a school. Gallaudet was impressed by the exhibition. In the spring of 1816, he visited the school in Paris and eventually invited Clerc to come back with him to the United States. The talented and ambitious Clerc saw that Gallaudet needed his assistance and was eager to help bring deaf education to the New World.

Clerc and Gallaudet sailed to America that summer. During the trip, Clerc tutored Gallaudet in sign language, while Gallaudet instructed Clerc in written English. Clerc studied assiduously, reading and keeping a journal. After drafting his daily entries, he would show them to Gallaudet, who made corrections. Clerc then wrote the amended text into his journal, which helps to explain

Laurent Clerc
(painting by Charles
Wilson Peale), 1822

why the version we have today is remarkably free of errors. After arriving in New York in August 1816, they spent the next seven months raising funds for their school. Using his newly-acquired English skills, Clerc wrote speeches for Gallaudet to read on his behalf to legislatures and civic groups. He also answered questions from the audiences; Gallaudet would sign the questions to him, and Clerc would write his answers on a chalkboard. Clerc's wit and intelligence rarely failed to sway onlookers, and their efforts were successful. On April 15, 1817, they opened the "Connecticut Asylum, For the Education and Instruction of Deaf and Dumb Persons" (soon to become the American Asylum) in Hartford, with seven students.

In January 1818, Clerc visited Congress with board member Henry Hudson to seek additional financial assistance for the school. Henry Clay, the speaker of the House, seated Clerc beside him, and during a recess Clerc conversed in writing with congressmen, in both French and English. The next day, Clerc visited President Monroe in the White House. His visits made an impression; in its 1819–20 session, Congress passed a bill granting land in Alabama to the school, and Monroe signed the bill into law. The land was subsequently sold for $300,000, enough to ensure the school's long-term financial stability.

On May 3, 1818, Clerc married Eliza Boardman, one of his first students. The marriage was by all accounts happy, and it provided a new incentive for Clerc to stay in America. The couple had six children, all hearing; four survived infancy. One, Francis Joseph Clerc, later became well-known among deaf people as an advocate and Episcopal minister.

In 1821, Clerc went to Philadelphia for eight months to help the Pennsylvania Institution get underway. Otherwise, he continued teaching at the American Asylum. In 1830, Gallaudet resigned from his position as school principal, an event that saddened Clerc. In 1850, graduates of the Hartford school held a convocation to honor Clerc and Gallaudet (see chapter eight). After Gallaudet's death in 1851, Clerc served as the president of an association to erect a monument in Gallaudet's memory. This group led to the formation, in 1854, of the New England Gallaudet Association of the Deaf, the first of many such deaf organizations. At the association's first meeting, a member introduced a resolution stating that "the memory of Professor Clerc is cherished with profound gratitude and affection by all American deaf-mutes." It was adopted unanimously.

After teaching over half a century in France and America, Clerc retired in 1858 at age seventy-three. He spent his retirement quietly in Hartford. In 1864, he gave a presentation at the inauguration of the National Deaf-Mute College (see chapter ten). He received an honorary degree from Trinity College in Hartford, as well as citations from Dartmouth College and the University of Lyons. He died on July 18, 1869, shortly after celebrating his golden wedding anniversary with his wife. In 1874, grateful deaf Americans unveiled a monument to Clerc at the American Asylum. Its inscription calls him "The Apostle to the Deaf-Mutes of the New World . . . who left his native land to uplift them with his teachings and encourage them by his example."

The selections here are mostly his early writings. His later speeches appear in part two.

Journal during Voyage from France to America

The following excerpts are from the journal Clerc kept during his fifty-two-day trip to the United States in 1816. In a brief notice at the beginning, Clerc writes that the work is "a Recital of all that I have done and seen, since my departure from Havre till my arrival in New York. I warn the Reader who may read this relation, that I have not written it for him, but for myself, and particularly to exercise and perfect myself in the English Language."

[*Tuesday, June the 18th.*] The ship named *Mary-Augusta*, the provisions all being ready in the morning of Tuesday the 18th of June 1816, we waited for nothing but the high water to take our departure. In fine, at three o'clock in the afternoon, the tide having risen, we left Havre, a pretty little City of France, surrounded by a crowd of spectators. The persons who knew us wished us a happy voyage and good health. We were in number six passengers without counting the Captain, whose name was Mr. Hall, and twelve strong and skillful sailors.

Friday, June the 21st. After breakfast, M. Gallaudet desiring to encourage me to learn good English, suggested to me the thought of writing this journal, and it is in consequence of his advice that I do it. I began it therefore on the spot and I wrote my diary of the 18th of June, which busied me all the day. It was a long time for so small a matter, but if you deign to consider that I was obliged, every moment, to seek in my dictionary the words which I did not understand, you would say of it, I am sure, that I could not do it more quickly. When I finished my first day, I presented it to Mr. Gallaudet, praying him to correct it. He did it with his ordinary kindness. Afterwards I wrote my work fair in my stitched book.

Saturday, June the 22nd. I passed all the morning up on deck to write my diary of the preceding days, and all the evening to talk with M. Gallaudet, who, at my request, gave me the description of an American dinner, of a marriage, and of the manners and customs of the inhabitants of that country; so that in arriving thither I may be familiar with them, and that the people may take me for a true American citizen and not for a stranger. This long conversation all amusing and interesting as it was, did not fail to fatigue us a little.

Wednesday, June the 26th. The whole day was bad, the weather always windy, the sea always agitated, the wind always contrary, so that we made but little way. My friend M. Gallaudet always indisposed, and all my companions melancholy. Indeed, all that were well were wearisome. Moreover, how much we wished to be in New York, but we ought to have patience. . . .

I talked a little with M. Wilder. We spoke at first of *Proctor*[1] and afterwards of marriage. He asked me if I should like to marry a deaf and dumb lady, handsome, young, virtuous, pious and amiable. I answered him that it would give me much pleasure but that a deaf and dumb gentleman and a lady suffering the same misfor-

---

1. Perhaps the title of a book.

tune could not be companions for each other, and that consequently a lady endowed with the sense of hearing and with the gift of speech was and ought to be preferable and indispensable to a deaf and dumb person.[2] Mr. Wilder replied nothing, but I am sure that he found my argument just.

Thursday, June the 27th. Conversation Between M. Gallaudet and Myself

M. Gallaudet: At what age do you think it will be best to admit the deaf and dumb into our institution?

I: You can admit at all ages those who will pay their board, because they will be able to remain there as long as they may wish. For those who may be at the expense of the Government, I think that it will be best not to admit them, except at ten years of age.

I: How long a time do you think that the Government will grant to the deaf and dumb persons who may be at its expense?

[Gallaudet]: I shall endeavor to have them continue 7 or 8 years. The children of the rich can stay longer. I shall write some few directions for parents who have deaf and dumb children, that they may teach them the alphabet and the names of material things before they come to us. What do you think of this? I mean for such as cannot be sent to us when young.

I: But if the children are ten years of age, the parents can send them immediately. If, on the contrary, the children are too young, that is, if they are 6 or 7 or 8 or 9 years of age, what you have just said will produce a good effect.

Saturday, June 29th. I presented my blotted paper to him with the same fearfulness which a scholar feels when he shows his lesson to

---

2. Since Clerc married Eliza Boardman, a deaf woman, two years later, his views on this subject would clearly change.

his master. In correcting my English, M. Gallaudet told me that I
began to make fewer faults than formerly, and that if I continued
to apply myself faithfully, in a short time I should not make any
more.

Tuesday, July the 2nd. I have forgotten to say in the beginning of
my journal that we have in our ship different species of living
animals for our daily nourishment, among which are six hogs, several ducks and several cocks and hens. We have also some canary
birds to tickle the ears of the passengers by the agreeable sound of
their singing. Ah well!! After dinner I was told that one was now
going to kill a hog. In truth, I saw two strong sailors seize the poor
animal by his feet, throw him down and thrust a large knife in his
neck. The blood flew and gushed—such a spectacle caused too
much pain.

Wednesday, July the 3rd. I . . . relaxed my mind in talking a moment
with M. Cowperthwaite:

M. Cowperthwaite: How long do you expect to stay in America,
   should you be so fortunate as to arrive there safely?

Answer: I hope to stay there three years. Then I shall return to
   France.[3] The time hangs heavy upon me here. I wish much to
   arrive at New York.

M. Cowperthwaite: How long have you been studying the English
   language?

Answer: I knew almost nothing before my departure from Havre.
   I had neglected to learn English when I went to London.

M. Cowperthwaite: I have seen your journal and I think that you

---

3. Again, Clerc would alter his plans. He remained in the United
States the rest of his life, returning to France for visits on three occasions.

make great progress. You have a very good instructor in M. Gallaudet.

Friday, July the 19th. Fair weather, a calm and peaceful sea, but not a breath of wind and consequently not the least progress. . . .

Thursday, August the 8th. Oh, great joy among us all! We are told that we are approaching America that if the wind continues we shall be in sight of New York in two days at latest. May God grant that this hope may be realized! But whatsoever He may please to command, we are all disposed to resign ourselves to His orders, and whatsoever may happen, I shall mention it tomorrow.

The end.

First Speech in America

In early September 1816, Clerc, Gallaudet, and Mason Cogswell (Alice's father) traveled to Boston to seek financial support for the proposed school. Clerc wrote the following address, which was read to an audience of civic leaders at the courthouse. He composed this speech just months after he began to study English seriously.

Gentlemen—you know the motive which has led me to the United States of America. The public papers have taught you it; but you do not yet know, I believe, the reason why I have come to Boston with Mr. Gallaudet and Dr. Cogswell, and why we have invited you to honor this meeting with your presence.

It is to speak to you more conveniently of the deaf and dumb, of those unfortunate beings who, deprived of the sense of hearing and consequently of that of speech, would be condemned all their *life* to the most sad vegetation if nobody came to their succor, but who entrusted to our regenerative hands, will pass from the class of brutes to the class of men.

It is to affect your hearts with regard to their unhappy state, to excite the sensibility and solicit the charity of your generous souls in their favor; respectfully to entreat you to occupy yourselves in promoting their future happiness. . . .

I was about twelve years old when I arrived at the Abbé Sicard's school. I was endowed with considerable intelligence, but nevertheless I had no idea of intellectual things. I had it is true a mind, but it did not think; I had a heart, but it did not feel.[4]

My mother, affected at my misfortune, had endeavored to show me the heavens and to make me know God, imagining that I understood her, but her attempts were vain; I could comprehend nothing. I believed that God was a tall, big and strong man, and that Jesus Christ having come to kill us, had been killed by us, and placed on a cross as one of our triumphs.

I believed many other droll and ridiculous things; but as one cannot recollect what passed in his infancy, I cannot describe them. I am sure that the deaf and dumb who are in your country, think as I once did. You must be so kind as to aid us to undeceive them. We shall cultivate their minds and form their hearts; but as the mind and heart cannot live without the body, you will have the goodness to charge yourselves, with your other countrymen, with the support of their bodies. In Europe, each nation, however small, has an institution for the deaf and dumb, and most of these institutions are at the expense of the government. Will America remain the only nation which is insensible to the cry of humanity?[5] I hope not, gentlemen; I hope that you will busy yourselves

---

4. Clerc embellishes the facts to call attention to the momentous effect that education had upon him; of course he could think and feel before he attended school.

5. With this appeal to his audience's national pride, Clerc sets a rhetorical example that subsequent deaf authors would follow.

with the same zeal as your neighbors, the good inhabitants of Connecticut. If the deaf and dumb become happy, it will be your joy to see that it is the effect of your generosity, and they will preserve the remembrance of it as long as they live, and your reward will be heaven.

Responding to Questions from the Audience

In November 1816, Clerc and Gallaudet traveled to Albany, New York, to raise funds for the proposed school for deaf students. Clerc gave a short address in the capitol to legislators, prominent citizens, and people from all over the state. Afterwards they asked him many questions. Gallaudet translated these into sign language, and Clerc wrote his answers upon a chalkboard.

Q: What is truth?

A: It is the conformity of an action with its fact, of what we say with what we have seen, or heard, or learned.

Q: How would you communicate the knowledge of God to a person deaf and dumb?

A: First, we will give them the knowledge of sensible objects, then pass to intellectual, and thence to the Supreme intelligence.

Q: What is the difference between religion and morality?

A: Religion is belief that there is a God in the world, and all the worship due to him. Morality has reference to manners & contains whatever is due from man to man, and whatever is enjoined by human laws & such as gain human esteem.

Q: Is there any universal language founded upon the principles of human nature? If so in your opinion, what is it?

A: The language of signs is universal, and as simple as nature herself. I think those who can gesticulate can be understood everywhere they go.[6]

Q: What is the difference in the manners and habits of the people of this country and those of the French people?

A: Your manners and habits seem to me more regular and simple, and consequently more salutary. Those of the French, though less regular and less constant, are nevertheless more elegant and polite, but you improve more and more every day and I hope you will be quite equal to them in a few years.

[*Editor's Note:* At a similar meeting in Philadelphia, more questions were asked.]

Q: By what means do you judge whether the operations of your mind are similar to those of persons who can hear and speak?

A: I can express my own ideas by writing, and as what I write is what you speak, I can judge that I possess the same faculties of mind as you do.[7]

Q: What are your ideas of music, and of sound in general?

---

6. Clerc's assertion that sign language is universal is typical of this period. He and other commentators seemed to include basic gestures and mime, which are universally intelligible, in their definition of sign language. However, actual American Sign Language, like other signed languages, has its own vocabulary, syntax, and structure, and thus is not readily comprehensible. For more on the romanticization of sign language as universal, see Douglas Baynton, *Forbidden Signs: American Culture and the Campaign Against Sign Language* (Chicago: University of Chicago Press, 1996).

7. Clerc's remark points to the crucial role that writing played in enabling deaf people to prove their intelligence and humanity to mainstream society.

A: I have no accurate idea of everything which relates to the sense
    of hearing, but if I may judge from what I have been told &
    what I have read, I may say that music is a concert of various
    sounds, emanated either from the voice or from some instru-
    ment, and which form a most agreeable harmony for the per-
    sons endowed with the sense of hearing. Sound is the feeling
    of the organs of hearing struck and moved by the agitation of
    clinking bodies, and which are causing an agreeable or dis-
    agreeable sensation on the ear.

Address to the Connecticut Legislature

*On May 28, 1818, Clerc and Gallaudet conducted a public exhibition
of their students before the governor of Connecticut, both houses of the
state legislature, and various citizens. Clerc prepared an address that
Thomas Hopkins Gallaudet read to the audience. An edited version appears below.*

Ladies and Gentlemen,

The kind concern which you were pleased to take in our public exhibition of last year, and the wish which you have had the
goodness to express, to see it renewed, have induced me to com-
ply with the request of the Directors of the Asylum, to deliver this
address. . . .

The language of signs . . . ought to fix the attention of every
enlightened man who makes it his study to improve the various
parts of public instruction; this language, as simple as nature, is
capable of extending itself like her, and of attaining the farthest
limits of human thought.[8] This language of signs is universal, and

---

8. In the preceding section, which does not appear here due to
space limitations, Clerc had discussed the history of deaf education in
France and the limits of oralism. On the purported universality of sign,
see note 6, p. 12.

the Deaf and Dumb of whatever country they may be, can understand each other as well as you who hear and speak, do among
yourselves. But they cannot understand you: it is for this reason
that we wish to instruct them, that they may converse with you
by writing, in the room of speech, and know the truths and mysteries of religion. . . . The arts and sciences belong to the mass of
physical or intellectual objects; and the Deaf and Dumb, like men
gifted with all their senses, may penetrate them according to the
degree of intelligence which nature has granted them, as soon as
they have reached the degree of instruction which Mr. Sicard's
system of teaching, embraces and affords.

Now, Ladies and Gentlemen, if you will take the pains of reflecting ever so little upon the excessive difficulties which this
mode of instruction presents, without cessation, you will not believe, as many people in this country do, that a few years are sufficient in order that a Deaf and Dumb person may be restored to
society, and so acquainted with religion as to partake of it with
benefit, and to render an account to himself of the reasons of his
faith. You will notice that the language of any people cannot be
the mother tongue of the Deaf and Dumb, born amidst these people. Every spoken language is necessarily a learned language for
these unfortunate Beings.[9] The English language must be taught
to the Deaf and Dumb, as the Greek or Latin is taught in the
Colleges to the young Americans who attend the classes of this
kind. Now, will you, Ladies and Gentlemen, give yourselves the
trouble of interrogating the professors of the Colleges, and asking
them the time required to put a pupil in a state to understand fully
the Greek and Latin authors, and to write their thoughts in either
of these languages, so as to make them understood by those who
would speak these languages, then you would agree with me that

---

9. By telling the audience that spoken languages, even in written
form, are necessarily foreign languages to congenitally deaf people, Clerc
introduces a theme in evidence throughout this collection.

the Greek or Latin would not be more difficult to be taught to the Deaf and Dumb, than the English; and yet to teach the Greek and Latin in colleges, the professors and pupils have, for a means of comparison, a language at hand, an acquired language, a mother tongue, which is the English language, in which they have learned to think: whereas the unfortunate Deaf and Dumb, in order to learn English, have not any language with which to compare it, nor any language in which they may have had the habit of thinking. These unfortunate have for their native language but a few gestures, to express their usual wants, and the most familiar actions of life. . . . I have the pleasure to inform you that the Deaf and Dumb of this country have very good natural talents, a great facility, and an unusual ardor in learning, and an intensity of application, which we have rather to moderate than to excite. . . .[10] From five to seven years only is the time we wish they may pass with us (especially if they come to the Asylum young), that they may truly improve in all the common branches of useful knowledge, after so painful and so hard a course of study, and that their teachers may see with satisfaction, that they have not sowed on the sand.

What must I think of the vain presage which some people draw from certain accidents, purely fortuitous! I compare these birds of good or bad augury, who imagine that the sight of Deaf and Dumb persons multiply them,[11] with those weak minds who fear beginning a journey on a Friday, or who believe that the meeting of a weasel, the overthrowing of a salt-box, and the salt

---

10. Clerc's belief in deaf people's capabilities challenges the conventional assumptions of the period. With the student exhibition following this address, he supported his claims with tangible evidence.

11. This superstition demonstrates how the schools helped to make deaf Americans more visible in society. When deaf people lived apart from each other, they were often hidden from view. Once they came together and signed in public, they became much more noticeable. Hearing observers must have wondered from where so many deaf people had suddenly appeared.

spread on the table, bring an ill-luck; or who fear hobgoblins, or who say that when there are thirteen persons at table, one of them is to die in the course of the year!

Every creature, every work of God, is admirably well made; but if any one appears imperfect in our eyes, it does not belong to us to criticize it. Perhaps that which we do not find right in its kind, turns to our advantage without being able to perceive it.[12] Let us look at the state of the heavens, one while the sun shines, another time it does not appear; now the weather is fine; again it is unpleasant; one day is hot, another is cold; another time it is rainy, snowy or cloudy; every thing is variable and inconstant. Let us look at the surface of the earth: here the ground is flat; there it is hilly and mountainous; in other place it is sandy; in others it is barren; and elsewhere it is productive. Let us, in thought, go into an orchard or forest. What do we see? Trees high or low, large or small, upright or crooked, fruitful or unfruitful. Let us look at the birds of the air, and at the fishes of the sea, nothing resembles another thing. Let us look at the beasts. We see among the same kinds some of the different forms, of different dimensions, domestic or wild, harmless or ferocious, useful or useless, pleasing or hideous. Some are bred for men's sakes; some for their own pleasures and amusements; some are of no use to us. There are faults in their organization as well as in that of men. Those who are acquainted with the veterinary art know this well: but as for us who have not made a study of this science, we seem not to discover or remark these faults. Let us now come to ourselves. Our intellectual faculties as well as our corporeal organization have their imperfections. There are faculties both of the mind and heart, which education improve; there are others which it does not correct. I class in this number idiotism, imbecility, dullness.

---

12. By suggesting that deafness could turn out to be an advantage, Clerc again questions traditional assumptions about deaf peoples' inferiority.

But nothing can correct the infirmities of the bodily organization, such as deafness, blindness, lameness, palsy, crookedness, ugliness. The sight of a beautiful person does not make another so likewise, a blind person does not render another blind. Why then should a deaf person make others so also: Why are we Deaf and Dumb? Is it from the difference of our ears? But our ears are like yours, is it that there may be some infirmity? But they are as well organized as yours. Why then are we Deaf and Dumb? I do not know, as you do not know why there are infirmities in your bodies, nor why there are among the human kind, white, black, red and yellow men. The Deaf and Dumb are everywhere, in Asia, in Africa, as well as in Europe and America. They existed before you spoke of them and before you saw them. I have read, in a certain account of Turkey, that the great Sultan knowing not what to do with the Deaf and Dumb of his empire, employed the most intelligent among them in playing pantomime before his Highness. The forty-two Deaf and Dumb, who are here present, except four or six, had never seen each other besides themselves.[13] Their parents probably imagined the same. It is not then the sight of them which can have produced them. I think our deafness proceeds from an act of Providence, I would say, from the will of God, and does it imply that the Deaf and Dumb are worse than other men? Perhaps if we heard, we might have heard much evil, and perhaps blasphemed the holy name of our Creator, and of course hazarded the loss of our soul when departing this life. We therefore cannot but thank God for having made us Deaf and Dumb, hoping that in the future world, the reason of this may be explained to us all.

The Bible, however, says that the doors of Heaven will be opened to no one, unless he has fulfilled the conditions imposed by Jesus Christ. If then, when the uneducated Deaf and Dumb appear before the supreme tribunal, they are found not to have

---

13. An indication of how isolated many deaf Americans were before the advent of deaf education.

fulfilled these conditions, they may plead: "Lord, we wished to learn to know you and to do what you had ordered; but it did not depend upon us. Our mind was buried in the deepest darkness, and no man raised or contributed to raise the veil which covered it, although it was in his power!"[14] But let us hope, Ladies and Gentlemen, that this will not be the case. You are at peace with all the powers of Europe, and nothing abroad requires any sacrifice of your finances. May this happy state of things, therefore, while it permits you to improve the agriculture and manufactures of your country, allow you at the same time to improve the welfare of some hundred individuals among your fellow-citizens! Doubtless you ought to use a wise economy in the distribution of the succor, for which the unfortunate sue from the national equity; doubtless you ought to refuse your charity to any establishment which, soliciting benevolence, would be a servant rather to pride than to humanity; doubtless you would have deserved well of your country by stopping with firmness, the first impulses of the sensibility of those among you who are ready to yield to pageantry and magnificence, that which ought to be granted only to the most urgent needs. But are these truths applicable to an establishment of a nature like ours? I believe I can deny it. About one hundred Deaf and Dumb [live] in the State of Connecticut, included in the two thousand spread over all parts of the United States, the greatest portion of whom are born in the bottom of indigence, and reduced to the most miserable condition, all deprived of the charms of society, all unacquainted with the benefit of religion, all more to be pitied than those who are bound by pure instinct, and holding nothing from man but the faculty of more lively feeling, ought

---

14. Clerc's appeal to Christian charity conforms to the religious environment of the time. Like Gallaudet, he calls on citizens to support the American Asylum so deaf people can learn the Gospel and be saved. In this way, he presents the school not only as the site of education and socialization, but also of Christian redemption.

they then to be still longer neglected, eternally forgotten! They suspect, doubtless, all the extent of the deprivation they experience; every day they lament their unhappiness; but this is invisible, and the comfortable voice of reason neither comes to soften the rigor of their fate, nor alleviate the weight of their misfortune. Yet do not they form, like yourselves, a part of human kind? Are not the unhappy authors of their existence, Americans like yourselves? On account of having not penetrated our benevolent views, some persons, instead of casting a kind look upon those poor Beings, rose against our project, but we are persuaded that their hearts belied their attempt, and that even at the moment in which they thought of opening their lips to remove from the great human family, Beings whom every thing commands you to introduce therein, their arms were involuntarily opened to carry them back to it.

An uneducated Deaf and Dumb is a natural man who attributes the whole good which he sees others do, to the personal interest which governs them; who supposes in others, all the vices which he finds in his own soul. Often prone to suspicion, he exaggerates the evil which he sees, and fears always to be the victim of those who are stronger than himself.

While casting your eyes on so afflicting a picture, do you not, Ladies and Gentlemen, feel a strong wish, that the art of instructing Beings as unhappy as the Deaf and Dumb, may receive all possible encouragement? Ah! what among the branches of your knowledge deserves more to interest Government and literary bodies of men, devoted by their profession, to patronize all that can render men better and happier.

One institution for them, in New England, would produce the most satisfactory result, and answer all your future expectations. In coming, thus, to lay our pretensions before so enlightened an assembly as this, we have not suffered ourselves to disguise the fact, that we should have for judges, persons to be regarded for their various and extensive information; but the desire of en-

riching our method of instruction with your observation has surmounted the fears which we had, at first, conceived. And we
presume to reckon the more on your indulgence, as the progress
of our pupils, which you are about to witness, are the fruits of
only one year's labor, and of the most constant and assiduous application.

Letter to Frederick A. P. Barnard

*In 1835, Frederick A. P. Barnard wrote to Clerc asking some complex
questions about deafness, language, and psychology. Only twenty-six
years old, Barnard had become interested in deafness several years before,
when he began losing his hearing while an undergraduate at Yale College.*[15] *Clerc wrote the following response.*

Dear Sir,

I received your letter just a week ago. Sickness in two
members of my family, Mrs. C. & Elizabeth,[16] impelled
me to lay it aside till the state of their health became less
alarming. Now I am happy to say that they both appear to
be out of danger, and I will not delay the answer which
you so much desire. . . .

I will . . . confine myself to answer the questions in
your letter, viz:

---

15. Since losing his hearing, Barnard had learned sign language,
taught briefly at the New York Institution, and published articles on deaf
education. He would go on to have a distinguished career, becoming a
noted scientist, the president of the University of Mississippi, and, later,
the president of Columbia University in New York City. As such, Barnard was the first deaf college president in America.

16. Clerc's wife and daughter.

Q: Do you habitually think in English, in French, or in the language of action?

A: I habitually think in English, and that, in the order of words in the English language. The reason is that being in a country where the language is daily spoken, I have acquired this habit. n.b. I habitually thought in French before I knew English and since I knew English, I continued for three or four years to think in French while writing in English or spelling on the fingers; that is, I translated French thoughts into English. Afterwards, I gradually acquired the habit of thinking in English, although I occasionally had recourse to the French to assist me.

Q: Can you, at will, adopt either of these modes of thoughts?

A: Yes, certainly—but separately & not at once.

Q: Do you find that you are able to think more clearly or more rapidly & more satisfactorily by means of signs than by that of words?

A: By means of signs. The reason is that I have plenty of signs at my command to express whatever I think, whereas I want words to describe it. I can then say with propriety that I want words to express signs, as you sometimes want words to express or describe feelings of gratitude, admiration, wonder or horror.[17]

Q: Do you learn to see words before you when you employ them as the instrument of thought, & if so, how? As written, printed, or spelled on the fingers?

---

17. Clerc shows again that sign language, rather than written French or English, is his most effective means of communication.

A: I do not always find words ready, but in general I seem to see them before me. As soon as I have sought them in my mind, in order to employ them, they usually present themselves as written, when I take up paper, or printed, when I open a book, but never as spelled on the fingers.

Q: Does your habit of thought accommodate itself to the circumstances in which you imagine yourself placed, & the individual with whom you think of conversing; that is: Do you think in signs when you imagine your-self before your deaf, & in words when you seem to be holding conversation with some servant?

A: Generally my habit of thought does accommodate it-self very readily, for when before my class, this idea which I have that they are deaf & dumb like myself, immediately leads me to think in signs if I have any thing to tell them in this way, & in words if it be my wish to have them put it in written language; and when before some servant with whom I am going to hold conversation, I usually think in words. I could not do otherwise.

I am afraid, my dear sir, that I have misunderstood some of your questions, & am aware that I have not ex-actly answered your expectations; but this is so puzzling a subject, that I am glad to dismiss it and to refer you to any other D[eaf] & D[umb] opinions more deeply versed in the sciences of metaphysics and logic than is yours truly.

LC

Autobiographical Sketch

In 1851, Clerc was asked to write a brief account of his life for inclusion in a book honoring Gallaudet, who had recently died. Clerc produced the following narrative.

I was born in LaBalme, Canton of Cremieu, Department of Isoro, on the 26th of December, 1785. The village of LaBalme lies twenty-six miles east of Lyons, on the east side of the Rhône, and is noted for its grotto, called "Latrottee de Notre Dame de la Balme." My father, Joseph Francis Clerc, a notary public by profession, was the mayor of the place from 1780 to 1814. My mother, Elizabeth Candy, was the daughter of Mr. Candy, of Cremieu, also a notary public. My father died in April, 1816, and my mother in May, 1818.

When I was about a year old, I was left alone for a few moments on a chair by the fireside, and it happened, I know not how, that I fell into the fire, and so badly burned my right cheek that the scar of it is still visible; and my parents were under the impression that this accident deprived me of my senses of hearing and smelling. When I was seven years, my mother hearing that a certain physician in Lyons could cure deafness, took me thither. The doctor, after examining my ears, said he thought he could make me hear, provided I would call at his office twice a day for a fortnight. My mother agreed to take me, so we called regularly every day and the doctor injected into my ears I do not know what liquids, but I did not derive any benefit whatever from the operation. And at the expiration of the fortnight, I returned home with my mother still as deaf as I was before.

I passed my childhood at home, in doing nothing but running about and playing with other children. I sometimes drove my mother's turkeys to the field or her cows to pasture, and occasionally my father's horse to the watering place. I was never taught to write or to form the letters of the alphabet; nor did I ever go to school; for there were no such school-houses or academies in our villages as we see everywhere in New England.

At the age of about twelve, that is, in 1797, my father being unable to absent himself from home on account of the duties of his office, at his earnest request, my uncle, Laurent Clerc, took me to Paris, and the next day I was placed in the Institution for the Deaf and Dumb. I did not see the Abbé Sicard, but I learned afterward that he was in prison for a political offense.[18] Mr. Massieu, deaf and dumb like myself, was my first teacher, and when the Abbé Sicard was set at liberty and had resumed the superintendence of the Institution, he took me into his class, and I was with him ever after.

Out of school hours, the Abbé Margaron, one of the assistant teachers, taught me to articulate together with a few other pupils. We learned to articulate pretty well all the letters of the alphabet, and many words of one and two or three syllables; but I had much difficulty to pronounce *da* and *la, de* and *do* and *to*, &c., and although Mr. Margaron made me repeat these words again and again, I succeeded no better. One day he became so impatient, and gave me so violent a blow under my chin, that I bit my tongue, and I felt so chagrined that I would try to learn to speak no longer.[19]

I applied myself to other things. I learned to draw and to compose in the printing office of the Institution till 1805, when I was employed as a tutor on trial, and in 1806 appointed a teacher with a salary of about two hundred dollars. In process of time, Mr. Sicard thought me capable of teaching the highest class, and I occupied that place when Mr. Gallaudet came to Paris. . . .

It was at the close of one of our public lectures that Mr. Gallaudet was introduced to me for the first time by Mr. Sicard, to whom he had previously been introduced by a member of parliament. We cordially shook hands with him, and on being told who he was, where he came from, and for what purpose, and on being

---

18. The Abbé Roch Ambroise Sicard (1742–1822) was the director of the National Institute for the Deaf in Paris and Clerc's teacher. Like many priests, he repeatedly had trouble with the French revolutionary government because he declined to take the oath of civil allegiance, which was required by the legislature but forbidden by the pope.

19. This moving anecdote helps further to explain Clerc's ardent belief in sign language over oralism.

further informed of the ill success of his mission in England, we earnestly invited him to come to Paris, assuring him that every facility would be afforded him to see our Institution and attend our daily lessons. He accepted the invitation, and said he would come in the ensuing spring. We did not see him any more, as we left London soon afterward. In the spring of 1816, according to his promise, he came to Paris, and glad were we to see him again. He visited our Institution almost every day. He began by attending the lowest class, and from class to class, he came to mine which, as mentioned above, was the highest. I had, therefore, a good opportunity of seeing and conversing with him often, and the more I saw him, the more I liked him; his countenance and manners pleased me greatly. He frequented my school-room, and one day requested me to give him private lessons of an hour every day. I could receive him but three times a week, in my room upstairs in the afternoon, and he came with punctuality, so great was his desire of acquiring the knowledge of the language of signs in the shortest time possible. I told him, nevertheless, that however diligent he might be, it would require at least six months to get a tolerably good knowledge of signs, and a year for the method of instruction so as to be well qualified to teach thoroughly. He said he feared it would not be in his power to stay so long, and that he would reflect, and give me his final decision by and by. In the mean time, he continued coming to receive his lesson, and we spoke no more of "how long he would stay" till the middle of May, when taking a favorable opinion, he intimated to me that he wished very much he could obtain a well educated deaf and dumb young man to accompany him to America. I named two young deaf and dumb men who had left our Institution a few years since, that I know would suit him, as they both had some knowledge of the English language, whereas I had none at all; but he answered that he had already made his choice, and that I was the person he preferred. Greatly astonished was I, for I had not the least expectation that I should be thought of. After a short pause, I said I would not hesitate to go if I could do it properly. I suggested to him the idea of speaking or writing to the Abbé Sicard on the subject, as I considered myself engaged to the Abbé. He said he would write, and accordingly wrote; but although his letter was never answered, we both inferred that Mr. Sicard's silence was rather favorable than otherwise. But in order to ascertain his views, I was requested to sound him. Accordingly I called and inquired in the most respectful manner whether he had received Mr. G's letter, and if so, what answer he had returned. I received but an evasive answer to my question; for he abruptly asked me why I wished to part with him. My reply was simply this, that I could without much inconvenience leave him for a few years without loving him the less for it, and that I had a great desire to see the world, and especially to make my unfortunate fellow-being on the other side of the Atlantic, participate in the same benefits of education that I had myself received from him. He seemed to appreciate my feelings; for after some further discussions on both sides, he finished by saying that he would give his consent, provided I also obtained the consent of my mother, my father being dead. I said I would ask her, if he would permit me to go home. He said I might. Accordingly I made my preparations and started for Lyons on the 1st of June, after having promised Mr. Gallaudet to return a few days before the appointed time for our voyage. I thought I was going to agreeably surprise my dear mother, for she never imagined, poor woman, that I could come to see her, except during my vacation, which usually took place in September; but I was myself much more surprised when, on my arrival, she told me she knew what I had come for, and on my inquiring what it was she handed me a letter she had received from Mr. Sicard the preceding day. On reading it, I found that the good Abbé Sicard had altered his mind, and written to dissuade my mother from giving her consent; saying he "could not spare me!" Accordingly my mother urged me hard to stay in France, but to no purpose, for I told her that my resolution was taken, and that nothing could make me change it. She gave her consent with much reluctance, and said she would pray God every day for my safety, through the intercession of La Sainte Vierge. I bade herself, my brother and sisters and friends, adieu, and was back in Paris on the 12th of June, and the next day, after having taken an affectionate leave of the good Abbé Sicard, who had been like a father to me, I went also to bid my pupils good-by, and there took place a painful scene I can never forget. A favorite pupil of mine, the young Polish Count Alexander de Machwitz, a natural son of the Emperor Alexander,[20] whom I knew to be much attached to me, came over to me and with tears in his eyes, took hold of me, saying he would not let me depart, scolding me, at the same time, for having so long kept a secret my intention to go away. I apologized as well as I could, assuring him that I had done so because I thought it best. However, he still held me so fast in his arms, so that I had to struggle to disentangle myself from him, and having floored him without hurting him, I made my exit, and the day following, the 14th of June, I was *en route* for Havre, with Mr. Gallaudet and our much honored friend, S. V. S. Wilder, Esq., who, I am happy to say, is still alive, and now resides some where in Greenwich, in this state. On the 18th of June, in the afternoon, we embarked on board the ship *Mary Augusta*, Captain Hall, and arrived at New York on the 9th of August, 1810, in the morning.

---

20. Czar Alexander I (1777–1825), the ruler of Russia, was deaf in one ear and, as he grew older, lost some hearing in the other. He had a long affair with the Princess Marie Antonova Naryshkina, who was born in Poland and lived in Russia as the wife of a prosperous prince. Naryshkina gave birth in 1803 and 1804; either of these children could have been the deaf student Clerc mentions here. However, scholars do not agree on whether these children were fathered by the czar or by one of Naryshkina's other lovers, so we cannot confirm or deny Clerc's claim that Count Machwitz was the czar's natural son. See Harlan Lane, *When the Mind Hears: A History of the Deaf* (New York, Vintage, 1984), 156, 433 n. 2.

Owing to adverse winds and frequent calms which usually occur at sea in the summer season, our passage lasted fifty-two days. It was rather long, but on the whole, the voyage was pleasant. A part of our time on board was usefully employed. I taught Mr. Gallaudet the method of the signs for abstract ideas, and he taught me the English language. I wrote my journal, and as I thought in French rather than in English, I made several laughable mistakes in the construction of my sentences, which he corrected; so that being thus daily occupied, I did not find the time to fall very heavily upon me. We formed plans for the success of the institution we were going to establish; we made arrangements for the journeys we expected to undertake for the collection of funds; we reformed certain signs which we thought would not well suit American manners and customs.

The weather was fair when we landed. Our first stops were directed to the store of Messrs. Wilder & Co., in Pearl street, thence to the customhouse, and thence we proceeded to the house of Mr. Gallaudet's father, in John street. I anticipated much pleasure in witnessing his joy at again seeing his parents, brothers and sisters after so long an absence; but I must acknowledge that I was rather disappointed; for I did not see any greater demonstration of welcome on both sides than the mere shaking of hands; little was I aware, at that time, of the difference between the French and American mode of saluting, especially with respect to the ladies. We stayed about ten days in New York. We met, or rather we called on several gentlemen of Mr. Gallaudet's acquaintance, who gave me a cordial welcome to America.

My first impression of the city was admiration of Broadway which appeared to me to be the finest street in the world, and my astonishment was great at seeing so much bustle in the streets, people in so great a hurry and walking so fast.

My second impression was the wearisomeness which the uniformity produced. Men, streets, squares, buildings, every thing was alike; all looked well, nothing appeared magnificent. I noticed neatness without elegance, riches without taste, beauty without gracefulness. I found that the happiness of the Americans was at their firesides with their wives, children and friends. They had few amusements, few spectacles and very few sublime objects capable of arresting the attention of a European; and such a one could not easily appreciate the extent of the private happiness of a people who were secure and not poor.

At length, we left New York for New Haven, where we made a short tarry, which I wished had been much longer; for I found it a delightful place. We called on President Dwight and some of the professors, who welcomed us.[21] We visited the college, the library and chapel. The next day, it being very pleasant, we took the stage for Hartford, where we arrived in the afternoon of the 22nd of August, 1810. We alighted at Dr. Cogswell's in Prospect street.[22] We found Mrs. Cogswell alone at home with her daughters, excepting Alice, who was then at school under Miss Lydia Huntley (now Mrs. Sigourney, our lovely poetess).[23] She was immediately sent for, and when she made her appearance, I beheld

---

21. Timothy Dwight (1752–1822), a well-known clergyman, was then near the end of his twenty-two-year term as president of Yale University.

22. Dr. Mason Fitch Cogswell (1761–1830) was a prominent surgeon and civic leader in Hartford whose daughter, Alice, was deaf. A strong supporter of deaf education, he developed a network of political and financial support to send Thomas Hopkins Gallaudet to Europe and, later, to help found the American Asylum.

23. Lydia (Huntley) Sigourney (1791–1865) was Alice's teacher in a public school while Gallaudet was in Europe learning about deaf education. She went on to become a popular poet, producing pious, sentimental verse that appealed to mid-nineteenth-century Americans. In 1853, she fondly recalled that Alice "was the darling of all." She wrote, "I was indebted to her for a new idea, that the hand and eye possessed an eloquence which had been heretofore claimed as the exclusive privilege of the tongue." See Lydia H. Sigourney, *Letters to My Pupils: With Narrative and Biographical Sketches* (New York: Robert Carter and Brothers, 1853), 251, 253.

a very interesting little girl. She had one of the most intelligent countenances I ever saw. I was much pleased with her. We conversed by signs, and we understood each other very well; so true is it, as I have often mentioned before, that the language of signs is universal and as simple as nature.[24] I had left many persons and objects in France endeared to me by association, and America, at first, seemed uninteresting and monotonous, and I sometimes regretted leaving my native land; but on seeing Alice, I had only to recur to the object which had induced me to seek these shores, to contemplate the good we were going to do, and sadness was subdued by an approving conscience. . . .

On the 15th of April, 1817, our school was opened with seven pupils, in the south part of the building now the City Hotel, and on the 20th, Mr. Gallaudet delivered an appropriate sermon on the occasion in the Rev. Dr. Strong's church.[25] In January, 1818, I visited Washington [D.C.] with the late Mr. Henry Hudson, to ascertain whether we could hope to obtain something from Congress for our Asylum. I attended the House of Representatives, and the Hon. Henry Clay, who was the speaker, politely offered me a seat beside him.[26] There was a recess of half an hour, and I conversed with several members of Congress, both in English and French. Afterward I visited the Senate chamber. The next day I had the honor of being introduced to President Monroe[27] at the

---

24. Clerc presumably used a lot of pantomime and gestures to communicate with Alice, who of course did not know formal sign language at the time.

25. Dr. Nathan Strong, the minister of the Center Church in Hartford, had died shortly before, so Gallaudet preached to the crowded gathering. He spoke on the many potential benefits of the new school.

26. Henry Clay (1777–1852) was a leading member of Congress during much of the first half of the nineteenth century. Later, he visited the American Asylum in Hartford.

27. James Monroe (1758–1831) was president of the United States from 1817 to 1825. He had met Clerc in 1817, when he visited the just-opened American Asylum while on a tour of New England.

White House, by Mr. Hyde de Neuville, the French ambassador, for whom I had a letter of recommendation from the Duke Mathieu de Montmorency.

The President received me with much affability and bade me "welcome to America," and said among other things, that he hoped I would receive great honor and much gratitude by doing good to the deaf and dumb. I carefully preserved the paper containing our conversation, but have mislaid it. I attended one of the levees with the ambassador and Mr. Hudson, and holding a paper and pencil in my hands, I had the pleasure of conversing with gentlemen and ladies.

In the session of 1819–20, thanks to the exertions of both our Connecticut senators and representatives, Congress granted us a township located in the state of Alabama, and President Monroe, with the benevolence which characterized him, readily sanctioned the act with his signature. . . .

In 1830, Mr. Gallaudet resigned his situation as Principal, notwithstanding my supplications that he would not.[28] We had been so intimate, so harmonious, so much attached to each other; we had labored together so many years; that I parted with him with unspeakable grief. . . .

L. Clerc

---

28. Thomas Hopkins Gallaudet (1787–1851), who suffered from illness throughout his life, apparently felt exhausted and unwell in 1830. He petitioned the school board for relief from daily teaching; when that request was denied, he resigned. He went on to write books on religion, help to found a women's seminary, and minister to the mentally ill, among many other activities.

2

JAMES NACK

(1809–1879)

James Nack was one of the first deaf people to publish a book in the United States. Born hearing in New York City on January 4, 1809, he grew up in an impoverished family. His older sister taught him at home, and he could read by age four. When he was eight, he was already showing skill at writing verse and rhyme. That same year, his life suddenly changed. He fell down a staircase and hit his head on a heavy fire screen, which left him unconscious for weeks and totally deaf. In 1818, Nack entered the newly-opened New York Institution for the Instruction of the Deaf and Dumb. He became increasingly interested in poetry, writing a complete tragedy when he was twelve. After leaving school at age fourteen, he began to produce romantic verse. One of these, "The Blue-Eyed Maid," caught the attention of Abraham Asten, a clerk of the city of New York. Asten befriended the boy and found him a job in a lawyer's office. Nack took advantage of the attorney's library, reading numerous books and learning several foreign languages on his own. Asten also introduced the prodigy to some of the city's leading poets and writers, who encouraged him to publish a collection of his work.

Nack's first volume, *The Legend of the Rocks and Other Poems,* appeared in 1827. It contained sixty-eight poems he had written before age eighteen, and received substantial attention. Hearing reviewers marveled at Nack's youth and talent, calling him an "intellectual wonder" and comparing him favorably to the young Lord Byron. The New York *Critic* commended his smooth and harmonious versification, which seemed all the more remarkable because of his deafness. Others praised the feeling in his work and wondered how Nack, as a deaf person "cut off" from society, could write so well about human emotion.[1] Nack became something of a sensation, and his poetry caused readers to reconsider their assumptions about deaf people.

In 1838, Nack married a hearing woman who had been a friend since childhood. They had three daughters. He supplemented his writing career by working as a legal clerk for over thirty years and translating literature from German, French, and Dutch. Nack represented one of the earliest success stories of deaf education in America. Leaders in later years would often cite him as an example of the potential many deaf people have. For example, in his 1854 essay calling for the establishment of a national college for the deaf, John Carlin refers to Nack as proof that "mutes of decided talents can be rendered as good scholars" (see p. 104).

Nack produced four volumes of poetry in all, but perhaps none was quite as influential as his first. His verse is typical of the sentimental style of the period, and may appear imitative and dated today. However, it marked an important step forward for deaf people. Nack showed that deaf authors were capable of producing

---

1. Quoted in Harry G. Lang and Bonnie Meath-Lang, *Deaf Persons in the Arts and Sciences: A Biographical Dictionary* (Westport, Conn.: Greenword Press, 1995), 270.

James Nack

that most difficult form of writing, poetry; he challenged stereotypes the public had about deaf individuals; and he no doubt
helped to inspire subsequent deaf poets like John Burnet (who was
Nack's close friend) and Carlin to write poems and seek to publish
their work.

The excerpt in this chapter is from "The Minstrel Boy," a
long poem of sixty-three stanzas that Nack composed when he
was just sixteen. It is one of his few works that deals directly with
deafness. Nack later wrote that he produced this poem at a time
when he was "peculiarly unhappy." In it, he mourns the loss of
his hearing and implores readers to extend their charity to "heathen" deaf people who do not know the gospel. Contemporary
critics praised it for its emotive power.

The Minstrel Boy

1.

And am I doom'd to be denied forever,
    The blessings that to all around are given?
And shall those links be reunited never
    That bound me to mankind, till they were riven
In childhood's day? Alas, how soon to sever
    From social intercourse, the doom of heaven
Was past upon me! and the hope how vain,
That the decree may be recal'd again!

2.

Amid a throng in deep attention bound,
    To catch the accents that from others fall,
The flow of eloquence—the heav'nly sound
    Breath'd from the soul of melody, while all
Instructed or delighted list around,
    Vacant unconsciousness must *me* enthral!
I can but watch each animated face,
And there attempt th' inspiring theme to trace.

3.

Unheard, unheeded are the lips by *me*,
    To others that unfold some heav'n-born art;—
And melody—Oh dearest melody!
    How had thine accents, thrilling to my heart,
Awaken'd all its strings to sympathy,
    Bidding the spirit at thy magic start!
How had my heart responsive to the strain,
Throb'd in love's wild delight, or soothing pain!

4.

In vain—alas, in vain! thy numbers roll—
    Within my heart no echo they inspire;
Though form'd by nature in thy sweet control
    To melt with tenderness, or glow with fire,
Misfortune clos'd the portals of the soul,
    And till an Orpheus rise to sweep the lyre
That can to animation kindle stone,
To me thy thrilling power must be unknown.

5.

Yet not that every portal of the mind
    Is clos'd against me, I my lot deplore;
Although debar'd by destiny unkind
    From one that never shall be open'd more,
Still from the lot at times relief I find,
    When science, I thy temple stand before,
Whose portal thou hast open'd, to my sight;
The gems displaying there enshrin'd in light.

6.

Blest Science! but for thee what were I now?
    Denied the rights of man, as to employ
Those rights incapable—mankind, if thou
    Hadst not aris'n the barrier to destroy,
No human blessings would to me allow;
    The sensual pleasures which the brutes enjoy
Alone were mine, than brutes a nobler name
Entitled only by my form to claim!

7.

Friends of misfortune's race, whose heart and hand
    Are never clos'd against affliction's prayer,
To heathens can your charity expand!
    Will you to them the gospel tidings bear?
And yet neglect your own, your native land?
    O shall the gospel be a stranger *there*?
Behold the Deaf and Dumb! What heathens need
More eloquently for your aid can plead?[2]

8.

Strangers to God!—And shall they still be so?
    Will you not lift a hand the veil to rend—
Their intellectual eyes to heaven throw,
    And lead them to a father and a friend?
Will you not snatch them from the gulfs of woe,
    To which they else unrescued must descend?
O save them! save them! that the Deaf and Dumb
May bless you in this world, and in the world to come!

---

2. Here Nack echoes not only Laurent Clerc (see p. 10, n. 5, and p. 18, n. 14), but also Thomas Hopkins Gallaudet, who called deaf people "heathen" in an 1824 sermon. It begins: "There are some long-neglected heathen; the poor deaf and dumb, whose sad necessities have been forgotten, while scarce a corner of the world has not been searched to find those who are yet ignorant of Jesus Christ." See Thomas Hopkins Gallaudet, "The Duty and Advantages of Affording Instruction to the Deaf and Dumb," reprinted in *The Deaf and Dumb, or, a Collection of Articles Relating to the Condition of Deaf Mutes,* ed. Edwin Mann (Boston: D. K. Hitchcock, 1836), 217.

3

JOHN BURNET

(1808–1874)

When Thomas Hopkins Gallaudet was sailing to America with Laurent Clerc in 1816, he told Clerc that he wanted to write "some few directions for parents who have deaf and dumb children." Gallaudet apparently never got around to publishing such a manual. That task fell to John Burnet, who composed a detailed essay for parents in which he admonished them not to neglect their deaf children. He explained how they could encourage deaf infants' natural instinct to sign and eventually teach them to read, write, and perhaps articulate. Burnet published the exhortative essay in his book, *Tales of the Deaf and Dumb* (1835). In other chapters, he decried prejudice, presented facts and statistics about deaf people, and offered original poems and stories that (he explained in an afterword) were designed to "awaken . . . an interest on the subject in the bosoms of many." This groundbreaking volume marked the advent of a talented deaf author.

John Robertson Burnet was born on December 26, 1808, in New Jersey. He grew up on his grandparents' farm. At age eight, he caught a fever that completely deafened him. Burnet never received formal schooling; his older sister Rachel educated him at home and he continued learning on his own, reading everything that came his way. When he was fourteen, Burnet's sister and friends began to use the two-handed British manual alphabet to communicate with him, which added to his ability to interact with others. He did not have much luck with speechreading, and his speech was of little use to him, except with those who knew him well. Curious about other deaf people, at age twenty-one Burnet visited the New York Institution for the Instruction of the Deaf and Dumb. There, he encountered sign language for the first time. Fascinated with the language and the deaf community at the school, he decided to apply to become a teacher. He was hired on a trial basis in 1831. However, Burnet was shy, unused to socializing much with others, and not yet skilled in sign or in disciplining students. As a result, he resigned toward the end of the academic year. In 1833 he began helping an uncle edit a Philadelphia newspaper, *The People's Friend*. He also conceived the idea of a book about the deaf community and, using the New York school as his headquarters, began securing subscriptions for it. Many teachers at the school took an interest in the project and encouraged him. *Tales of the Deaf and Dumb* appeared in 1835, when he was just twenty-six years old. The book gave what was easily the most comprehensive overview of deaf Americans to date. It sold well, and Burnet earned enough money from it to pay off his grandfather's debts and assume sole management of the family farm.

In 1839, Burnet married Phebe Osborn, a graduate of the New York school. They adopted a hearing daughter, who delighted her parents by becoming quite proficient in sign language. Over the next decades, Burnet worked on the farm, studied, and continued his literary efforts. A productive author, he regularly published articles in the *American Annals of the Deaf,* the *North American,* and periodicals for deaf readers. He consistently promoted deaf education, both in his writing and by meeting in person with state legislators. Burnet maintained close ties with the

New York Institution for the rest of his life. Tired of physical farm labor, in 1868 he agreed to become a correspondence clerk at the school. Soon thereafter, he accepted a position as a full-time teacher, and he continued teaching for the next six years. In 1871 he received an honorary degree from the National Deaf-Mute College (now Gallaudet University) in recognition of his achievements. He died in 1874.

The writings included here are all from *Tales of the Deaf and Dumb,* Burnet's most influential work. In addition to the essays, there is an excerpt from a long poem, "Emma," which is notable for its positive, unpitying portrayal of a student at a deaf school. The short story, "The Orphan Mute," is probably the first published piece of fiction by a deaf American. Burnet wrote that he was surprised that few, if any, novelists had tried to portray a deaf person, and hoped that his own "humble attempts" would inspire more to do so. "Here," he stated in his afterword, "is an unexplored field, worthy of the genius of a Cooper, or an Irving."

What the Deaf and Dumb Are before Instruction

Of all the long catalogue of infirmities which flesh is heir to, deafness is the one which is least apparent at first sight, and which least affects, directly, the vigor of the bodily or mental faculties, and yet there is no other infirmity, short of the deprivation of reason, which so completely shuts its unfortunate subject out of the Society of his fellows. Yet this is not because the deaf are deprived of a single sense; but because the language of the hearing world is a language of sounds. Their misfortune is not that *they* are deaf and dumb, but that *others* hear and speak. Were the established mode of communication among men, by a language addressed not to the ear, but to the eye, the present inferiority of the deaf would entirely vanish; but at the same time, the mental and social condition of the blind would be far more deplorable, and their education far more impracticable, than that of the deaf is now.[1] It would be as hopeless as that of the deaf, dumb, and blind is at present.

Those who have appealed to public sympathy in behalf of the deaf and dumb, have given highly colored and often exaggerated pictures of their sad condition when abandoned without instruction.[2] That condition is certainly, without exaggeration, sufficiently deplorable; and has in too many cases been rendered far more deplorable by the influence of prejudices, which, not content with shutting out the deaf and dumb from all intellectual enjoyment, have averted from them all the kindly feelings of the human heart, and denied to them an equal measure of civil justice! Superstition has regarded them as beings laboring under the curse of heaven; and the benevolent de l'Epée[3] remarks that, in his time, parents held themselves disgraced by the fact of having a deaf and dumb child, and concealed it from the eyes of the world, to vegetate in a cloister; a lot, compared with which, the customs of those barbarous nations which are said, even at this day, to put them to death as soon as their infirmity is known, would be mercy.

That men should so long have regarded the deaf and dumb as little if any superior to the brute, ought, perhaps, to excite less

---

1. With this example, Burnet suggests that much of deaf people's "inferiority" is socially constructed, that is, more a product of the environment in which they live rather than any biological characteristic.

2. We can perhaps see such exaggeration in the language of nothingness, savagery, and heathenism used to describe uneducated deaf people throughout this volume. As a person who never formally attended school himself, Burnet was perhaps sensitive to such hyperbole, although he, too, occasionally gives in to such rhetorical flourishes.

3. The Abbé Charles-Michel de l'Epée (1712–1789) was a French priest who began teaching deaf people in Paris in the late eighteenth century. A strong proponent of sign language, he helped to popularize deaf education, published numerous treatises, and founded the National Institute for the Deaf, which Laurent Clerc later attended.

surprise than regret, when we consider that the natural and almost inevitable effect of such prejudices is to degrade those who are so unfortunate as to be the objects of them, as low as the image of the Creator is capable of being degraded. It is only when attended to with care, and treated with kindness by those to whose care and kindness providence has committed him, that the deaf mute can be expected to exhibit those proofs of intellectual and moral qualities, which give the lie to prejudices by displaying indisputable traces of the Creator's image. Finding himself, on the contrary, as he too often does, not only neglected, but an object of aversion, marked out by the unanimous consent of the world as a victim at the altar of prejudice, is it strange that the solitary mind of the mute should sink in this unequal struggle? that his unaided faculties should succumb under the mountain heaped on his devoted head? And then, that same *prejudice* whose hand crushed him to the dust, justifies her deed by pointing to the degraded condition to which she has herself reduced him!

We are indeed compelled to deplore the blindness of human nature, when we find even the families which contain deaf and dumb persons affected with such prejudices. The birth of a deaf and dumb child is, under any circumstances, a heavy affliction; but its weight is incalculably increased by the influence of neglect on the character of the child. In such cases the fearful effects of the prejudices or neglect of his friends, recoil, with indeed some show of justice, upon themselves. Nor are the effects of the unrestrained indulgence of misjudging kindness much less deplorable. It is certain that however *unfortunate* the ignorant deaf and dumb may be, they are not so *unhappy* as their families. These last ought to instruct them for their own sakes, if not for less selfish considerations. And, severe as the task may seem, I venture to assert that, as no labor could be better employed, so none would be more richly rewarded.

Still, despite the withering influence of coldness or neglect, the deaf and dumb not unfrequently display most undeniable proofs of intelligence and sensibility. Though compelled to begin, as it were, even at their birth, the world for themselves, and to acquire by their own unaided efforts, all that they can acquire of that intellectual wealth which has been accumulating from generation to generation, and to which hearing children are, as it were, born heirs, they often do acquire a stock of knowledge, which, however scanty when compared with that of those who hear, is truly wonderful when we reflect under what disadvantages it was gleaned. To expect that a solitary mind should acquire a knowledge of all that is useful to know, is to expect that the labors of a solitary bee should fill the hive with honey.

I shall not attempt to give an elaborate dissertation on the character of the deaf and dumb before instruction. It may be sufficient to say that their characters are such as might be expected in minds constituted like our own; but not, like our own, cultivated and corrected.[4] That is, that they display the characteristics of untaught *childhood*; not, as many by a strange propensity to degrade their own species would make us believe, of *apes* or *monkeys*. Such an opinion is not surprising in the vulgar, who are accustomed to think the power of speech the only difference between man and the ape; but we can not repress our surprise and indignation, when we find it gravely asserted and maintained by men, in other respects sensible and intelligent; even by not a few who have aspired to the first rank in Philosophy. It is certain that the deaf mute has received a mind and a heart from nature, in which the seeds of bright talents and warm affections are as frequently implanted, as in the minds and hearts of speaking children; and only need as diligent cultivation to quicken them into as luxuriant growth. There is, therefore, nothing wonderful or mysterious in the art of instructing the deaf and dumb. If instruction has wonderfully improved their mental faculties, it is because those faculties were

---

4. Since Burnet was hearing until age eight, he distinguishes himself from those who are "deaf and dumb."

formed capable of improvement. The teacher can no more create a mind where a mind is wanting, than the workman can manufacture a watch without the steel, the brass, and the silver.

Let the deaf and dumb, then, be regarded as your own brethren, differing from yourselves only in being less instructed, because ignorant of the language of those around them; and ignorant of that language, only because the ear, the great avenue through which language and knowledge is acquired, is, with them, sealed forever; and consequently only requiring to be taught that language under its written form, a form addressing itself to the eye, to enable them to compete with yourselves (except where a knowledge of sound is required), in all the various divisions of the intellectual field.

On the Early Domestic Education of Children Born Deaf

The number of the DEAF AND DUMB, those most unfortunate beings who, by the deficiency of a single sense, seem to have been rendered, in a great measure, outcasts from society, is much greater than any one ventured to suppose. . . . By the census of 1830, the United States then contained six thousand one hundred and six Deaf and Dumb persons, and if this number has increased with the rapid increase of our population, which is very probable, it must now amount to nearly seven thousand. The subject, therefore, of these remarks, namely, the means which even their own parents and friends may successfully use to rescue these unfortunate beings from the ignorant and degraded condition to which they are too often consigned, is not interesting merely to the curious, or to the professed teacher of the Deaf and Dumb. It comes home to the firesides of *five thousand families* in our land; it makes a direct appeal to the *hearts* of *five thousand* mothers; nor is it without interest to all—for no condition or situation in life is exempt from this desolating calamity; and who among my readers can say that their own families may not be so afflicted? . . .

The increasing attention which of late has been paid to the peculiar claims of the Deaf and Dumb, is as pleasing to the philanthropist as it is honorable to the enlightened benevolence of the present age. Only twenty years ago, there was not a single school for the thousands of our own deaf and dumb population, and only about twenty-five for the tens of thousands in Europe. Now there are about *one hundred and thirty* institutions for the Deaf and Dumb in the world. Our own country presents *six* well conducted institutions, which now dispense the blessings of education to about *four hundred and fifty* of our fellow beings who, without education, would be, even in this land of Christianity and civilization, condemned for life to a lot worse than that of the most ignorant savage. . . .

Though so much has been done for them, nothing, at least in this country, has yet been done to remedy this greatest of all their wants. We leave these immortal minds to vegetate for the first twelve or fifteen years in utter darkness, and then we expect to teach them in the space of four or five years, not only all that others acquire by study, but also till that incalculable mass of information which, with those who hear, accumulates in the memory without a sensible effort on their part, not only from the conversations in which they take part, but still more from those daily and hourly remarks to which they are accidental listeners. Were it possible that the thousand active scenes of twenty years could be rehearsed in the school room during five, still how much will the representation fall short of the impressive force of the reality!

Hence it is, and the remark cannot be too emphatically made, that if we would raise the deaf mute to a level with his well educated hearing and speaking brothers and sisters, we must begin his education, like theirs, at home in the family and social circle, and as early as theirs begins; that is, as soon as he is capable of distinguishing the persons and objects around him.

Yet important as this principle is, it is a lamentable fact that
deaf and dumb children receive, for the most part, no education
whatever while they remain at home; and thus their teachers have
to cultivate in their minds, not only a soil untilled, but, as might
naturally be expected, overgrown with weeds and briers.

If, as a distinguished foreign teacher remarks, we must often
blame the *negligence* of parents and relatives, the evil proceeds still
oftener from their ignorance of the proper means to be employed.
. . . No books, however, have yet been published in this country,
from which parents could learn what ought to be done and what
has been successfully done in similar cases; to supply, in some measure, this great defect is the object of the following remarks.

During the first months of existence, there is no perceptible
difference between the hearing child and one born deaf. . . . In a
few months, the mind, growing with the growth and strengthen-
ing with the strength of the body, begins to arouse from this le-
thargic slumber; to attend to and distinguish the diverse sensations
that assail it on every side; to discover by the success of those first
efforts which nature, or rather instinct prompts, its power over the
muscles of the body, and to exercise that power, first as a means of
supplying its few wants, and then for the mere pleasure of exercising it and acquiring by its means a knowledge of the forms and
qualities of the objects around it. Among these powers it finds that
of producing vocal sounds, and from the time it makes this discovery, the difference between the hearing child and the child deprived of hearing begins; a difference, small indeed at first, but too
often destined to widen into an almost impassable gulf.

The same lesson of experience that teaches the mind of the
child its power over the arm, which it can by an effort of the will
cause to stretch forth and grasp an apple, teaches it that it possesses
the like power over the muscles which produce sounds. The child
begins to imitate by a sort of sympathy those words which he
hears his mother pronounce to him, and learns their meaning by
her looks and gestures. His ear informs him when his imitation has

been successful and teaches him how to correct his pronunciation. "Thus he goes on without attending to those motions of the throat, tongue, and lips which produce sounds, but regulated solely by the ear, from indistinct prattlings to the acquisition of intelligible speech" the noblest faculty of man.★

The deaf child has the same power of producing sounds, and, in fact often exercises it without knowing it. But experience can never inform him of its existence. . . . Hence the deaf child *remains* dumb, while his hearing brothers *learn* to speak.

Still, the deaf and dumb child understands, in common with his hearing brother, by the instinct of sympathy, the looks and gestures with which his mother accompanies her words; and if she would only continue to talk to his eyes, and to teach him signs as she teaches his hearing brother words, a language would soon be established between them, not only sufficient for all the wants of childhood, but capable of expanding with the development of the child's understanding, and of aiding that development as much as the language of sounds aids his speaking brother's.

But, unfortunately, the mother too often forgets that she possesses *two* languages, one for the *ear* and the other for the *eye*. Hence when she first makes the agonizing discovery that her child is deaf and will become dumb, she thinks the misfortune irremediable. She recalls to mind the appalling and all but impassable gulf which, after years of neglect, separates the mind of one born deaf from the cultivated and enlarged mind of his hearing brother, and she imagines that this vast gulf is already fixed between her and her deaf child. How lamentably is she mistaken! The gulf is scarcely opening, it is but a step to cross it, and it is in her own power, if not wholly to close it, at least to prevent it from opening wider. But, ignorant of this, strangely ignorant too that she *has*, daily and hourly, held intelligible communication with her child through those signs which nature teaches; the mother, when she

---

★*Edinburgh Encyclopedia* [Burnet's note].

finds that the ear, the customary door of communication which she seeks to open between mind and mind, is closed forever, instead of returning to the *first* and in fact *nearest*, though less convenient passage, the eye, sits down in despair and abandons the mind of her child to the solitary darkness of its "prison house of clay". . . .

To the neglected deaf and dumb child, the universe, material and moral, lies in the chaotic darkness and confusion of chance: the future is to him without hope, indeed he scarcely suspects its existence. Still by his own unassisted efforts he acquires some faint glimmerings of that knowledge which an immortal mind only can acquire, and we find by the signs which he invents to overcome the barrier between himself and the speaking world, that he has been an accurate observer within his own narrow sphere. Yet when so neglected, his early condition must be dark and desolate indeed. He almost necessarily becomes selfish, for those who find none to sympathize with them, can hardly be expected to feel sympathy for others. He becomes also suspicious, for he cannot but observe Himself often the subject of conversations held in his presence. Hence it is no wonder if he is often self willed, and irritable. He must also feel himself painfully inferior to his speaking brother. He can form no idea of the nature and uses of the books, papers, slates, &c. with which the latter is so familiar, and for his acquaintance with which he is praised and rewarded. He attempts in vain to comprehend the motives of those gatherings of men together to discuss private or public affairs, or to worship the Giver of all good. He feels himself in short, in almost every thing which distinguishes the man from the animal, an outcast from society, or barely admitted to sit down at its threshold. Neglect has now done her fearful work, a mighty chasm separates him from his speaking brethren, and the world says it is because he is deaf; not so; IT IS BECAUSE HE WAS NEGLECTED. . . .

The remedy, the *only*, but an *efficient* remedy for the misfortune of the *deaf*, is, *By making their eyes supply the place of ears*. This short and simple sentence contains the whole art of instructing the deaf; an art which so many consider a mystery, and its success a sort of miracle. . . .

This golden rule kept in view, in every thing else the early education of the deaf is one with that of the hearing. . . . Let the mother only attend to the first signs of her deaf and dumb child as carefully and assiduously as she would attend to the first prattlings of a speaking one, and she will soon find the former as able to make his wants distinctly known as the latter. . . .

Nature, however unindulgent she may seem to the deaf and dumb, has not proved herself such a cruel stepmother as to throw these children of misfortune upon the world without a language. The ability of any human being to exchange with its fellow beings the most common and necessary ideas, does not depend on the mutual knowledge of certain signs previously agreed on, whether we suppose those signs to be, addressed to the eye or to the ear. On this point I have taken the opinion of men eminently acquainted with the subject, and they agree that all that is necessary in order to establish a mode of communication by signs with a deaf and dumb child, is to encourage the child himself to make signs, by attending to and imitating his first efforts.

His first signs will naturally be the expression of his physical wants, but precisely in proportion as he finds himself encouraged and attended to, he will enlarge his vocabulary of signs, till it becomes fully adequate to the expression of all his ideas, whether those ideas be few or many in number.

It is not because deaf and dumb children were born, more than others, with any peculiar facility for making signs, that we counsel their friends to learn signs from them. Hearing and speaking persons, as well as the deaf and dumb, have received the language of signs from the hand of nature; but having acquired and exclusively used, in speech, a more perfect and convenient language, they have forgotten this natural language and must submit to learn it again from those who, having learned no other language, have had no opportunity to forget it. *Rules* may, however, be given. . . . That some signs, as, for example, the signs for hunger and thirst, the expression of anger and threatening, or of good will and compassion, are universally intelligible, no one will doubt; and the extent of this *universal language* is much greater than most people imagine. How often do we read in the narratives of travelers and navigators, of interviews between parties, neither of whom know a word of the other's spoken language, in which however, matters of the highest importance, involving the welfare or perhaps the existence of one or both parties, were discussed by means of natural signs. In such cases, the value of some previous skill in sign-making becomes strikingly manifest. . . .

Let those then, who would acquire this language (I address myself more especially to MOTHERS and SISTERS, who, if any are, are capable of becoming *ears to the deaf and a tongue to the dumb*), attend to these few simple directions.[5]

Endeavor, as far as in you lies, to forget *words* and think only of *things*, become for the time dumb, if you would converse with the dumb.

Study the spontaneous expressions of the feelings and passions in the countenance, and in those gestures which nature prompts us to make whenever words seem inadequate to the full expression of our feelings or thoughts.

Form in your own minds clear and well defined ideas of the forms, qualities, and uses of those objects, and of the characteristic circumstances of those actions, which you would represent by signs.

Cultivate the faculty of IMITATION.

This last direction is the key to the whole art of making signs. We imitate the spontaneous expression of sentiment in the coun-

---

5. By writing particularly to mothers and sisters, Burnet reminds us that women usually had primary child-rearing responsibilities in the antebellum United States.

tenance and gestures, and all men understand, for nature operates with the savage of America or Africa, with the barbarous Malay and half civilized Chinese, in the same manner as with the polished European. We delineate the forms and uses of objects and imitate the actions of others, a sort of pictures, whose parts indeed vanish as soon as seen, but after a little practice, the memory will retain and combine them and they will be as intelligible as if their outlines were fixed on paper.

Those who, visiting an institution for the deaf and dumb, or witnessing the conversation of two intelligent mutes, have gazed bewildered on the thousand changing motions through which every thought of the mind flashes and disappears; or who, desiring to study the language of signs in its improved form, have looked at the mass of signs flitting before them, with as much dismay as if they were to be compelled to count and individually recognize a swarm of bees, will be surprised to find that the whole language may be resolved into elements so simple and so few in number.[6] Yet so it is; all these signs are only living pictures, in which a few of the outlines being traced, the mind of the spectator supplies the rest.

It is not to be supposed that the language of signs at the beginning of its use, or even after considerable cultivation, will compare either with speech, or with that beautiful, expressive, and figurative language, which, in a community of intelligent mutes, fully supplies the place of speech.[7] The language of signs which a deaf and dumb child shall devise for the expression of its own ideas will

---

6. In producing these vivid descriptions of watching rapid signed conversations in confusion, Burnet doubtless drew upon his own experience of first encountering American Sign Language as an adult, at age twenty-one. His depiction contradicts the frequent claim during this period that sign language is universal (see p. 12, note 6).

7. Burnet contrasts a deaf child's home signs with the beauty and eloquence of American Sign Language, which can only be truly learned by interacting with other ASL users.

be, at the beginning, circumscribed as the narrow circle of ideas of which it is the expression. But precisely in proportion as the ideas of the child become more extended, more just, or clearer, its language of signs, if any one will attend to them, will become more copious, significant, and precise. . . .

A few examples to show how a language of signs is formed and improved, may be both interesting to the curious and useful to the friends of deaf and dumb persons.

If a deaf and dumb child has been accustomed to drink *milk*, for example, from a bowl with a spoon, the first sign by which he asks for *milk* will most probably be the imitation of the action of holding a bowl, and carrying milk to the mouth with a spoon; when afterwards he wishes to refer to giving milk to a pig, he will still figure the bowl and the spoon for milk; but if you take him to the farm yard and show him the process of milking, he will readily consent to substitute the motion of the hands in milking for his former sign; by which change there will be an improvement both in propriety and precision, as will be evident when we would refer to giving milk to a kitten, a calf, &c. or when we would speak of any thing besides milk which is eaten from a bowl with a spoon. . . .

To a person of an inquisitive and philosophic mind, it will be a highly curious and interesting task to trace the manner in which a language is thus gradually formed. Circumstances merely accidental and temporary will often be found to exercise a great influence on its formation. The child will note individuals by some accidental peculiarities of features, dress, or manner; as, a scar on the cheek, a garment of an unusual fashion, a stoop in the gait, a habitual action, &c; and these signs will generally remain after the peculiarities which gave rise to them have passed away, and will not infrequently become generalized by becoming applied to a whole class resembling the individual to whom they are first applied, or in any way connected with him. When President Monroe (says Mr. Barnard), visited the Asylum at Hartford, he wore a cocked hat of the old fashion; and it was by reference to this article of dress that he was ever afterwards distinguished among the pupils. The same sign has since been generalized, and applied to all Presidents, whether their functions are political or otherwise. A similar instance is related by M. Paulmier, an associate of Sicard in the Royal Institution at Paris. A pupil from near the city of Rouen, in Normandy, had unusually large eyes. A reference to this feature naturally became his distinctive sign among the pupils, and was, by a metonymy, applied to the city from whose environs he came. Afterwards, when several generations had successively entered and left the school, and the recollection of the pupil with the large eyes was wholly lost among them, they still continued to figure large eyes for the city of Rouen.[8]

If it should happen that the deaf and dumb child should see a laborer come to his father's wood pile regularly every Saturday afternoon, and cut up, with a saw, wood for the week, he will, most probably, imitate the action of sawing wood to denote not only the saw, or the wood, (adding some other distinctive sign, as that of gathering up an armful for the latter), but also the wood-sawyer, the woodpile, and every Saturday afternoon.

The degree of copiousness and precision which the sign dialect of a solitary mute will acquire, will vary with the capacity of the inventor, and still more with the degree of attention which is paid to his signs by those around him. A language being the medium by which ideas are conveyed from one mind to another, the co-operation of at least *two* minds is necessary to the formation or development of such a medium. Certain it is that if sufficient attention is paid to the signs of a deaf and dumb child, they will become adequate to the expression of all its ideas, and may be made a medium of imparting new ideas to a far greater extent than

---

8. These examples illustrate the fascinating ways sign languages can develop from the iconic and literal to more generalized, arbitrary symbol forms.

is usually supposed possible under the circumstances. Pupils have been educated in our institutions for the deaf and dumb, who have obtained an amount of information decidedly superior to that of most persons who hear, wholly through the medium of natural signs.

The signs which are most generally wanting to the language of an uneducated mute, are those which express general or abstract ideas, and, particularly, those which serve to express intellectual or moral judgments. . . . It is certain that the mute's moral and intellectual conceptions will become much more distinct when he has learned to express them by some sign, whether natural or arbitrary. These delicate shades of thought flit through the mind so rapidly that they almost escape observation, and if observed are soon forgotten, unless they are associated with something more permanent and tangible. Thus by giving signs to such immaterial ideas, we may be said to give them a body.

The signs which express ideas beyond the material world must, of course, be either arbitrary or figurative; and in the natural language of signs, that part which expresses such ideas is figurative to a very remarkable degree.

To create such signs, it will be, for the most part, sufficient to excite in the mind of the child the idea to which you would induce him to give a sign, or to place him in circumstances in which that idea must necessarily be excited. . . .

Suppose for example, you would elicit a sign to express the ideas of likeness and unlikeness, some such process as the following might be employed.

Suppose you have several sets of books, each set distinguished by a difference in size or binding; place them all promiscuously on a table, the several volumes of each set at a distance from each other; then busy yourself to re-arrange them in sets, and invite the deaf and dumb child to assist you. Thus employed to arrange objects by their resemblance, he cannot avoid conceiving the ideas of resemblance and difference, and in the process you will readily

obtain, if you seek for them, such gestures as seem to him adapted
to express those ideas. If his signs should not be satisfactory you
can bring him to use any signs which seem to you more convenient or expressive; as for example, by placing side by side the two
fore-fingers, between which there is a perfect resemblance.

We will here give a few of the signs used in deaf and dumb
institutions to express intellectual and moral notions, as examples
of the manner in which some signs are formed.

From time immemorial the heart has been supposed to be the
seat of the affections, and the brain of the understanding. Hence
many figurative signs are derived. A deaf mute presses his finger
on his forehead, accompanying the action by a look of intelligence
to signify, I understand; he draws his hand across his brow, with a
corresponding expression of countenance, to signify, I have for-
got, &c; and he generally accompanies the natural signs for passions and emotions by the laying his hand on his heart with an
appropriate manner and emphasis.

Some signs are more purely figurative. The sign for the *past* is
made by pointing back (over the shoulder most commonly); for
the *future* by extending the hand *forward*; for *now, to-day, ready,* and
other ideas involving *present* time by presenting the hands with an
emphatic motion on each side of the person (that is neither back-
wards nor forwards, i.e. neither past nor future). The sign for *always,* &c. is made by describing several circles in quick succession.
Here, it will be seen, signs originally denoting ideas of space are
applied to time. Portions of time are easily expressed by referring
to the course of the sun, or of the hands of a watch, or to any
event which the child's experience has taught him will occur at
regular intervals.[9]

Still more figurative does the language of signs become when
we apply it to the expression of moral notions. Almost the only

9. Many of these descriptions of signs will be familiar to modern
ASL users.

natural signs for such notions are those for good and bad (expressed by gestures of approbation and disapprobation, more or less emphatic); but, adopting a figurative expression from speech, we use signs describing a straight line, for many ideas which involve the notion of *right*, and signs describing a crooked line for their opposite ideas. Thus *truth* is expressed by laying the finger on the lips, and then throwing it straight forward; and on the other hand, falsehood is expressed by running the finger across the lips in a contrary direction, and generally in a crooked line.

But to attempt to describe a language of signs by words, or to learn such a language from books, is alike to attempt impossibilities. Those for whose benefit I write will stand in no need of such descriptions if they have followed my reiterated advice to attend to and encourage a deaf and dumb child to make signs, and to imitate his signs, and endeavor to converse with him, and to give him new ideas through this medium.

If this course shall be faithfully followed, the deaf and dumb child, unless indeed he is affected with idiotism, will be able to express *all* his ideas, almost as clearly and intelligibly to one acquainted with his signs, as a speaking child of the same age can do. He will prove himself equally fond with the latter of telling what he has *seen* or *heard by the eyes*, and of asking questions about the nature and uses of all the things he sees, and about past and future events. . . .

In this manner, which any intelligent mother will easily understand and apply to other cases, the deaf and dumb child may be introduced, step by step, only by the means of signs, to a knowledge of all that a child of his age can know.

But there is still one thing wanting, and that one thing is of the utmost importance. It is a KNOWLEDGE OF WORDS, without which he can never converse, save with the few who understand his signs, and must thus remain a helpless dependent on the kindness of friends whom fortune may snatch from him. A knowledge of words, also, is necessary to enable him to have recourse to books, those never failing companions which are never weary of conversing even with the deaf. Give him but the key of this grand storehouse of knowledge, *written language*, and you put all at once the mind's wealth in his reach. No longer dependant on the leisure or the kindness of a few for information, he can then riot at will among the intellectual stores of successive centuries.

But this is an enterprise of no common magnitude. The ordinary passage by which hearing children are admitted to this great storehouse of knowledge, is irrevocably barred to the deaf at birth. Spoken language is an open sesame whose magic power causes the door of this storehouse to fly asunder; for the deaf and dumb a passage must be cut through the wall itself.

Let the reader figure to himself a language (like the Chinese) in which each idea is expressed by an arbitrary character, or, still worse, by an assemblage of arbitrary characters, in an order too, very different from that in which the words of his own language are arranged, and he will have some idea of the difficulties which attend the acquisition of a written language by the deaf and dumb.[10]

Still, the difficulties though great are not insurmountable, and were they greater, they ought not to be permitted to weigh a feather against the advantages which the mute will receive from access to books, and the possession of a mode of communicating his ideas, common to all in his country. The writer of this, deaf from his early infancy, would not relinquish his knowledge of written language to gain the wealth of the Indies, or even to recover the faculty of hearing. . . .

To give a deaf mute from birth a perfect knowledge of a writ-

---

10. Like Laurent Clerc, Burnet compares deaf Americans learning English to hearing people studying a foreign language. By stating "in order . . . very different from that in which the words of his own language are arranged," Burnet implicitly acknowledges that sign language has a grammar and structure quite different from English.

ten language is an enterprise which may be compared to digging into a mountain for treasure which we know to be concealed *somewhere*. The depth is considerable, and those who begin at random, throwing up the earth in fifty places, will scarcely ever find enough of the treasure to reward their labor.

I will point out the place where you must begin to dig. By persevering efforts you will go deeper and deeper, meeting at every turn of the spade encouraging indications of final success, and throwing up constantly larger and larger fragments of the great treasure beneath. Though you may not, perhaps, fully succeed, yet you will in a very great degree facilitate the labor of the regular instructor, when the child passes under his care. . . .

The *Manual Alphabet* is a very useful instrument in teaching words. It is a mode of spelling words on the fingers, not only more convenient, but after practice, more rapid than writing. It can be used at all times and in all places; sitting or standing, walking or riding at meals, and in a thousand circumstances in which writing would be very inconvenient, and even impracticable. A still greater advantage is that it can be used like natural signs, in an intercourse between two persons at a considerable distance. It requires far less light than writing for its employment, and can even be used in the dark by holding the hand of the *speaker* between the hands of the person spoken to. The latter can thus, with a little practice, distinguish the letters by a sense of touch, a fact of which I have often had proof. Lastly, it assimilates much more directly to speech than writing can be made to do. The interlocutors can sit facing each other, and observe each other's countenances and gestures while *speaking* (if I may use the word for this silent manner of expressing words).

The child may be early made familiar with the positions of the Manual Alphabet, and may be taught to spell a number of words on his fingers before he is able to read or write them on paper. After this, to teach him the written or printed alphabets, is only to teach him that a certain position of his fingers corresponds

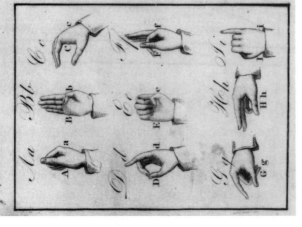

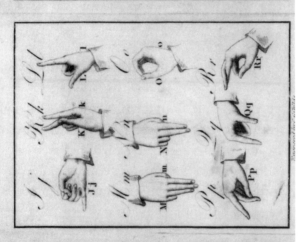

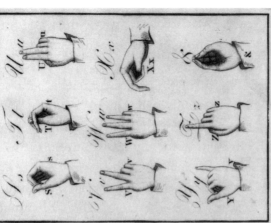

In his preface, Burnet wrote, "The engraving of the manual alphabet which accompanies the work, will enable any person to acquire the art of talking with the fingers in a few hours, and a few weeks practice will give a surprising degree of expertise in its use."

to a particular letter. . . . [*Editor's Note:* Burnet goes on to give detailed directions on how to teach a deaf child to read and write words.]

These general hints will perhaps be sufficient, because, though I give directions for beginning the mute's education at home, I would by no means dispense with his being sent, when of suitable age, to a regular institution for the deaf and dumb. . . . If public schools and experienced teachers are necessary for speaking children, they are doubly necessary for the deaf and dumb. The instruction in written language, therefore, which the mute receives at home, ought to be considered as only the foundation of a fabric to which the experienced instructor is afterwards to put the finishing hand. . . .

Articulation and Reading on the Lips shall now receive a brief consideration.

These are, beyond all question, the most valuable accomplishments which a deaf and dumb person can acquire. They restore him more effectually than he can be by any other means restored to the ordinary intercourse of Society, by giving him the power of conversing with the speaking world in a mode, which, though in his case not free from difficulties, still exacts less effort than any other on the part of his neighbors, who, I am sorry to say, are too seldom inclined to give themselves trouble for his sake. Hence he will become, by more frequent practice, far more familiar with words, and will thus be more likely to reach that great end in his instruction, an end which too few educated mutes have ever attained, the ability to read books with ease, pleasure, and profit. Some have even thought that his physical development was rendered more perfect, and his health improved by the free play of the chest and vocal organs consequent on the habit of utterance. Certain it is that the deaf mute taught to speak passably, and to read on the lips, is far less dependant on the kindness and sympathy of others, than his brethren in whose education these branches have been neglected.[11] With these last, even the very cultivation of their intellectual faculties seems, when they leave the society of their school-mates and go forth into the speaking world, to increase their dependence, as it gives them a keener relish for social enjoyments whose gratification must depend on the willingness of others to be at some inconvenience on their account. No teacher of the deaf and dumb has ever denied the value, to them, of the accomplishments of which we are speaking; and experience has abundantly shown that their acquisition is, in most cases, practicable to a very considerable degree. That they are still, in so many schools for the deaf and dumb, including all in this country, entirely neglected, is to be ascribed to the lingering effects or the early prejudices of instructors, or to their desire to give the ideas of their pupils a more than ordinary range and expansion, and to the scantiness of the period to which the education of the deaf and dumb is almost always restricted, making it difficult, if not impossible, to attend at the same time to the early development of their ideas, and to the giving them the power of vocal speech. Though this branch of instruction, more than any other in the education even of the deaf, demands the perfect work of patience, yet I will not suppose that any instructor, having by heart the very choice of a profession devoted himself heart and hand to one of the noblest labors of Philanthropy, will shrink, merely on account of its difficulty, from that labor which alone can be said to crown his perfected work.

True it is that he can never hope to give the deaf the *correct, emphatic,* and *euphonious* utterance of those who hear; he must be content if their articulation is intelligible. And it is equally true that reading on the lips cannot wholly supply the sense of which

---

11. Because he grew up hearing, Burnet no doubt was especially aware of the value speech could have. Although he supported sign language, he expressed cautious hope in oral education, as did several other deaf Americans during this period.

the deaf are deprived. It exacts, for its exercise, light, proximity to the speaker, and a direct view of the countenance. But why speak of the boundaries which limit our utmost ability to remedy the deficiencies of Nature, when we are yet so far from having attained them? . . .

I think it possible that the mother may teach her deaf and dumb child, as early as she would a hearing one, to imitate a few words, such as *papa, mama,* and &c., so as to be intelligible to her, by making it observe the motion of her lips, and in particular, making it *feel* the emission of breath, and the vibration in the throat which accompany the utterance of a sound. It is as natural for a deaf child to utter cries as it is for a blind one to move its limbs; and not more difficult to teach the former to speak, than to teach the latter to walk. The mother certainly ought to make the trial. . . . [*Editor's Note:* Here Burnet provides elaborate instructions on teaching a deaf child to speak—placing the hand on the speaker's throat, before the speaker's mouth, and so forth.]

A consideration which greatly enhances the importance of teaching articulation to the deaf is found in the fact that many children who pass for deaf-mutes are only *partially* deaf.[12] Such will readily hear *noises*, while they cannot distinguish *spoken words*. It has been found that this is, in many cases, because finding it difficult to distinguish words, they neglect to listen. With them sounds, though heard, excite only the same confused sensation which all feel in endeavoring to listen to the rapid utterance of a strange language. Experiments made at the Parisian Institution on several such, have proved that they may be brought to distinguish sounds by only *accustoming them to listen;* and that in teaching them to *speak,* they are often, to a considerable extent, taught to hear. . . .

---

12. By addressing the various situations of partially deaf and late-deafened people, Burnet calls attention to the range of auditory status within the signing deaf community.

The case of those who lose their hearing after learning to speak shall now be considered. . . .

It repeatedly happens that children who lose their hearing after learning to speak become in time dumb; and in all cases, unless particularly attended to, their articulation becomes more and more indistinct as they grow up, till at length none but those who are in the habit of hearing them speak can understand them.[13] In this point of view, the reader will easily conceive how important it is that children should be early taught to read. If able to read before the loss of their hearing, they will soon learn to write, and will thus, without particular instruction, possess all those advantages which can only be restored to the really dumb by a laborious process of instruction. Cases are not very rare in which persons who have lost their hearing after learning to read, have afterwards by their own efforts, assisted only by books, acquired an amount of information, and a knowledge of language far greater than it is generally practicable to impart to a person deaf and dumb from birth.

But supposing that the child loses its hearing before learning to read, retaining, however, the power of speech, still his case admits a much easier remedy than that of one *dumb* as well as *deaf.*

It is only necessary to bear in mind the rule I have already laid down, a rule applicable as well to the case of those who become deaf at any period of life, as of those who are born deaf; viz: *To make their eyes supply the place of ears.*

None but the *deaf, dumb and blind* are beyond the benefit of this principle, and that case is fortunately as rare as it is well nigh irremediable. . . .[14]

---

13. Burnet himself apparently experienced this type of speech deterioration.

14. Burnet is of course mistaken to present deaf, dumb, and blind people as almost hopeless cases, but perhaps can be pardoned since that situation was rather rare. When his volume appeared, Julia Brace (1807–

I will conclude this subject with one more remark. Many parents whose children have been bereft of hearing, have, with much pains and expense, tried, and tried in vain, every remedy which reason, experience or even quackery could suggest, while at the same time the simple and certain means of *making the eyes supply the place of ears* have been neglected. Without trespassing on the province of the physician, I would observe that, though deafness has been some times relieved by medical means, yet the success of those means is, in most cases, extremely doubtful; but that the means which I have pointed out for restoring the deaf to the blessings of social intercourse, are within the reach of all; and, if properly and perseveringly used, will in no case fail to produce valuable results.

The Orphan Mute

On a beautiful sunny afternoon in June, a group of happy children set out, with light hearts and smiling faces, on a strawberry excursion. At some distance from their little village, there was a deserted and ruinous house, around which were a few fields abounding in strawberries, the whole embosomed in woods, but near a public road. Thither the children proceeded, but had hardly entered the fields when they were alarmed by mournful cries, which quickly caused them to huddle together in a group, like so many frightened sheep, and retreat towards the road. A consultation now took place, what course they should pursue; some were for continuing their employment in the fields farthest removed from the place where the cries were heard, others, especially the girls, were for running home to get help. But a manly and intelligent boy of ten,

---

1884), a deaf-blind woman, was impressing observers with her achievements at the American Asylum. Others, such as Laura Dewey Bridgman (1829–1889; see p. 96, n. 3) and Helen Keller (1880–1968), later achieved more fame.

insisted that it was only the cry of some child, who had been picking strawberries like themselves and had lost itself, or perhaps got hurt; he, therefore, proposed that they should proceed towards the spot, and himself volunteered to lead the way. A few of the boldest took courage by his example, and following, they found a little girl apparently about six years old, seated on a stone, and sobbing bitterly. As the party approached, she started up and fled like a wild bird. The suddenness of her flight astonished the party, and most of them, doubting whether the being they saw was not a being of another world, the rather as her dress was unusual and her countenance remarkably beautiful, were disposed to retreat. George Wilson, though as we have already said only ten years old, and younger than many of his companions, had been too well instructed to experience any idle terrors of ghosts and fairies. Leaving his hesitating companions to their own course, he instantly darted forward in pursuit, and soon overtook the timid and exhausted child.

As he caught her in his arms, he endeavored to sooth her alarm by the kindest looks and words; whether it was the former or the latter, the little stranger soon ceased sobbing; and looking eagerly into his face, suffered him to lead her back to his companions, who had now begun to advance. The sight of so many strange faces seemed to renew her alarm, but she seemed now to have a perfect confidence in her conductor, and while the rest gathered around her, she clung tenaciously to him. George, proud of this mark of confidence, offered to carry her home to her mamma, but to all his offers and enquiries, she made no other reply than by looking anxiously in his face. Much puzzled by her silence, the children made several fruitless attempts to make her understand. Various solutions were proposed for her conduct. Some thought that she might be of a French family, which was said to live within a few miles, and some inarticulate sounds, which she attempted to utter, being entirely unintelligible to the children, were believed to be indubitably French. George Wilson, to whom she still continued to adhere as a protector, notwithstanding the endeavors of the girls to entice her away, declared that he would immediately return to the village with her, and take her to his father's; the rest being much too intent on the anticipated pleasures of the afternoon to accompany him, he proceeded on his humane errand alone. His mother was much surprised to see him return so soon, and so strangely accompanied. On hearing the story she highly praised the manly conduct of her son, and promised to take care of the interesting child till she could ascertain to whom she belonged. As she really found it impossible to make the child understand her, and as there actually was a French family within two or three miles, she considered it very probable that the little girl belonged to this family, and had strayed away and lost herself, as often happens to children. "When your father, George," said she, "comes home he will ride there, and inform them; in the mean time you may go back and pick your strawberries." A piece of cake and a toy reconciled the little stranger to her new protector, and George set off to rejoin his companions, with that lightness of heart which ever attends the consciousness of doing well.

George Wilson was an only child, his parents were pious, intelligent, and though by no means wealthy, yet independent and highly respected. His mother in particular, was a woman of a very superior mind. Under her watchful and enlightened care her son grew up, a model of youthful excellence. Possessed of naturally quick parts, his acquirements were beyond his years; his naturally warm and impetuous feelings had been carefully directed to the side of honor and generosity; and the bright promise which he gave of talents and virtue, and future eminence, daily gladdened the hearts of his parents.

Mr. Wilson arrived late in the evening, and his son immediately assailed him with an account of his adventure, and entreated him to ride to Monsieur Dupin's. His father being much fatigued, and not wishing to go that evening, directed him to call one of their neighbors who had lived some time in the French family.

The neighbor soon arrived, and at once ascertained that the child did not belong to them. To this George objected that she spoke French. The neighbor, who professed to some smattering of French, accordingly addressed the child in that language, but finding it impossible to make her understand, she declared that the girl was dumb, and deaf too. This George rejected indignantly, and seemed inclined to ascribe the assertion to anger at the child's disproving her pretensions to an accomplishment of which she was very vain. His parents, however, who had already a suspicion of the truth, immediately adopted the opinion of their neighbor, and by various experiments, soon convinced him of its correctness.

The next day Mr. Wilson made diligent enquiries, which were continued some time without gaining any intelligence of the child's friends. An advertisement was also inserted in the newspapers, mentioning, among other circumstances, that she had a remarkable scar behind her right ear. All they could learn, however, was that a person had been seen in a riding chair, accompanied by a child, driving towards the place where she was found; and it soon became the general opinion that she had been intentionally abandoned. In the mean time, the little foundling, by her beauty and helpless condition, no less than by the native goodness of heart she discovered, and the signs of intelligence she displayed, which seemed extraordinary in one of her years and misfortune, twined herself more and more round the hearts of the whole family, till the old people became indifferent to, and George absolutely fearful of, the success of their enquiries.

Some weeks having elapsed without bringing them any intelligence of the child's friends, Mrs. Wilson declared her intention to adopt her as her own daughter, and give her the name of Mary, after an early and unfortunate friend, whom, she said, the child strongly resembled. From that time, the little deaf and dumb girl became a cherished and a happy, yea, a happy member of the family. Whenever George was not at school, they were inseparable

companions, and when he returned, she would endeavor to inform him of all that had passed in his absence. As her signs were
sure of being kindly and patiently attended to, they daily became
more expressive; and George and herself soon acquired a degree
of mutual intelligence which often afforded matter of deep won-
derment to the gossips of the village. Sometimes she would endeavor to relate something that happened before he found her in
the strawberry field; she would point to her adopted mother, and
then to a chest, and would close her eyes, and incline her head,
and cover her face with a white handkerchief. This seemed to be
a scene which had made a strong and durable impression on her
memory. At other times she would point to the scar behind her
ear, and would intimate that she had been overrun in the road, by
a carriage; of which she seemed to have such an instinctive dread,
that she never ventured in the road alone without looking carefully around her. From this circumstance Mrs. Wilson imbibed an
opinion that she had lost her hearing by such an accident, and
this suspicion was strengthened by observing that, whenever her
feelings were strongly excited, she would utter sounds that
strongly resembled words; and she thought she could distinguish
the word mother, among others.

    We will now take our readers by a short cut, to a point of
time, eight years removed from that at which we set out. We will
introduce them to Mr. Wilson's parlor, on a winter evening. A
noble looking youth of eighteen, was reading the newspaper to a
lady who seemed to be his mother. As he read, his mother
glanced, with an air of apprehension, to a beautiful and dark haired
girl of fourteen, who sat knitting, yet at that moment, intently
watching the countenances both of the reader and listener. She
caught the glance, and as George raised his eyes from the paper,
he met the earnestly enquiring eyes of Mary, and the glow on his
cheek deepened. With a look and gesture of irresistible entreaty,
Mary applied for an explanation. George extended his arm
towards the east, and seemed as if pointing to a distant place, then

pointing to herself, he described with his finger, the tie of her bonnet, and placing his finger alternately on his ear and his lips, he finally joined his hands together. Mary quickly put her hand to her head with the motion of putting on a hat, and with an enquiring look, also placed her fingers on her lips. George shook his head, and moved his lips as if speaking.[15] Mary looked down upon her work, but her color deepened and her bosom heaved. Mrs. Wilson seemed to observe the couple with increased anxiety and inquietude.

The communications which we have occupied some minutes in describing, passed in less than as many seconds. If after all our pains, the reader is so dull as not as not to know what passed on the occasion we pity him, and advise him to reflect what kind of beings wear bonnets, and what is meant by joining hands (and hearts); and if he cannot then understand, we shall set him down as incapable of comprehending or relishing our story.

The next day, Mrs. Wilson took an opportunity of seriously proposing to her husband that they should procure for Mary the benefits of the State laws, which humanely provide for the education of the indigent deaf and dumb. Mr. Wilson was easily persuaded and promised to exert himself for that purpose; but George, when apprised of the scheme, warmly opposed it. He could teach Mary himself, he said, and in fact he had already taught her many words. An incident, however, happened, which by changing his situation and prospects, changed in a great measure the current of his thoughts. His mother's only brother, who

---

15. More than any other author in this anthology, Burnet repeatedly tries to convey some sense of sign language and gesture in his writing. Here he illustrates the advice he has made in the preceding essay; George and Mary readily converse through a home sign that they apparently have developed on their own. However, Burnet stretches our belief since George's signs for "girl," "deaf," and "marriage" resemble established ASL signs.

had been for many years engaged in commercial pursuits abroad, during which time she had scarcely ever heard of him, unexpectedly returned with considerable wealth, and having lost his wife and children in a foreign climate, he declared his determination to adopt his nephew and give him a collegiate education. Mr. and Mrs. Wilson, of course, most gladly embraced the offer, which seemed almost to realize all their dreams of their son's future career, which, however, they were not destined to see further fulfilled; so often are we called away from this world, when our cup of joy seems fullest. Before George departed for College, he was enjoined the task of reconciling Mary to her own removal to an Asylum, which George himself now warmly advocated, though to his surprise, his mother seemed to have lost her zeal in the cause. The necessary steps, however, had been taken, and there could be no reasonable excuse assigned to justify delay.

To reconcile Mary to the step was indeed a difficult task, and probably none but George would have been able to effect it. What arguments he used we cannot say, but they were, at least, powerful enough to succeed. Deaf mutes have hearts as well as others, and perhaps George informed her that the young lady whose marriage he read of in the newspapers, had been educated at a deaf and dumb Asylum, certain it is that, when she found George was leaving home, she became willing and almost anxious to go too.

The day of parting arrived, and George took leave of his friends, parents, and Mary, and left his home with some regret indeed, but with high hopes and bright anticipations. Perhaps he experienced the most regret at parting with Mary. Ever accustomed to give way to the unchecked current of her feelings, she now wept in uncontrollable affliction. The motives which could induce George to leave her, she could not comprehend, and he in vain endeavored to explain them. The grave and anxious faces of the family, as the hour of parting drew near, naturally impressed her with the idea of misfortune impending; and her vision into futurity was far too limited to look beyond present affliction, or to consider it as the means of future happiness. The only idea she could form of George's employment at College was that he was going to spend his time chiefly in looking over books. She had often seen him reading with an intensity of interest that made even her conversation an interruption. On such occasions she would watch the changes of his countenance as he hung over his book, and weep in the full bitterness of feeling to find herself incapable of sharing what seemed to be his dearest enjoyment. Not perhaps, at any other time, did the consciousness of her deprivation seem much to alloy her happiness. With the young companions of her childhood, she was always an object of interest, and was invariably treated with kindness. She joined in their sports, and was generally preferred to a distinguished place. Her misfortune, joined to her sweetness of temper, her personal charms, and that quickness of intellect, which, when coupled with her misfortune, always excites surprise in common minds, rendered her universally an object of pity and admiration. She was often, indeed, a spectator of pleasure she could not comprehend, and mirth she could not share, but then she could always turn to her adopted brother, with the feelings of a wild bird, flying from the company of those of other species, to a mate, of its own kind. But when that adopted brother too, devoted himself to pleasures which she could not share or comprehend, she seemed to feel the full extent of her misfortune. It was this feeling which George availed himself of to reconcile her to her own banishment from home. How another could teach her better than George, she could not comprehend, but George assured her that it was so. Perhaps he informed her that the mute whose marriage he read of, had been so taught. At any rate George himself was leaving home for instruction, and it almost seemed to associate them, to suppose that she should leave home too, for the same purpose, though in a different direction.

Though George did not succeed in explaining to her the motive of their separation, he at least succeeded in assuring her that they should meet again. Perhaps his looks and gestures spoke an-

other promise to her heart, but as George himself would have
been puzzled to reduce it to words, we shall not attempt it; of its
nature the reader may judge by the fact that it seemed to reconcile
Mary to the idea of going among strangers, from which, at another
time, she would have recoiled with the instinctive timidity of a
fawn or wild bird. At parting, George gave her a beautiful pocket
testament, with a red cover, which she had often admired, assuring
her that she would one day be able to read it.

★ ★ ★

One day in May, a respectable elderly couple, accompanied by
a beautiful girl of fourteen, called at the Asylum at ———— and
were received by the Principal with his wonted courtesy. He ascertained at a glance the character of the party. The appearance of
the elders forbade the idea that they had called for the gratification
of idle curiosity. And there was an expression of eager and
trembling curiosity, the natural effect of mingling hope and fear,
in the quick glances with which the girl seemed to study, furtively
indeed, the lineaments of his own countenance. Shaking the hands
of the old people, he advanced towards her, observing, I suppose
you have brought me a new pupil. We have sir, replied our old
friend, Mr. Wilson. Mr. P. with his kindest look and manner took
Mary's hand, and asked her a few questions in the language of
mutes, in which he was deeply skilled, concerning her former employments and her present feelings; enquired if she could write,
and if she was desirous to learn, and assured her of his pleasure to
have her among his pupils. The benevolence which beamed in his
countenance seemed in a great measure to remove her fears, and
when she found herself enabled at once to hold intelligible intercourse with a stranger, and one too, of an age which she had hitherto deemed unapproachable to her, her heart, which had been
fluttering in her bosom like a frightened bird, seemed to rest with
a feeling of confidence. By the Matron to whom she was now
introduced, she was received with equal kindness; and during the

half hour that her adopted parents remained, she continued entirely at her ease.

After being conducted by the Matron to view the internal arrangement of the building, and into the school rooms to witness the progress of the pupils, they took their leave. Then it was that Mary's newly acquired confidence seemed to forsake her, when she saw her old friends departing, and herself left among strange, though kind faces; she sunk on a seat, covered her face with her hands, and wept long and bitterly. The Matron considerately permitted her to give a free course to her feelings, but when she became more composed, took her hand and conducted her to the girls' sitting room. On entering, Mary at first shrunk instinctively, and with an additional feeling of desolation, from a group of unknown faces and the curious eyes which were turned upon her.[16] But it was not long before she became interested in what was passing around her. She saw many girls, nearly of her own age, in groups, evidently engaged in interesting conversation; but she looked in vain for any motion of the lips. Those hidden thoughts which had been wont to pass from mind to mind, in such an invisible manner as to elude all the vigilance of her senses, seemed now to have become visible and palpable. The air was literally swarming with the creations of the mind; events past and future, thoughts, feelings and wishes, seemed floating around her, and that knowledge which she had hitherto sought so eagerly, and often so vainly, now knocked continually for admittance.

As the Matron placed her in one of these circles and withdrew, the various groups gradually merged in one, of which she became the center. A hundred welcomes were given, and a thousand questions asked and answered, till the questioners, having gratified their curiosity, separated by degrees, and returned to their several

---

16. Such grief was not uncommon among new arrivals at the schools, who had to undergo the trauma of separating from their family for the first time, and often did not understand why.

employments, leaving their new associate interested, pleased, tranquil, delighted, almost happy.

We are not going to give a particular account of her progress at school. The instructions of George had not been lost on her; she could write her own name, and the names of most common objects, and many detached words; these advantages, aided by a natural quickness of perception and an ardent thirst for knowledge, rendered her progress unusually rapid, and she soon became a favorite with her teachers.

That she was happy at school, it is hardly necessary to take the trouble to attempt to prove. Who, that has long lived among a people of an unknown language, is not happy when he arrives among a community whose language he understands? Who that has long felt himself painfully inferior in mental acquirements to those around him, that has long hungered and thirsted in vain for knowledge, is not happy when he finds himself brought at once to the gushing springs of science when the whole world is opened to his vision, and the pages of history unrolled before him? Who that has gazed upon the works of nature, and asked in vain, how these things are; that has seen a whole congregation join in prayer and praise; has looked upon their faces, beaming with the feelings of devotion, and felt that all this is above his comprehension— would not be happy if the being and attributes of the Creator were revealed to him, if he could himself join understandingly in prayer and praise to him? Such had been, and such now was Mary's lot. Reader, do not you think she was happy? Yes, she was happy. Only one circumstance brought with it an alloy. She never heard from her early friends, and often keenly felt their neglect; not knowing that those who had brought her to the Asylum, were now no more.

★ ★ ★

"It is surprising that we have never heard from Miss Wilson's friends since she came here," remarked Mrs. P. to her husband, as they sat in their private parlor after the school was dismissed.

"Though they informed us that she was only an adopted daughter, yet they seemed to feel much affection for her, and, interesting as she is, I could not have thought it possible that they should, for nearly four years, entirely neglect her." "I have been much surprised at it myself," returned her husband. "I have several times written to their address, but have received no answer. Miss Wilson's time, as a State pupil, expires in a few weeks, and I often feel considerable anxiety respecting her future fortune." "But at all events," remarked Mrs. P., "she will not want friends." "She shall not," replied Mr. P. and continued, "Her early history seems to be mysterious. I have directed her to write what she could remember of it, which I will read to you."

Account of Myself

When I was a little girl, and began to remember, I lived in a little white house, with a lady who was very kind to me. One day I was playing in the road, and a man drove his wagon, that ran over me, and crushed my head, and I was near dying; yet I got well, but I was deaf and dumb. The kind lady often wept over me much, and she was pale and sick. One day I saw her lie in a coffin, she did not look at me or move, and I cried very much. A gentleman took me away, and he rode with me some days in a chair. He set me down, and I picked some strawberries. The gentleman got in the chair, and left me. I cried after him, but he rode away fast. I felt very much afraid, and I sat down and wept. A good boy found me, and led me home to his parents. They pitied me, and took care of me, and I was very happy. I was always pleased to play and converse with my young friends, but was often envious and sorry because they went to school and learned, and I was ignorant. Then my friends began to learn me to write, and I was very glad. Then they said I should come to the Asylum to be taught; but I was afraid and did not wish to leave my home.

They told me that I would learn to read fast, and that they would often come and see me. Then I felt willing to come. When I came to the Asylum I was very happy to converse by signs, and to study many things. I soon began to read the books. I often thought of my friends, but they did not come to see me, nor write to me, and I sometimes felt very unhappy, because they neglected me. But I hope that my teachers and directors will be my friends. And I am happy to think that I have learned about God and the Bible, and that God is good, and will be the friend of the friendless, and the father of the orphans. And I will try to be good, that I may not displease him.

MARY WILSON[17]

The reading of this simple and affecting composition brought tears to the eyes of the amiable lady, and Mr. P. himself was much affected. Just then a knock was heard at the door. Mr. P. opened it, and ushered in a young man of prepossessing appearance and manners. He apologized for his intrusion, observing that he had called to see an old friend, among his pupils, one Mary Wilson. Pleased at so extremely opportune an adventure, Mr. P. desired his guest to sit down, while he would go and call her. While he was gone on this friendly errand, the stranger explained to Mrs. P. the cause of the apparent neglect with which Mary had been treated, by mentioning the deaths of those who had placed her in the Asylum, within a few weeks afterwards. The only other person who claimed particular interest in her welfare, had been pursuing his studies in a distant college, and during the vacations, obliged

---

17. Mary's essay resembles many student essays from the period that appear in the schools' annual reports. It is typical in its heartfelt, simple English, its narrative of coming to school, and the religious references at its conclusion.

to attend on his uncle, on whom he depended for support. But having now left college, and begun the study of the law in the office of an eminent practitioner at ———, he had lost no time in calling to enquire for her.

We must now change the scene. In another room of the Institution, there were collected about forty females, chiefly from ten to twenty years of age. They were all neatly dressed, and displayed contented and happy faces. Their employments were various, some were engaged in the manual occupations of their sex, some were reading, some eagerly conversing on the news of their little world, and a few looking from the windows with the curiosity natural to their age and sex, and perhaps with no small relish of the beauties unfolding under the warm sun of April. Among the whole there was, perhaps, a larger share of personal attractions than could often be met with among the same number promiscuously assembled; but one young lady, apparently about eighteen, instantly struck the eye by the unrivaled symmetry of her form, and the charms of a countenance, which, though not perfectly regular, yet beamed alternately with intelligence and sensibility. It seemed in fact a transparent covering for her heart and mind. But at the moment at which we introduce the reader, there was an expression of seriousness and sadness in her eyes, which were intently bent on the pages of a little red covered book, and thence occasionally seeking the columns of a dictionary.

The door of the room opened; twenty eyes immediately glanced towards the respected form of their principal. He placed his finger behind his right ear, and every eye which saw the action instantly turned on the young lady we have attempted to describe.[18] Intent on her book, she did not immediately perceive the

---

18. The principal's gesture, based on the scar behind Mary's ear, is her name sign. Burnet might subtly be paying tribute here to Laurent Clerc, whose name sign—a brushing of the two forefinger tips on the right hand down the right cheek, near the mouth—also came from a scar, which he had received from a fall into a fireplace as an infant.

signal, but those near her were prompt to inform her that she had been called. When Mr. P. saw that he had caught her eye, he beckoned her to follow, and in answer to her enquiring glance, locked his fingers together, the established sign for a friend; then holding up one finger, and extending his palm towards herself he pointed to the parlor below. They were already through the door, but the gestures we have attempted to describe, were caught and repeated by those near the door; and in a few seconds all in the room knew that Miss Wilson had been called to the parlor to see a friend.

Mary followed her teacher with such feelings as a young, ingenuous, and warm hearted girl might be supposed to feel, who, believing herself for years neglected by her earliest and most valued friends should find herself suddenly summoned to their presence. As they descended the stairs, she ventured to inquire whether the friend who awaited her was one of those who accompanied her to the Asylum four years before. He shook his head and intimated that it was a young man, adding at the same time some of those gestures and imitative variations of the countenance, which are frequently used by deaf mutes to give an idea of the personal appearance of strangers, but which we should vainly attempt to transfer to paper.

Mary's heart fluttered, and her head grew dizzy. Mr. P. perceiving her emotion, kindly took her arm, and they entered the room. A single glance told her that her suspicions were correct. She saw the companion of her childhood, changed indeed, and improved in manly beauty, but not disguised from the penetrating eye of one long accustomed to mark the human countenance. As George looked on the tall and elegant girl before him, he could hardly believe that it was the same he had left four years before, almost a mere child. But quickly recovering himself, he came forward, and took her hand with a warmth which spoke more to Mary's heart than any words could have expressed. In the confusion of the moment, he spoke to her audibly, but smiling at his mistake, he endeavored to recall those almost forgotten looks and gestures which he was wont to employ years before, but in this mode of communication he soon found himself embarrassed. Reflecting, however, that Mary had now learned to write, he immediately produced his pencil and pocket book, and seating himself by her side, soon explained to her the melancholy cause of the apparent neglect with which she had been treated.[19] He now found no difficulty in making her understand the motives which had led to their separation, and the nature of his present employment. Eager to ascertain the improvement of her mind, he conversed with her at some length, and his questions were always answered with a readiness and intelligence which both surprised and delighted him. In historical and geographical knowledge she scarcely yielded even to himself; and though almost entirely unacquainted with the fictions of poetry and romance (for there are too many truths which require to be imparted to the minds of the deaf and dumb, to permit any part of the limited period allotted to their education, to be devoted to fiction), she evidently possessed both imagination and sensibility. Astonished and delighted by her improvement, and fascinated by her replies, which evinced a heart wholly uncorrupted by intercourse with the world, and deeply imbued with the truths of religion and morality, George protracted his visit as long as he could with propriety. And he afterwards called at the Institution as often as he could find leisure and a decent pretext. He now began again to acquire the eloquent and poetical language of gestures, which he often found to express his feelings at least to Mary, much more forcibly and clearly than words could do, and when his skill in this language failed, the manual alphabet was an interpreter always ready at his fingers' ends.

★ ★ ★

---

19. Again, we see writing acting as a bridge between deaf and hearing people.

"What a lovely girl she is," said George to himself one day, as he left the institution, "what a beautiful form, and a face like heaven's bow in showers, round which her dark hair flows like the streaming clouds, as Ossian says. And then what grace and propriety in all she says or does: what a highly gifted mind she must possess, to have acquired, in four years, larger and better arranged stores of knowledge than many, with every advantage, have acquired in twenty years. In a few days, Mr. P. says, her time as a State pupil will expire. Where can she then go. My parents alas! are no more; my uncle is a single man, and of a morose temper. And this lovely, intelligent, helpless, and warm hearted girl, clings to me as her only friend, as she did when I picked her up among the strawberries. Shall I leave her fragile form and susceptible heart to the cold charity of the world! No! I will devote my life to her; I will be her protector." And with these generous feelings he sat down to write to his uncle. To this uncle he had been much obliged. By him he had been placed in a situation where he could gratify his passion for knowledge, and where the powers of his mind had room to develope themselves. By him he had been assisted along the rugged path to fame, which his ardent genius longed to essay. And this uncle, though constantly impressing on him the necessity of depending on his own exertions for the acquisition of fame and fortune, still held out the idea that his nephew would be his heir. George, therefore, felt it to be incumbent on him to gain his uncle's consent, if possible, though when he reflected on the subject, he felt almost hopeless of obtaining it. He sat down, however, and summoned all his powers to represent the case in such a light as would be the most apt to make an impression on his uncle. He painted in glowing colors the personal and mental charms of Mary; he described her destitute and helpless condition, and mentioned the early ties which had connected them, and finished by declaring that with such a being he could enjoy more domestic happiness than with any other, and in the most respectful manner implored his uncle's consent.

While George is waiting for an answer to this letter, we will suspend the course of our narrative to give the reader some account of his uncle. . . .

[*Editor's Note:* Here Burnet makes a long digression about James Morris, the uncle. We learn that he was a dissipated, reckless young man who pursued wealth. His love for a woman named Mary Harris was rejected; she married a Charles Melville, and he swore revenge. He cultivated the friendship of Charles and drove him to ruin and death. Mary Harris was devastated and died soon after her husband. Morris offered to care for her young daughter, who had recently recovered from an illness. What became of the child was not known, but its death was soon announced.]

It was from such a man, still engaged in the pursuit of wealth in one of our great commercial cities, that George awaited a reply to his romantic epistle.

The reply at length came, and we here lay it before our readers.

Dear Nephew,

I have received your letter, and perused it with much surprise, that you should think of marrying before you are established in your profession, and especially that you should think of marrying a dumb woman. I am at a loss to conceive what pleasure you could find with such a companion for life. As to what you say of her person, I hope you have more good sense than to be taken by a mere outside; and as to the improvement in her mind, which you say has taken place, I am quite incredulous. I have seen some deaf and dumb persons who have been educated, and none of them are able to express any but the most simple ideas. Surely such a girl, no better than a well-taught parrot, a mere beautiful automaton, cannot be a proper companion for a man who is to rise in the world by the exertion of his talents. But I have other reasons for refusing my consent. I have already fixed my mind on your union with the daughter of an old friend, a girl of high accomplishments and immense fortune. I expect you to come hither immediately, when I will introduce you to her. I have spoken to Mr. ———, an eminent lawyer in this place, who has agreed to receive you into his office. As to the concern you express for the future fortune of the dumb girl, if her good qualities are such as you represent, the directors of the Asylum will no doubt provide her a place in some respectable service. Trusting to your prompt compliance with my wishes, I remain your affectionate uncle,

JAMES MORRIS

So, exclaimed George, as he threw down the letter, and paced the room in an agitation he could not control, so the old gentleman is to choose me a wife, ugly and silly she may chance to be; when old men choose for young ones, they look to nothing but money. And then Mary, how coldly and contemptuously he speaks of her. A well taught parrot! a mere automaton! heavens! and she is to go to service, to bake, and scrub, and wash, but it shall never be. I have promised to be her protector, and I will keep the pledge. Her happiness or misery is in my hands, and I will not trifle with the deposit. I care not for the loss of my uncle's fortune. The sale of my father's farm will support us for the present. My profession is open before me, I will hew my own way to fortune and distinction. No votary of fashion, no vain, gaudy butterfly, no mawkish sentimental girl for me. Give me the pure heart, the warm, unadulterated feelings of nature. Give me above all, a wife whose heart is wholly mine, no flower that every fly may buzz round, and sip its sweets; no coquette, whose heart has fluttered for half a hundred lovers, no compound of vanity and caprice, concentrated all in self, to whom a husband, like a reticule, is only a necessary appendage. No, I would have a wife for myself, and not for others, a companion to whom I shall be all the world, who will cling to me through all the changes of fortune, with devoted love; I had almost said with idolatry.

With these feelings, the reader will not be surprised to hear that George Wilson soon called on the principal of the Asylum on business of importance. And that in a few weeks he left ———, not to wait on his uncle, but to establish himself in some town in the West, where a favorable opening might offer for a young lawyer.

★ ★ ★

One evening in June, a riding chair was seen winding along the banks of the Passaic, and evidently keeping as much in a westerly direction as the sinuosities of the road would permit. It contained a gentleman and a lady. The latter was of surpassing beauty, and her fine, and most expressive countenance, was continually lit up with new pleasure at every change of the prospect. Though neither of them were heard to utter audible sounds, it was plain that there was no want of intelligible communication between them, and thoughts often shone through a single look and gesture, which long sentences would have failed adequately to express; and occasionally they seemed to converse by what one, unacquainted with the manual alphabet, would have considered only a rapid quivering of the fingers; but which to their practiced eyes, left the traces of letters, words and sentences, as clearly as if impressed on paper. It was now near the close of the day, and the gentleman was beginning to consider where they should stop for the night, as no inn appeared in view, when the road suddenly merged into another, and they came in full view of a neat whitewashed cottage, over whose windows roses twined in luxuriant wreaths; to the right lay a garden, to the left, an orchard, and beyond the cottage a beautiful meadow sloped down to the bank of the Passaic; on the opposite side of the river was a dense forest, and beyond, the brow of a mountain of considerable elevation, rose high over the tops of the lofty trees, and now glowed in the rich hues of sunset. The scene was one of the most beautiful they had passed, but instead of gazing on it with her wonted delight, Mary (we trust the reader has already recognized her) seemed to regard it with a feeling of bewilderment. She pressed her hand to her forehead, as if endeavoring to recall almost forgotten impressions, and then again surveying the scene, her doubts seemed to dissipate. Pointing over her shoulder, as the deaf and dumb are wont to do when they would refer to the past, she referred George to the time when she was a child, before she had been picked up in a strawberry field, and then pointing to the cottage in view, she intimated that there her infancy had passed, there the kind lady had wept over her, and there she had seen her laid cold and pale in a coffin. It is impossible to describe the feelings of George at this discovery; the mysterious circumstances in which Mary had been found had taken a strong hold on his imagination, and he had often a kind of vague expectation that they would one day be explained. Checking his horse, he resolved to apply at this cottage for accommodation for the night. A girl appeared at the door, and introduced them into the parlor, where sat a venerable old lady in an easy chair. At their entrance she rose to receive them, and Mary and herself seemed mutually struck with surprise. George keenly remarked this circumstance, and after apologizing for their intrusion, and preferring his request for a lodging for the night, which was courteously granted, he endeavored to ascertain if Mary and their hostess recollected each other. Mary's recollections of the old lady were evidently very dim, but she thought she had often seen her, and been kindly treated by her. The old lady looked in considerable surprise at the evidently intelligible communications between the strangers, in a manner which she could not understand. George observing her surprise explained to her that his wife was deaf and dumb. The old lady's interest in her evidently increased, and she inquired her name. "I do not know her real name, Madam," replied George, "she was found abandoned by her friends, and my mother gave her the name of Mary." "Mary," said the old lady, "is a very appropriate name, she is the very image of my daughter-in-law, who bore that name. She died many years ago, and left a girl, which, if it is alive, would be about the age of your lady." "Is the child dead then?" asked George. "It was taken away, on its mother's death, by an uncle," replied the old lady, "and he informed me that it died soon after; but I have sometimes had doubts of it. The child was in the way of his possessing a considerable fortune, and he might have made way with it." "Was the child deaf?" enquired George. "It was not by birth, but shortly before its mother's death, it was overrun by a wagon, and I know not if it ever recovered its hearing." George's heart palpitated violently as he asked, "Did the child bear any visible marks of the accident?" "Yes," replied she, "a large scar here," as she spoke she placed a finger behind her right ear. Mary, who had been intently watching the speakers, saw the action, and removing her own glossy ringlets, she exhibited the scar deeply indented behind her own ear. The old lady tottered forward, examined the scar a moment, looked intently in Mary's face, and then caught her in her arms. Enough, the orphan child of the unfortunate, Mary Melville, was recognized by her grandmother.

Our story now hastens towards a conclusion. George listened with astonishment to the narrative of the old lady, and the strong suspicions which rested on his uncle of having caused the child to be exposed in some remote place, concluding doubtless, that as the child could give no account of itself the truth would never be discovered. Leaving Mary at the white cottage he returned to ———, in order to take measures to ascertain the truth of that suspicion. An accident which we have not time to describe, threw in his way the wretch who had been the accomplice of the villainies of the once dissipated James Morris. Now at the extremity of his career, he was willing to make his peace with Heaven, by atoning, as far as possible, for at least one of the injuries he had done. He confessed that he had been employed by Morris to make way with his sister-in-law's child, but chose rather to abandon it in a distant and solitary place. Armed with this testimony, George easily induced his uncle to avoid a public exposure by giving up the patrimony which he had so unjustly withheld from his niece. And thenceforward George and Mary lived chiefly at the white cottage, happy, and conferring happiness on all around them.

Emma

The following excerpt is from Burnet's ten-page narrative poem, "Emma." It tells of a young girl who becomes deaf due to illness. Initially confined to a gloomy life of isolation, Emma's prospects brighten when, at age fourteen, she goes to a residential school for deaf students.

> . . . An edifice I see,
> A noble monument of charity,—
> That near the new world's great commercial mart,
> In its unostentatious grandeur tow'rs apart.
> I see an hundred of the deaf and dumb,—
> Collected from full many a distant home,—
> Within this noble pile,—whose walls—to them
> Open'd another world,—a fairy realm;
> A realm of a new language,—all their own,
> Where mind was visible,—and knowledge shone,
> As the bright all revealing daylight shines
> To the poor native of Cracovia's mines,★
> When, first emerging from his regions dim,

★ In the salt mines of Cracow in Poland, it is said, many persons have been born and passed all their lives without ever seeing the light of day. [Burnet's note.]

The broad,—bright world above seems heaven to him.
And there is a fair girl, —whose eyes seem red,—
Nor yet the tears are dry so lately shed—
Sad had been Emma's parting hour,—and when
She saw strange faces all around her,—then
Her heart shrunk back with desolating chill,
Nor, for a time, would its wild throb be still.
But round her kind hearts from kind faces beam'd,
And the soul's sunshine on her spirit gleam'd,
That melted all her doubts and fears away,
As morning fogs fade in the blaze of day,
Soon her once cag'd and insulated mind
Rejoices in communion with its kind.
She *now* no longer feels herself alone,
Her knowledge but what could be glean'd by one.
But the mind's commerce, *here* set free from thrall,—
Makes each one's store become the wealth of all,
Here, from the speaking limbs, and face divine,
At nature's bidding, thoughts and feelings shine,
That in thin air no more her sense elude,—
Each understands,—by each is understood.
Here can each feeling gush forth, unrepressed,
To mix with feelings of a kindred breast.
Here does her teacher's skilful hand unroll
The curtain that hung round her darken'd soul,—
Revealing all the secret springs that move
The once mysterious scene, around, above,
Here, when the sense is pall'd,—she learns t' enjoy
And revel in delights that never cloy,—
To spurn this clog of clay and wander free
Through distant ages,—o'er far land and sea.
Collecting, one by one, each precious gem
That decks of science the bright diadem.
Till her mind,—rev'ling in the stores of thought,—

Ceases, almost, to murmer at its lot!
Nay more—her teacher,—pointing to the skies,—
Unrolls the sacred volume to her eyes,—
The charter of her immortality,
That teaches how to live, and how to die;—
Bids virtue lean on him who died to save,—
And look from earthly woes beyond the grave!
   Lo! in those walls a congregation met,
A hundred mutes in silent order set,—
A congregation met for praise or pray'r,
And yet no voice,—no song,—no sound is there.[20]
Yet not from the heart's thoughts ascends alone
That pray'r or praise to heavenly mercy's throne;
The teacher stands, to pray or teach, and all
The eyes around drink in the thoughts that fall,
Not from the breathing lips,—and tuneful tongue,—
But from the hand with graceful gesture flung.
The feelings that burn deep in his own breast
Ask not the aid of words to touch the rest;
But from his speaking limbs, and changing face,—
In all the thousand forms of motion's grace,
Mind emanates, in corruscations, fraught
With all the thousand varied shades of thought.
Not in a cloak of words obscur'd, confined—
Here free conceptions flash from mind to mind,
Where'er they fall their own bright hues impart,—
And glow,—reflected back—from ev'ry heart!

---

20. Such chapel services often had a powerful impact on hearing
visitors to the schools. Lydia (Huntley) Sigourney wrote in 1845: "It is
touching, even to tears, to see the earnest attention of that group of
silent beings, the soul, as it were, sitting on the eye, while they watch
every movement and sign of [the minister's] hand." See Lydia H. Sigourney, *Scenes in My Native Land* (Boston: James Munroe and Co.,
1845), 242.

4

JOHN CARLIN

(1813–1891)

John Carlin was not only one of the most accomplished deaf Americans in the nineteenth century, but also one of the most contradictory. A successful artist, writer, and lecturer, he was ambivalent about his deaf identity. He lost his hearing in infancy, used sign language, married a deaf woman, and spent most of his life among deaf people, working for their benefit and urging them to improve themselves. Yet at times he showed contempt for deaf people and sign, saying he preferred to associate with hearing individuals, who seemed to him more proactive and who had "superior knowledge of the English language." In a society where hearing people had most of the status and power, perhaps such expressions of what we might today call self-hatred should not surprise us. Carlin is but an extreme example of how many nineteenth-century deaf Americans sometimes felt torn between the deaf and hearing worlds.

Born on June 15, 1813, in Philadelphia, Carlin was the son of an impoverished cobbler. His younger brother, Andrew, was also deaf. As a child, Carlin wandered the city. When he was seven, he

was one of a group of deaf street children taken in by David
Seixas, a crockery dealer, who took care of them and organized a
school that became the Pennsylvania Institution for the Deaf. One
of Carlin's first teachers was Laurent Clerc, who served as acting
principal of the school in 1821–22 to help it get underway. (Carlin
would later count Clerc among his warmest friends and paint several portraits of him.) Carlin graduated in 1825, at age twelve. He
began to study drawing and painting under various teachers. Since
his father could not support him, he worked as a sign and house
painter to pay for his art education.

In 1838, Carlin went to Europe for more formal study of art.
In London, he examined ancient artifacts in the British Museum;
in Paris, he studied portrait painting under Paul Delaroche. He
illustrated in outlines several epic poems, including *Paradise Lost*
and *Pilgrim's Progress*. At the same time, he worked on his own
verse, but described himself as discouraged with the results. In
1841 he returned to New York, where he opened a studio and
began producing miniature paintings on ivory. He was quite successful, with many diplomats and other public figures commis-
sioning him for paintings. Jefferson Davis, who was then the
Secretary of War, asked him to paint his son. Carlin developed
friendships with Horace Greeley and William Seward, among others. In 1843, he married Mary Wayland, a graduate of the New
York school; they had five children.

With the encouragement of the poet William Cullen Bryant
and others, Carlin continued to write verse. He studied rhyming
and pronunciation dictionaries and was soon publishing poems in
various newspapers. "The Mute's Lament" appeared in the first
issue of the *American Annals of the Deaf and Dumb* in 1847. The
editor admiringly remarked that a congenitally deaf person writing
melodic English poems was such a rarity that it could be compared
to a person born blind painting a landscape. The poem's bleak
portrayal of deafness reveals Carlin's mixed feelings about his identity. Such sentiments were by no means uncommon. Nack offers

John Carlin, c. 1845

a similarly gloomy view in "The Minstrel Boy," and other writers in this collection—including Clerc, Jewel, and Searing—present a vision of becoming hearing in heaven.

Beginning in the early 1850s, Carlin took a more active interest in deaf people's public affairs. He helped to raise $6,000 for St. Ann's Episcopal Church for the Deaf in New York, the nation's first church for deaf parishioners. He contributed a side panel to the monument for Thomas Hopkins Gallaudet, showing Gallaudet teaching fingerspelling to deaf children. He also began to publish essays on deaf education. Unlike most deaf adults, Carlin was somewhat opposed to sign language in teaching. Although he himself did not speak or speechread, he advocated speechreading and fingerspelling in the classroom, for he thought these were the most effective ways for deaf children to acquire English. Again, we should remember that while Carlin was perhaps more extreme, he was not the only deaf person to hold such views.

Carlin frequently gave lectures at deaf events. His long signed speeches, full of learned allusions and quotations, made him something of a deaf Edward Everett (examples of his speeches appear in part two). He was among the first to argue for a national college for the deaf, demonstrating his firm belief in deaf people's potential. At the inauguration of the National Deaf-Mute College in 1864, Carlin was the main speaker and received the college's first honorary degree in recognition of his services to the deaf community.

When photography made his painted miniatures obsolete, Carlin turned to painting landscapes and portraits. He produced several important works, including *After a Long Cruise,* which was later purchased by New York's Metropolitan Museum of Art. He continued writing; in 1868 he authored a children's book, *The Scratchsides Family.* He also published articles on architecture and lectured on such diverse topics as geology and New York's Central Park. In 1864 he founded the Manhattan Literary Association of the Deaf, the first such organization in the country. He also helped to raise funds for the Gallaudet Home for Aged and Infirm Deaf. Carlin died in 1891 at age seventy-eight.

The Mute's Lament

I move—a silent exile on this earth;
As in his dreary cell one doomed for life,
My tongue is mute, and closed ear heedeth not;
No gleam of hope this darken'd mind assures
That the blest power of speech shall e'er be known.
Murmuring gaily o'er their pebbly beds
The limpid streamlets as they onward flow
Through verdant meadows and responding woodlands,
Vocal with merry tones—*I hear them not.*

The linnet's dulcet tone; the robin's strain;
The whippowil's; the lightsome mock-bird's cry,
When merrily from branch to branch they skip,
Flap their blithe wings, and o'er the tranquil air
Diffuse their melodies—*I hear them not.*
The touches-lyric of the lute divine,
Obedient to the rise, the cadence soft,
And the deep pause of maiden's pensive song,
While swells her heart, with love's elated life,
Draw forth its mellow tones—*I hear them not.*
Deep silence over all, and all seems lifeless;
The orator's exciting strains the crowd
Enraptur'd hear, while meteor-like his wit
Illuminates the dark abyss of mind—
Alone, left in the dark—*I hear them not.*
While solemn stillness reigns in sacred walls,
Devotion high and awe profound prevail,
The balmy words of God's own messenger
Excite to love, and troubled spirits soothe—
Religion's dew-drops bright—*I feel them not.*
From wearied search through long and cheerless ways
For faithless fortune, I, lorn, homeward turn;
And must this thankless tongue refuse to breathe
The blest word "Mother" when that being dear
I meet with steps elastic, full of joy,
And all the fibres of this heart susceptive
Throb with our nature's strongest, purest love?
Oh, that this tongue must still forbear to sing
The hymn sublime, in praise of God on high;
Whilst solemnly the organ peals forth praises,
Inspired and deep with sweetest harmony!
Though sad and heavy is the fate I bear,
And I may sometimes wail my solitude,

Yet oh, how precious the endowments He,
T'alleviate, hath lavished, and shall I
Thankless return his kindness by laments?
O, Hope! How sweetly smileth Heavenly Hope
On the sad, drooping soul and trembling heart!
Bright as the morning star when night recedes,
His genial smile this longing soul assures
That when it leaves this sphere replete with woes
For Paradise replete with purest joys,
My ears shall be unsealed, and I shall hear;
My tongue shall be unbound, and I shall speak,
And happy with the angels sing forever!

Advantages and Disadvantages of the Use of Signs

Fully sensible how grave and momentous the nature of the ground is, along which I am about to tread, it will be my special care to render every argument in favor of my theory, perspicuous and worthy of consideration, at the same time avoiding any thing that may savor of dogmatical conceit or pedantry. . . . With the system of instructing deaf mutes in articulation, carefully and philosophically expounded by Messrs. Weld and Day, who visited a few years since the principal institutions of Europe, we rest perfectly satisfied in the conclusion that is not the one which has long been or desideratum.[1] It has been to us a source of surprise and regret to see so much voluntary blindness and infatuation with which the German and other professors have continued, and are still continuing the system, utterly regardless of the strong and natural antipathy of their pupils to it, and also of the truth that they have made little progress in literature.

---

1. Lewis Weld, of the American Asylum, and George E. Day, of the New York Institution, visited Germany in 1844 to observe the methods of oral deaf education used there. They agreed that such techniques were not effective and should not be utilized in the United States.

That the American system, adapted after the Abbés de l'Epée and Sicard's, has proved itself superior to any already known, except the French, none can have reason to deny; nor can he ever disagree with me that the manual alphabet, being the principal branch of our system, is the best and surest channel of knowledge and communication for the deaf and dumb; nor can he offer any dissent to the fact that the language of signs, properly used, is indispensable to their mental improvement in the school-room and chapel. The latter is indeed an immense advantage offered to them to facilitate their intellectual power of comprehending even the most difficult principles of the English grammar, if clearly and plainly explained—otherwise had it been, without that necessary assistance, that a deaf-mute pupil would have been a great wonder—worth exhibiting in the Crystal Palace, if he could form in a short time clear and correct ideas of new words spoken by digital gyrations only![2] Yet I regret to say the beautiful language of signs has given them grievous disadvantages to experience. . . .

The speaking person's mind enjoys all the wonderful powers of his five senses: besides its power of thought and reasoning, it *sees* all things pertaining to nature, and art, *hears* all the sounds and noises, *smells*, *tastes*, and *feels* all that have even long before passed through the organic channels. Hence, deriving from its constant repetitions of hearing words spoken, his superiority in language over the deaf mute. The speaking blind has but four senses. Unless he had lost his sight in his youth, his mind can convey no clear, decided idea of nature with all her beauties of form and color. But yet, by his mind's constantly hearing words spoken, he has indeed gained a vast advantage over the poor deaf mute in the power of language. The celebrated Laura Bridgman, whom all know, has

---

2. The Crystal Palace was the centerpiece of the 1851 Great Exhibition in London. Constructed in less than one year, the building housed thousands of exhibits of new and unusual things, including much of the latest industrial technology.

but three senses to enjoy.[3] Her two lost senses (of seeing and hearing) which deprived her mind of the privilege of seeing nature,
persons and things, and hearing words, (what a sad spectacle her
case presents!) have increased the strength and inquisitiveness of
her sense of touching. Here I respectfully invite your attention to
this fact that, by her mind's long practice in *feeling* the raised letters
of her few books and words in the manual alphabet spelt within
her hands, she has acquired a superiority in language over most of
the deaf and dumb community. . . .*

On a new pupil's first entrance in the institution, his mind is
all blank, though it retains in remembrance a few objects at his
home and other places; but the longer he remains in his new
home, the more stored it gets with new objects, faces and signs.
As the pupils uniformly converse with each other in the language
of gestures, almost without the use of dactylology, the said pupil's

---

3. Laura Dewey Bridgman (1829–1889) was the famed deaf-blind
student of Samuel Gridley Howe, who patiently taught her English.
First, Howe attached labels with raised letters to common objects. Then
he cut these labels and mixed up their individual letters; Bridgman gradually learned to rearrange them in their proper order. When she finally
understood that the letters were a means to communicate with others,
she made rapid progress. Bridgman increased her vocabulary and then
was taught the manual alphabet. She could soon spell very quickly with
her fingers. Charles Dickens visited Bridgman in 1842 and was impressed. He includes an account of her in his *American Notes*.

*When I and my wife visited her a few years ago, we were struck
with the ease and rapidity of her spelling forth words, and the correctness
of their grammatical construction; and I, incited by curiosity, asked her
amiable and patient benefactress if she ever made signs in explaining new
words to her sightless pupil. She answered Oh no—*Not at all*; but it
however cost her much pains to make her comprehend the meaning of
a word by means of a sort of synonyms. It strikes us that she has no idea
of signs except by a very few plain ones necessary for her immediate
wants. [Carlin's note.]

mind, being constantly in contact with them, naturally receives and retains the impressions of what his eyes have seen, and of course is overloaded with signs, while but few words—one word to twenty signs—are treasured therein. At all times, in the daylight or in the inky of darkness of the night, and every where, it sees nothing but gestures perpetually swinging, advancing, retreating and flourishing in the air. O, would to heaven that but half of these images haunting his brain were of the fingers moving in our own as well as the English manual alphabet, and of the printed or written letters![4]

Here I pause, and ask if the *learned* signs are his natural, vernacular language? If so, what is Laura Bridgman's—certainly not of signs? What has rendered her superior to most of us in written language? Believe me to say that I candidly admit the necessity and indispensability of gestures to his mental improvement. Yet, what has always led him to commit such grammatical errors and blunders as to raise a flush of mortification and vexation in his teacher's face? It is the exclusive preponderance of *superfluous* signs, impressed on his memory, which bewilders and entangles his ideas intended to be written down or spelt on the fingers. Nevertheless I am happy to mention that there are among us several mutes of superior intellectual capacities, who, having labored incessantly and with signal success to treasure so many words and rules of the English language as to countervail their mental signs, are able to convey their ideas in writing with almost as much ease and fluency as any speaking persons do.

There are four kinds of signs: the NATURAL, the VERBAL, the PANTOMIMIC, and the INDIVIDUAL. Of these the verbal is the most

---

4. Carlin refers here to fingerspelling, the practice of manually spelling out the letters of English words, which is a distinct part of American Sign Language. In modern ASL, fingerspelling is used to give proper names and to express certain other words. By the "English manual alphabet," Carlin presumably means the two-handed British alphabet.

necessary and appropriate to the pupil's faculty of comprehension. It is eminently qualified for defining all necessary abstract words and the principles of the English grammar. The natural signs, by their beauty, grace and impressiveness, have a tendency to encourage his predilection for them and excessive indulgence in their use, and, by their being mostly superfluous, to retard his intellectual progress.[5] The pantomimic are sometimes useful in depicting passions and imitating others' actions for his edification—yet his teacher should be extremely sparing and circumspect in their use at school. The individual, with a few exceptions, are wholly superfluous and nonsensical. What! our new pupils are to be marked like sheep by individual signs ridiculous in the extreme—as for one, the right fore finger pressing the shut right eyelids, a compliment by no means agreeable to him or her—for another the fore finger pushing the nose's end upward, signifying that he or she has a pug nose, and so on with others.[6] No such thing is ever known in the public schools, seminaries and colleges. Among the few exceptions, those for God and the Savior are proper in the chapel. Of the pantomimic, I deem it a duty incumbent upon me, notwithstanding my extreme repugnancy, to remark the fact that in some public exhibitions (particularly of one of our leading institutions), those signs have been used to excess: though a few *recherché* specimens of some little mute boys' powers of mimicry might perhaps suffice to render the whole exhibition attractive and interesting, the little theatrical representations displayed by young ladies would not seem to be in keeping with the high position the institution has been enjoying; and I question the propriety of making little mute girls, being non-professors in religion, to repeat the

5. Like many of his contemporaries, Carlin uses a narrow definition of "intellectual," one that privileges skill in written English and discounts facility with ASL.

6. A protest against the common deaf practice of creating name signs based on people's physical appearance.

Lord's prayer in beautiful, graceful and measured gestures before the gaping spectators. The Lord's prayer is a solemn incense of the soul to our Heavenly Father, and not a show to court human admiration and applause.

I might be asked how the superfluity of signs could be effectually remedied, and I would with due respect submit a *modus operandi* to your consideration. When new pupils enter into the institutions next year and in the succeeding years, give them no individual signs—but impose on them a *habit* of spelling their names, though, for the reason of old habit, the old pupils must still retain their individual signs—yet they themselves, as well as their teachers are also to spell the new ones' names. The new ones will in one month or two be able to spell their own as well as the others' names. Thus, this new habit you will undoubtedly perceive will tend to increase their mental sight of dactylological images. Besides, all the signs should be given them to comprehend what the words they represent are, and, after they are repeated twice or thrice in order to make their impressions firm in their memory, they (the signs) must be discarded for ever (I mean in the school-room). For example—the teacher is to represent the word LION, by an impressive sign or a picture if within his reach, and then substitute in its place, and use always and uniformly the digital characters: thus, his pupils will be *habituated* to see the word LION, spelt on the fingers. Again, for "a strong lion," he is to define this abstract adjective by a gesture, and afterwards repeat the word by the fingers. It is to be remembered that the articles should be distinguished by the teacher's expressions, which his pupils, proverbially quick-sighted, will readily interpret; as for the article A or AN, his face should present an *indefinite* and unfixed expression; and for THE, the expression should be *definite* and intensely fixed in attention to any particular object either visible or imaginary.

Were I to give more examples *ad infinitum*, it would require to fill a volume; but I trust these examples already shown are suffi-

cient for the purpose; and I sincerely hope that all the instructors
will heartily undertake the arduous and somewhat fatiguing task
of spelling words to their pupils after their respective signs are
given.[7] All for their intellectual good. May God speed their success!

The National College for Mutes

The human mind is one of the most precious of all things
with which man is endowed by his Maker. Its mysterious nature
has through all ages been studied and explored by hosts of
philosophers. . . .

Taking in consideration the great variety of minds, arising
from the physical formation of the brain, and the effects of climate,
disease, parental negligence, etc., it would be at variance with the
logical principles of physiology, to suppose that *all* speaking and
hearing persons have minds equally capable of superior culture, or
that *all* the minds of the deaf and dumb are incapable of higher
training. Yet, though there can be found no difference between
speaking persons or deaf mutes, of the higher class, in imagination,
strength of mind, depth of thought and quickness of perception,
it can not be denied, however repugnant it may be to our feelings,
that the deaf mutes have no finished scholars of their own to boast
of, while the speaking community present to our mental vision an
imposing array of scholars; as the two Websters, Irving, Prescott,

---

7. Carlin's proposal is an antecedent of later trends. Beginning in
1878, proponents of the Rochester Method employed fingerspelling almost exclusively in the classroom. Students and instructors at Gallaudet
College used fingerspelling a great deal well into the twentieth century;
Gallaudet alumni were somewhat notorious in the American deaf community for fingerspelling extensively. Fingerspelling retains a certain air
of learning, and occasionally even pretension, in the deaf community
today.

Anthon, Maury, Mott and other Americans known in the literary and scientific worlds, besides the host of learned men of Europe.[8] How is this discrepancy accounted for, seeing that the minds of the most promising mutes are eminently susceptible of intellectual polish? Does it not show that there must be in existence certain latent causes of their being thrown in the shade? Is it not within the range of our researches to solve the mystery in which they are enveloped?

There are in the great deaf-mute family several graduates, whose intellectual soil, being but partially cultivated at the institutions, by reason of their limited term of pupilage, has returned to its *status quo*; and the germs of knowledge, notwithstanding the favorable signs which they once gave of healthy vegetation, have in some cases withered away, and in others made but little progress toward maturity, which we may with propriety attribute to the baneful effects of their incessant toil in trades detrimental to their superior minds. Respecting certain persons of this same class, they have, since their discharge from school, succeeded in making respectable scholars, and that without their having ever been under the proper and practical husbandry of experienced preceptors. Indeed their great successful efforts in obtaining the object of their longings, under such adverse circumstances, are a striking illustration of the excellent maxim: "Perseverantia vincit omnia."[9]

It must, however, be borne in mind, that they are few in num-

---

8. By listing prominent scholars and including foreign phrases in this essay, Carlin displays his own academic accomplishments and, not incidentally, deaf people's intellectual potential. Here he refers to Noah Webster (1758–1843), lexicographer and author; Daniel Webster (1782–1852), statesman and orator; Washington Irving (1783–1859), writer; William H. Prescott (1796–1859), historian; Charles Anthon (1797–1867), classics scholar; Matthew Maury (1806–1873), oceanographer and naval officer; and probably Lucretia Coffin Mott (1793–1880), an abolitionist and suffragist orator.

9. "Perseverence conquers everything."

ber, and that they have come far short of the mark—the front
rank of the learned—toward which their hearts have long been
yearning. Why have they come short of the point which the
speaking scholars have gained, even without such efforts, as the
former have made in their undertaking? It is simply because they
have no universities, colleges, high schools and lyceums of their
own, to bring them through the proper course of collegiate education to a level with those human ornaments of the speaking
community, who are indebted to the existence of their own
above-named temples of learning, for their superior attainments
and for their consequent reputation and success in literary, scientific and civil undertakings.

The question, whether there is any possibility on the part of
able masters to develop the intellect of their prominent mute
scholars to its fullest scope, were their term of pupilage extended,
and their course of studies semblant to that generally pursued at
colleges, may be answered in the affirmative; for, with the gracious
permission of my excellent friend, Mr. Isaac L. Peet, the able preceptor of the High Class at the New York Institution, than whom,
as one fitted for that arduous avocation, the directors thereof could
not have made a better selection, I have made careful and impartial
investigations of the progress his scholars have made in their
studies.

Notwithstanding their having been but one year and a half in
the High Class, they have, in their pursuance of the higher
branches of education, pushed on with prodigious strides toward
the goal, where merit, honor and glory wait to be conferred upon
their brows. They are now drinking in the beauties of rhetoric,
astronomy, chemistry, the Old Testament Scriptures—with reference to literature, geography, history, civil polity and ethics—
history, geography and algebra, unfolded and explained by their
teacher, with examples, analogies and the like, expressly to
sharpen, strengthen and make exquisite their cognoscitive faculties. Whence came their evident success in what naturally appears

difficult for them to acquire within so short a time? Allow me to assert, with a certainty of the fact, that the secret of their success lies in their knowledge of the superiority of their minds, the value and importance of such a department, which they have had the good fortune to obtain permission to occupy, and the brevity of time allowed for their whole course of study. Hence, their ambition being aroused and encouraged most judiciously by their preceptor, in his endeavors to elevate their minds to the standard of speaking scholars, they have studied, and still study *con amore*, and with all possible diligence, even under many discouraging difficulties which most of our instructors of deaf mutes are enabled by their long experience to trace to their source.

Besides those of the New York High Class, I have learned with much satisfaction that the scholars of the Hartford High Class have made such progress as to encourage our hopes of the ultimate success of that department of higher mute education.

Notwithstanding the acknowledged excellence of that department, and its system which is arranged expressly to accelerate the progress of its scholars in knowledge, it is still but a step, which invites them to ascend to the college, where they may enter upon a still more enlarged scale of studies, and then retire with *honorary degrees*. But alas! no such college is yet in existence.

Apropos of High Classes in the Institutions, I am fully convinced by what I have seen, of their being absolutely indispensable to the intellectual improvement of all their most intelligent pupils, therefore I earnestly recommend them to those which have none of the kind.

The question: Is a college absolutely necessary for gifted mutes? may perhaps create some discussion, *par écrit* in the *Annals*, and *viva voce* at our next convention, in which arguments *pro* and *con* will be duly given so as to lead to a conclusion, whether or not the deaf mutes should be *blessed with that precious boon*.

With a view of securing its establishment, I shall here state a few arguments, which I trust will meet general approbation; but I will be happy to read, weigh and analyze opinions unfavorable to the subject in question, and to acquiesce in them, if they fully convince me of their correctness.

1st. Universities, Colleges, Free Academies and High Schools have been built. For whom? For speaking persons of fine minds. For what? For their intellectual culture to the utmost degree. Why should not *one* college be reared in fair proportions to elevate the condition of our most promising deaf mutes and semi-mutes, seeing that they have a just claim to the superior education enjoyed by the former?

2d. Those of those who speak and hear have indeed produced eminent men. So will our "National College," also. I do not pretend to say that the mutes will be equal to the speaking in the extent of their learning and in the correctness and elegance of their language;[10] but if proofs be needed to give conviction of the truth of my assertion, that mutes of decided talents can be rendered as good scholars as the Barneses, Macaulays, Lamartines and Bryants, I will readily refer to Dr. Kitto, of England, the celebrated biblical commentator, Messieurs Berthier and Pelissier, of France, the former a successful biographer, and the latter a fine poet; our own Nack and Burnet, both excellent authors and poets, and Mr. Clerc, who is the only mute in this country enjoying the honorary degree of Master of Arts, to which he is fully entitled by his learning and long experience in mute education.[11] It is worth remembering that those gentlemen have never been educated at colleges.

---

10. By "language" Carlin means English. Since English is a foreign language to congenitally deaf people, he suggests they will never quite match hearing people in their English fluency.

11. William Barnes (1800?–1886), British philologist and poet; Thomas Babington Macaulay (1800–1859), British historian, author, and statesman; Alphonse-Marie-Louis de Prat de Lamartine (1790–1869), French poet; and William Cullen Bryant (1794–1878), American poet and editor. John Kitto (1804–1854), a British biblical scholar and author, became deaf at age twelve. He published an acclaimed autobiog-

3d. The proposed ALMA MATER will be the only real nursery, under whose fostering care we may have reason to believe will be produced mute sages and distinguished men of all professions—especially civil engineers, physicians, surgeons, lawyer and statesmen, who will thereby be restored to society, from which they have been isolated, by reason of the nature of their misfortune, and of the poverty of their minds.

4th and lastly. The establishing of a National College for mutes, being the first of the kind in the world, will perpetuate the gratitude of its hundreds of students, and add fresh luster to the halo of glory encircling our blessed republic; a country distinguished for the beauty and solidity of her federal and state governments, her unrivaled prosperity in commerce and domestic enterprise, and the great number of public and private acts of benevolence, consummated by her enlightened citizens.[12] The importance of such an establishment can not fail to be obvious to all thinking minds; and, furthermore, all whose hearts are ever alive with a generous desire to promote the welfare of the class of beings referred to, will not fail to consider it a duty, as imperative in its call as laudable in its execution, to carry into full effect that grand desideratum. . . .

Perhaps the *Annals*, in succeeding numbers, may be the most proper medium of maturing our deliberations in this matter, before our next convention comes; and on that occasion we may

---

raphy called *The Lost Senses* in 1845. Jean-Ferdinand Berthier (1803–1886), who either was born deaf or became deaf at a young age, published papers and books in defense of deaf people and sign language. In 1849 he was elected to the Societé des Gents des Lettres, France's most distinguished literary fellowship. Pierre Pélissier, totally deaf from childhood, published a well-received book of French poetry in 1844.

12. Like Clerc (see p. 10, n. 5), Carlin appeals to American patriotism by arguing that deaf education will make the United States a greater country.

accomplish what is binding on us to promote the well-being, intelligence, happiness in social ties, and prosperity in business of
those beings to whom the blessed auditory sense is denied by our
Heavenly Father, for certain reasons which it is always difficult to
fathom.

5

EDMUND BOOTH

(1810–1905)

Unlike the other authors in this volume, Edmund Booth spent most of his adult life on the American frontier. A tall, imposing man, he moved out west to Iowa when he was twenty-nine. Like many settlers, he did a variety of jobs. He helped construct buildings, worked on a farm, held several minor government positions, and even sought gold in California. In 1856 he began a long career in journalism, editing the *Anamosa Eureka,* a weekly Iowa newspaper. Despite his somewhat isolated location, he also actively participated in the deaf community, writing on deaf issues and working for the advancement of deaf people.

Booth was born on August 24, 1810, in Chickopee, Massachusetts. His family had a farm. When he was four, his father caught "spotted fever" (most likely meningitis) and died suddenly. Booth contracted the same disease, which left him blind in one eye and partially deaf. At age eight, he lost the remainder of his hearing. His mother taught him to read and write, skills he cherished throughout his life. When he was sixteen, Booth learned about the school for deaf students in Connecticut. He applied, was accepted, and—over the protests of his uncle, who wanted him to stay and do farmwork—went by stagecoach to Hartford.

Later, he recalled how it felt to encounter signing deaf people for the first time. "It was all new to me . . . the innumerable motions of arms and hands," he wrote. "I was among strangers but knew I was at home."[1] His teachers included Laurent Clerc and Thomas Hopkins Gallaudet. He excelled at his schoolwork; before he graduated, he was invited to become an instructor. He taught for seven years. One of his pupils was fourteen-year-old Mary Ann Walworth, his future wife. In 1839, he resigned because of pneumonia, a dispute over pay, and a desire to see the world.

Booth traveled 1,300 miles to Iowa, where Walworth lived with her family. He worked building a sawmill, a dam, and houses. The following year, he and Walworth were married. They would eventually have four children, three of whom survived infancy (the youngest, Frank, later became the superintendent of the Nebraska School for the Deaf. Ironically, he was a rigid oralist, banning sign language from the school although both of his parents used sign to communicate). To support his family, Booth worked at different times as county recorder, postmaster, and as a clerk for the Iowa House of Representatives. He also had a small farm.

In 1848, Booth decided to join the California gold rush. He left his family with his brother and departed with another deaf man, identified only as Clough. The trip took six months. Booth stayed in California five long years, during which time he and Mary Ann maintained a remarkable correspondence. One of these letters is excerpted here. The letters demonstrate again the important role writing played in connecting deaf people who were separated from each other. Booth did not find enough gold to become wealthy, but he did earn a significant sum. At his wife's plea, he

---

1. Quoted in Harlan Lane, *When the Mind Hears: A History of the Deaf* (New York: Vintage, 1984), 233.

Edmund Booth

returned to Iowa in 1854. Two years later, he became editor of the *Anamosa Eureka*, making it a strongly abolitionist paper in the years before the Civil War. In 1862 he purchased the paper and gave up farming. He continued editing the paper until his retirement in 1895.

In the 1840s, Booth helped to convince the Iowa legislature to provide for sending deaf children to the Illinois School for the Deaf. Later, he played an instrumental role in lobbying for the Iowa State School for the Deaf. He penned many articles for deaf publications; the essay on emigration included here appeared in the *American Annals of the Deaf* in 1858. In its lean, practical style, it typifies Booth's writing. Booth also took part in the debate over a deaf commonwealth (see chapter ten). In 1880 the National Deaf-Mute College awarded him an honorary degree in recogni-

tion of his "high attainments as a scholar and as a journalist." The
same year, he helped to found the National Association of the
Deaf. He was nominated for the presidency of the new organization, but he gracefully declined in favor of a younger man. Booth
died in 1905, at age ninety-four.

Letter to Mary Ann Booth

*While Booth prospected for gold in California, his wife and children re-
mained in Iowa. At the time of this letter, Booth had not seen his family
in over three years.*

Chili Camp, Tuolumne Co., California
Jan. 21, 1852
My Dear Wife,

Your letter of Nov. 17th was brought to me from So-
nora last night by Mr. Buck, one of my partners. I was
most heartily glad to receive it and equally glad to hear
that at last you and the children are in your own house
and living by yourselves and so comfortably. I hope you
and they will continue to live pleasantly and comfortably.
We do not fully know the value of a home till we leave it.

Everything that tells me of home is intensely interesting; and I hope to be there next summer. It is not probable
that I shall be rich, but my coming will have done some
good in enabling us to live more easy and comfortably.
You need not feel any concern about what others say in
regard to my not being able to come home. It is all folly.
Your statements about others who return with nothing
make me laugh, but it is in the nature of the thing; for
gold digging is much like lead digging—uncertain. I can
find gold in a thousand places within a mile, but in few

cases would it be rich enough to pay for digging. I have made but little in the past two months. In Dec. rain most of the time, and prospecting took up the rest of the month. In January (this month) we worked while we had water, and joined a sluicing company—to wash with a sluice 500 feet long with a torn at the tail—but we had not sufficient water. A race has since been finished, five miles in length, to bring water from Sullivan's Gulch, but we cannot get it till another heavy rain.

Last night two more men joined our company, so we are four in all, the lawyer & Englishman having left us during the last rain to work their own claims at Yankee Hill. All my partners are from Boston. All came together around the "Horn"—arriving, when I did, in '49 after eight months' voyage. All are married. One has four children, one three and one has lost his only child. . . .

We have sold our mule and cart and have some talk of buying another because the rain holds off so long. It costs as much to board a horse as to board three or four men. What we most want is frequent showers of rain all winter and spring. . . .

I cannot give up the idea of removing you all at some future time to Cal. At present, things are too unsettled. This will not continue so forever. Gen. Wilson—well-known in Dubuque, etc.—came here on a pleasure trip, and probably likewise from curiosity, and the wonderful climate took away his head. He has done what he would not do in regard to Iowa or Wisconsin, viz., made Cal. his permanent home. . . .

Thomas[2] is a brave boy, but he must not use his courage rashly. He is not old enough and must not cut down trees yet. The danger is always great and requires the great-

2. Booth's oldest son, approximately eleven years old at the time.

est caution. Many men (not boys) have been killed by the trees, which they were cutting, falling on them. He must be careful likewise not to cut his legs or feet when chopping wood. I am glad he helps you and is useful and obedient. Every man is made for some use; and he will find it more pleasant to be useful than to be otherwise. Let him help you cultivate the garden next spring and summer. I will give him a dollar for his biggest melon.

I hope you will keep in good heart & comfortable. Make home pleasant to the children that they may love their home. Use the money in the way you think best. Get fresh beef, etc., and salt it yourself; it is more healthy than pork, and much better for children—also dried apples, etc.

I will remain in this country six or ten months longer.[3] I do wish it would rain. I could make twenty dollars a day if we had rain. We cannot haul the best dirt to water because the mountains are in the way. The gulches where is water are dug out. In a few years men will make but two or three dollars a day except in quartz. I have an offer of a share in a quartz mine for $50—good but no machinery to work it. May accept it; think I shall and afterwards sell again.

Love to all,
Edmund

On Emigration to the West by Deaf Mutes

The following article was written when Booth was living in Anamosa, Iowa.

---

3. The indeterminacy of Booth's plans shows clearly in this letter, in which he considers returning home in the summer, moving his family to California, and now staying almost another year.

About eighteen months ago a friend of mine (S. A. L.), formerly a pupil of the American Asylum, paid a visit, at my request, to this part of the country, with a view of removing his family here, in case he was satisfied with the appearance of things and future prospects. After several days' observation, and when he had become well posted in regard to the advantages of a removal to and permanent settlements here, he, seated quietly in his chair, awoke from a brown study of some minutes duration, and turning to me, with a sad, reproachful look, asked why I had not some years sooner informed him of the advantages of removing to the West?

The question, and especially the manner of his putting it, came upon me with something of an electric shock. I had long known that, as a general rule, a deaf-mute could, if he had learned a mechanical trade and was skillful, industrious and temperate, do better here, in a worldly point of view, than he could in the East. Here he could have equally good and sometimes better wages. He could live cheaper, and buy land at a rate which, compared with eastern prices, is nearly nothing. These reasons inclined me to advise educated deaf-mutes to come West; but another and a darker side of the picture deterred me.

I came here over eighteen years ago, when wolves, deer, rattlesnakes and Indians were far more numerous than white men. The land all belonged to government or to the Indians, and every white man was a "squatter" from necessity, as no land was in the market. The times, too, were emphatically hard times, as they are now. . . .

To advise deaf-mutes to come at such a time, seemed to me of doubtful propriety. The danger was not that they would not find work and good wages, for there were an abundance of both. It was that they would fall into the loose habits which then prevailed among a loose and more miscellaneous population than, as a general rule, we have now. Another reason I had. I was certain some would be dissatisfied; for, unless a man has more romance, or

courage and energy, than fastidiousness in his composition, a frontier life is not to him a bed of roses, and you, Mr. Editor, will
readily understand that it is not very pleasant, after inviting a man
to the best feast that caterer ever prepared, to find him complaining at every turn of his knife and fork.

Within the past five years, things have greatly changed. Population has poured into the West as it never poured before. Iowa
has grown at the rate of a hundred thousand annually, and now
numbers over six hundred thousand. So it is with other and contiguous States. Railroads are stretching in every direction. Cities
and towns are building every where, and not men enough to build
them. The great influx of emigrants has created a proportionate
demand for lands, and where advantageously situated in regard to
railroads, etc., the price has ran up to a point almost fabulous.
True, the financial revulsion has brought it down, and in measure
checked many works of improvement and a multitude of wild
dreams, yet it is only for a few months or years at most. The land
grants by Congress will insure the completion of the main lines of
railroad; and the stream of emigration must enlarge with the coming spring, forced to do so by the contraction in the East, and by
the ready facilities now provided for removing West. Why should
not many educated deaf-mutes follow the general rush?

And now let me speak seriously to them. Brethren! If you
have farms that are productive, and are thus or otherwise well off,
or have aged parents who depend on you, I cannot say, come
West. There is a class of persons among the hearing as well as
among deaf-mutes, who for want of active habits, energy, judgment, or some other quality, never make their way in the world.
These may better their condition by coming West, but they need
not expect to become wealthy. It might be cruel to suggest to such
the old proverb: "Blessed is he that expects nothing, for he shall
not be disappointed."

There are those among you skillful in the use of the plane
and the saw, the plow and other implements of labor, who are

industrious, temperate, hopeful, and possessed of a reasonable share of common honesty and common sense, who would be largely benefited by a settlement in or near some of our Western towns. Mechanics, such especially as carpenters, builders, cabinet-makers, etc., are in great demand. The many thousands of people pouring in, need houses and household furniture, and this offers you abundant opportunity for work, and at as good or better wages than most of you receive in the East. And while you are at work, you are living cheaper, and, by the use of economy and good judgment, you are enabled to purchase real estate, build houses of your own, and grow with the country.

With all these fair prospects laid before you, truth requires me to state that, just now, it is "hard times" with us, as with you in the East. "The people's money," as certain politicians call it, and "bank rags" have become scarce. The highest price paid now for wheat is fifty cents per bushel, in trade, for no one will give money for it at this time. In fact, wheat has become a superabundant article, as have most other agricultural products. Therefore, if you come at the present time, you must expect to take pay for work, as we all do, not in money, but in trade, until times improve.

Should you decide to remove westward, make up your minds at the same time to depend each on himself. I have known hearing men come West, and expect their friends or neighbors to give them fifty acre lots, town lots, houses, etc., for nothing. Such men are of no value in any sense and it were better that they stayed in the East. They do not consider that these friends and neighbors have struggled for years through privation, hardship and difficulties, until have made themselves what they are. Do not waste weeks and months hesitating where to go. Go anywhere, if the work to be performed suits you. Towns spring up every year, and almost every where; and at all such places mechanics are wanted. If you are not a mechanic, and intend to engage in agriculture, still go any where, and engage in such work as offers, until you can learn about the country and determine where to purchase land

for a farm. In any cases, it is better to buy an improved farm, if
you have money, than to buy wild land. In the former case you
will at once have a home and the products of the farm. In the
latter, you must build, plow and fence, and wait eighteen months
or two years before the farm begins to pay for cost in money and
labor. Hence, if you have the means, it is cheapest to purchase a
farm already under way. In settling in Iowa, or any one of the
prairie States, do not, as some do, grumble about the scarcity and
high price of timber. A few acres of timber is all that a family
needs; and as it is not so abundant as prairie, it of course commands a higher price. I haul my fencing staff five miles and do not
consider it much of a hardship. Men are here who go further than
that for firewood and fence and building materials.

Let me suggest to deaf-mutes coming West, that perhaps it
were not the wisest plan for a large number to settle in one town,
if all are of the same trade or mechanical occupation.[4] They may,
as the saying is, eat up one another. In the winter season, when
building operations are suspended, the amount of work for each
may be small. The country is vast in extent, and the amount of
room abundant. Do not crowd into one spot. Do your work well
and faithfully; be honest and temperate; be good citizens, and you
will command respect and confidence, and will make friends
among the best people of your locality, wherever it may be. If you
fail in that, the fault must be your own, for men usually, everywhere, see and appreciate real worth. It may be delayed for a
while. It may be hidden under a cloud, but it will almost certainly
come out clear in the end. If, then, you stand high in the community, the merit is yours. If you stand low, the fault—not always it
may be, for there are men who are never understood, if understood ever, until they are dead—is most generously yours.

A common question with persons removing West is, "Is this

---

4. Booth repeats this opinion more forcefully when arguing against
the idea of a deaf commonwealth (see chapter ten).

location or that healthy?" It is a question which makes an old Western settler smile, if he does not involuntarily laugh in your face. Every locality in the West is liable to afford its inhabitants a taste of the fever and ague. It is true that some places have little of it, but the stories that fever and ague is a disease never known in such and such a place, are moonshine. The elevated grounds away from water courses or ponds and marshes are the most healthy. But some persons I have known exposed for many years to the miasma of the marshes, and they were never affected in any way. It depends much on a person's constitution, temperament, or something else which the doctors with their finespun theories do not appear to understand, and I do not pretend to be wiser. . . .

I ought to state, before closing this rather long communication, that, as a general rule, shoe-makers do not fare as well in the West as men engaged in other active occupations. The cause lies in the cheapness of shoes of Eastern manufacture, and in the high price of leather in this region, owing to the fact that the country does not produce the kind of barks used in tanneries.

In conclusion, I would suggest to those New England deaf-mutes who may decide to remove to the prairie regions, that they will find it preferable to settle in Northern Illinois, Southern Wisconsin and Minnesota, and Northern and Central Iowa. Further North, there is more cold than most of them would desire. Further South, the soil has more of clay, and the people are more generally from the South and less from the Northern States.

6

ADELE M. JEWEL

(1834–?)

Adele M. Jewel's work provides a rare glimpse into the life of a lower-class deaf woman before the Civil War. Jewel (née George), a homeless woman in Michigan, wrote primarily to earn money to support herself and her mother. Her pamphlet, *A Brief Narrative of the Life of Mrs. Adele M. Jewel (Being Deaf and Dumb),* was printed for her by a local publisher, and she apparently sold it herself on the streets to passersby.[1] Despite undergoing hardships, Jewel displays vivacity, faith, and determination in her writing. Her account of growing up apart from other deaf people, attending a residential school for the deaf, and learning American Sign Language gives us concrete illustrations of some of the general trends that other writers discuss in this collection. Moreover, Jewel provides the only reference to deaf African Americans in these pages, pointing to the existence of that overlooked group.

We do not have much information about Jewel beyond what

---

1. Because the only existing copies of the pamphlet use her married name, we do not know the original title of her autobiography.

appears in her pamphlet. She was born deaf in Cincinnati in 1834. Her parents doted on her, their only child. When she was three, Jewel and her family moved to Michigan, where they eventually acquired a farm. About nine years later, her father suddenly became ill and died. Jewel and her mother sold the farm to pay off debts and moved to Jackson, Michigan, where they eked out a living by sewing and performing any other work they could find. In Jackson, Jewel met another deaf person for the first time. Almena Knight not only became Jewel's friend, but also taught her ASL and inspired her to attend the state's residential school for the deaf in Flint. With financial assistance from some local citizens, Jewel was able to enroll. She flourished at the school, learning to read and write and becoming part of the community she found there. In a preface to *A Brief Narrative,* a "friend" describes Jewel as an accomplished young woman after she gained an education: "[She is] interesting and communicative . . . conversing rapidly, in the sign language, to those who understood that method of speaking, or writing in a clear and graceful hand with a pencil, to others."

Despite such progress, Jewel was compelled to withdraw from school when she caught a severe illness that ruined the sight in one of her eyes and damaged her health. Since her mother was now an invalid, the two had trouble supporting themselves; they lost their property and became homeless. In these critical circumstances, Jewel came up with the idea of writing her story and selling it to the public. The plan worked, and she evidently was able to earn enough money to secure a living and a home for herself and her mother. Jewel most likely published this first version of her narrative in the late 1850s, when she was in her mid-twenties. She added to the work and sold slightly expanded editions in subsequent years.

After publishing the material excerpted here, Jewel married and had three children: a deaf son and two hearing daughters. However, the marriage ended unhappily. We do not have any

details. We do not even know if her husband was hearing or deaf.
In the preface, the "friend" calls it only "an unfortunate marriage." Jewel herself says "I have drank bitterly of the cup of sorrow, since my marriage; but I cannot here speak of the trials that
have fallen my lot." We can only speculate about the events that
so distressed her. As a single mother, Jewel again relied on her
pamphlet to raise funds to support her family. She earned enough
money to send her deaf son to the Michigan school in Flint, which
she had attended herself. Unfortunately, we have no record of
what became of Jewel in her later years.

A Brief Narrative of the Life of
Mrs. Adele M. Jewel

The history of my life is made up more of thought and feeling
than of incidents and events. It is brief and simple, and yet may be
interesting to those who are curious enough to know how the
world and its experiences are regarded by one who can neither
hear nor speak. . . . I was born deaf, on the 15th of November
1834, in the city of Cincinnati, though I do not remember much
before our removal to Detroit, in the year 1838. Among my early
acquaintances was a little girl nearly my own age, Charlotte Monroe. We became warm friends from the first, and were seldom
separated from morning till night. Our plays, our toys, everything
we had, was shared in common; and by the use of our own
signs—a language taught by nature—we understood each other
very well. They tell me that she ran in to her mother, saying, in
a voice of gladness, "Ma, I can talk deaf and dumb as good as
Dellie."

My father had a tame black bear chained up in the yard. He
was harmless, at least, we believed him so, and were not afraid to
play near him, and even sometimes to pat him on the head—I and
my little friend Lottie. But he soon taught us not to be quite so
familiar. We used to feed him apples and cake, and were delighted

when we could make him show his teeth, or climb the pole, or rear upon his hind legs. One day (I shall never forget that) I had a piece of cake in my hand, which I held temptingly before him, though I had no intention of dividing with him, and frequently disappointed him by drawing it back. He became enraged at last, and seizing me in his arms, he tore my clothes off in an instant, and would have killed me had not my shrieks brought me instant relief. My father dared not keep so dangerous a pet, and soon disposed of him. . . .

When a few years older, my parents removed from Detroit to Grass Lake, on the Central Railroad. There I found myself among strangers, and longed for the friends of my other home. It seemed as if no one would ever understand me as Lottie did, and I missed her sadly. But I was not long left to pine in solitude. Dear Polly Ann Osgood, I soon learned to love her as well. We grew up together like sisters. How many delightful rambles we had about the fields and forest, gathering berries and other fruits, and weaving the sweet wild flowers into garlands to crown our heads; and although I could not hear the warbling of birds, my little friend did, and she tried to make me understand it. . . .

My young mind was filled with thoughts all unexpressed and inexpressible. Deep, fervent and glowing, I longed to worship *something*, I knew not who or what. My dear mother was constantly importuned with questions, who made the grass and the flowers and all the living creatures that throng the earth? . . .

Oh how I yearned for the knowledge to illumine my darkened mind. My mother, as well as she was able, explained to me that One who dwells above made them all; and that I must kneel and raised my eyes, hands and heart in adoration. Oh, I thought "If I *could* only see him." But since I have been able to read His Holy Word, I have learned more of Him. I have learned to worship Him in spirit and in truth. . . .

While dwelling in Grass Lake an event took place that I shall never forget, the remembrance of it even now fills me with horror. My father used sometimes to pour powder upon the hearth to make it flash for my amusement. I think he did not know what a mad-cap I was, or he would hardly have thought it prudent to set me such an example.

One day I was left at home alone, and I got the powder, and sprinkling it about the floor set it on fire. It flashed in earnest, setting fire to everything. I had on a flannel dress, fortunately, or I might have flashed with the rest. But I caught my little dog in my arms, and drew my father's trunk to the door. It was very heavy, and I could not lift it over the sill. So I was obliged to leave it and run more than a quarter of a mile to the house of the nearest neighbor to give the alarm.

When they reached the house the roof had fallen in, and the house with all its contents was consumed. When my mother and father came home, there was no home to receive them. My dear father had taught his foolish little dumb girl a trick that had robbed him of it; though they did not know it then. I could not explain the cause of the fire, and they were so happy to find that I had not also perished in the flames, they thought little of their great loss in the house, though many valuable papers and other articles were destroyed which were never replaced. After I learned to write, however, I gave my mother a faithful account of my part in the affair.

When about twelve years of age I was sent to a common school. I tried as hard as I could to learn, but it was a dry, tedious process, as my teacher was not qualified to instruct the dumb, and I gave it up in despair; feeling, oh how bitterly, that I was not like the rest and could never hope to acquire much knowledge.

I had an uncle who wished to take me to the Deaf and Dumb Asylum in New York; but my father's health was fast failing, and as I am an only child, my mother could not endure the thought of separation and that project was also relinquished. And I, much as I longed for a more enlarged and cultivated sphere, much as I hungered and thirsted for a high knowledge of the world in which

I lived, was brought up wild and wayward, with no definite understanding of my relation to the world, or the duties required of me. . . .

About this time it became evident to all—all but me—that my father's days on earth were numbered. I had never seen a person die, and death to me was a subject upon which I had never thought. To *die!* what was it? I saw the change upon his face. I saw the last dying glance of his eyes as the film gathered o'er them. I felt the last grasp of his icy fingers—then he lay cold and motionless. It was a sight so terrible that I clung frightened to my mother. And yet I could not believe that I must give him up. I believed that change only temporary. It seemed to me that he would rise up again, and speak to us, and live as before. But long hours and days passed away and the change came not. Then they placed his rigid body in a long box, and screwed the lid down tightly, and buried him up in the earth.

What did it all mean? . . . They tried to explain to me that some part of him was still alive and gone to God. But I shook my head. No, God lives up in the sky, and I saw him buried in the ground, I said. . . . That was my first sorrow. But after a little while my dearest friend, Polly Ann, sickened and died also. She was taken away and buried, and I became so hopeless and disconsolate that I hardly cared to live myself. I was sullen, gloomy and resentful. I refused to look upon the lovely face of nature and take heart for the future. All things had ceased to charm me—"what are they all good for if we must die and leave them?" I thought. It seemed to me that if God could do as he pleased with all the world, he could not be good to deprive the poor little mute of some of her dearest friends, rendering her life so dark and cheerless. . . .

After my father's death, my mother and myself were left quite alone and found it hard to get along on the farm. So we sold it, and after paying all the debts contracted during his long sickness, there was little left for ourselves, and we moved to Jackson, where we endeavored to obtain sewing or any kind of work that would enable us to get an honest living. We lived in that city three years and during that time found several good, true friends who did all they could to aid us. Here I formed the acquaintance of a young lady also deaf and dumb, who had been educated at an Asylum in Ohio. She was the first mute I ever saw and the mysterious ties of sympathy immediately established a friendly feeling between us. I was surprised and delighted at her superior attainments.

She could write a beautiful hand on her slate to those who knew not the use of signs, and in a little while taught me the sign language by which we conversed very easily together. We enjoyed many pleasant seasons together, and I shall always count among my dearest friends, Miss Almena Knight, the name of this young lady. . . .

After I saw Miss Knight I grew very anxious to become a pupil at Flint.[2] Some friends who felt interested in my welfare, obtained my mother's consent and assisted me to go. Thanks for the instructions received of Miss Knight, I succeeded in making myself understood, and from being an entire stranger, soon became as a member of one large family. My instructors found me an "apt scholar," and when I had been there ten weeks, I sent home a written article of my own composition. My friends were surprised and pleased at the rapid progress I had made.

Elsie Fairbairn was my especial friend among the pupils; we became warmly attached and seldom separated. The parents of friend "Eppy," as I called her, were also true friends to me, and did many things to show their kindness to myself and mother. . . .

During my stay at Flint I was taken with inflammation in my eyes, causing me great suffering and destroying the sight of one.

---

2. The Michigan school was established by an act of the state legislature in 1848, but it did not open until six years later, in 1854, in a rented house in Flint, Michigan. Jewel, then close to twenty years old, must have been in one of the school's first classes.

My health became poor, and I was obliged to withdraw from the school. I resigned my place with much regret, as I still felt greatly deficient in useful knowledge. The loss of my sight is a great loss to me, still I am thankful for the blessings I do enjoy; for though poor and with slender means of support, I have laid up my treasures in Heaven; looking forward to that glorious time when the mute tongue shall burst forth in strains of love and praise to its Creator in a world of peace and joy. When the lame can walk, the blind shall see, the deaf hear, and the dumb shall speak. All will be right there—no aching heart, no saddened countenance. What a comfort it is for me to believe thus!

Part Second

Dear Reader:

Let me add a few more pages to the brief sketch you have just read of my life, which was written over four years ago. It was a great undertaking for me to publish for perusal by the public a history of my life, and then offer it for sale. I shrunk from it, and could never have done so, had it not been really necessary for me to do something for my own maintenance. But though sometimes chilled by averted looks and want of sympathy, I have found many ready and willing to extend the helping hand; many earnest, true friends who have aided and encouraged me. The son of Mr. Barns, my former publisher (who is a true gentleman, has also been afflicted with deafness, though not mute), and the printers in the *Tribune* office, made me a present of the first thousand copies of my little book and a few dollars in money to help me on. Words fail to express my gratitude for this kindness, but I shall ever cherish for them the most grateful remembrance. By this means I was enabled to secure a home for myself and mother. . . .

And now I will tell you what I have seen in my

travels. . . .[3] Thank Heaven for sight, precious sight! To the deaf it is both hearing and speech. I have only the full enjoyment of one eye—the other is still so dim that I cannot distinguish objects with it. But the sight I do have is invaluable to me. Some of my blind friends seem very cheerful, and even happy. Yet pleasures which sight secures can never be theirs. The faces of beloved friends, beaming with smiles of affection—the green fields—the beautiful flowers—the trees waving in the summer winds, white with blossoms or laden with ripe fruits—the broad, winding river sparkling in the sun, while boats of every shape and size glide over its bosom. . . . The most wonderful sight I ever beheld, a sight that made me tremble and worship God, was the Falls of Niagara. Such a great river, pouring over such a descent! It made me dizzy to look at it; and it shook the earth far and near. . . .

At the Suspension Bridge we found an Asylum for the deaf, dumb, and blind.[4] It was a private school kept by Dr. Skinner and his wife. The Doctor had been blind two years—his wife, though she could see, was a mute. This worthy couple, though white themselves, were deeply interested in the poor colored children afflicted like themselves, and their pupils are all colored.[5] Those who could

---

3. We are left to wonder how Jewel, who was evidently quite poor, managed to afford such trips.

4. A celebrated suspension bridge spanned the Niagara River near the Niagara Falls. Constructed by John Roebling between 1852 and 1855, it is no longer extant today. We unfortunately have no further information on the Skinners or their school.

5. This comment is the only mention of deaf African Americans that I could find in deaf writing before 1864. As this gap suggests, people who were black and deaf were frequently neglected in antebellum America. In the South, teaching an African American (deaf or hearing) to read and write was illegal in every state except Maryland and Ken-

see had bright sparkling eyes, and were quiet and respectful. The blind were very tidy and attentive. They all
seemed very contented and happy, and it was interesting to
see the dumb scholars converse with their blind associates.

The institution is supported partly by donations and
contributions from those who sympathize in the good
work, and partly by the publication of a paper—the work
is done by the pupils who are printers and compositors.

We came away much pleased with our visit and praying for success and prosperity of the Asylum, and for the
welfare of the generous instructors and founders.

[*Editor's Note:* Jewel goes on to relate her other travels,
describing Wyoming, the Allegheny Mountains, Seneca
Falls, etc.]

Arriving in Genoa, we went to visit uncle's family,
who received us with much joy, and my young cousins
did all they could to make our visit pleasant. We remained
a week, and when we set out on our return my aged
grandfather and his wife accompanied us and spent the
winter with us. . . . [Now] my mother and myself are left
alone again.

Two years ago the Principal of the Indiana Asylum sent
me an invitation to visit the institution and remain a pupil.

Miss Almena Knight accompanied me. We had a very
pleasant visit, and were treated with great respect by the
teachers. The process of teaching is similar to that of Flint;
and the exercises in the school were very interesting. We
remained, however, but a few days, for I was not able to
meet the expenses of tuition there.

---

tucky. In the North, when deaf African Americans did receive an education, it was usually in a segregated school, such as the private one that
Jewel describes here.

And now for the present, dear readers, adieu. At some future time I may tell you more. My home is not yet free from incumbrance, and could I emerge from indebtedness, I shall be forever grateful to all who, by purchasing my little book, enable me to do so. It is still a great trial for me to offer my book for sale, for though on one hand I meet with sympathy and kindness, on the other, coldness, slight, and discouragement chill me. Still I will hope for the best. May the dear Lord, who was ever a friend to the poor, bless ever the tender, generous heart, is the sincere and constant prayer of

Adele M. George[6]

---

6. Somewhat curiously, Jewel signed her maiden name, Adele M. George, at the end of this account, even though she retained "Adele M. Jewel" in the narrative's title. Perhaps she went back to her maiden name following her separation from her husband.

7

LAURA REDDEN SEARING

(1840–1923)

Laura Searing was born as Laura Catherine Redden, in Somerset County, Maryland on February 9, 1840. She became deaf at age eleven due to meningitis. By that time, her family was living in St. Louis, so she enrolled in the Missouri School for the Deaf in Fulton. She wrote the essay included here when she was just eighteen. It appeared in the *American Annals of the Deaf*. In it, she offers some perceptive observations on the relationship between deafness, sign language, and writing.

After graduating in 1858, Searing found work as a columnist and assistant editor for a St. Louis religious newspaper, *The Presbyterian*. She also contributed articles to the *St. Louis Republican*. She became engaged to a St. Louis Presbyterian minister, but instead of marriage chose to go to Washington, D.C., as a war correspondent. There she interviewed President Lincoln, General Ulysses S. Grant, and members of Congress. In 1862 she published her first book, *Notable Men in the House of Representatives*, under the pen name of Howard Glyndon, which she used throughout her career. An ardent Unionist, Searing also started writing patriotic poetry. In 1863, her poem "Belle Missouri"—written in response to

"Maryland, My Maryland"—was set to music and became a popular battle song among pro-Unionists. The following year, her
book of war poems, *Idyls of Battle,* appeared and was well received.
President Lincoln was among the people who bought the volume.

Searing's subsequent career was equally distinguished. She
spent several years in Europe as a foreign correspondent. Her writing appeared in such diverse publications as the *New York Times,
Harper's,* and the *Atlantic Monthly.* In 1876, she married a hearing
attorney, Edward W. Searing, and settled in New York. They had
one child.

Searing advocated the teaching of speech in schools for deaf
students. Yet embarrassed by her own strained and unnatural
speech, she refused to speak for years, preferring to write or sign
instead. As an adult, she was a pupil of Alexander Graham Bell,
who helped her to regain confidence in her voice, although she
never learned to speechread.

In 1889, Searing delivered a lengthy dedicatory poem in sign
and voice at the unveiling of the Gallaudet statue on the campus
of the National Deaf-Mute College. She published more than two
hundred poems and five books during her career. She spent her
final years in California.

A Few Words about the Deaf and Dumb

It is one of the most interesting sights in the world to watch a
mute, whose mind is just beginning to come out of its dormant
state, after he has mastered the first rudiments of instruction, and
is beginning to comprehend what is taught him. The countenance
before so inanimate and vacant, becomes bright and intelligent.
His movements are quick and nervous. His eye, sparkling with
awakened thought, is ever turning to some new object of which
he would seek information. It seems as though he can not learn
fast enough. Life wears a new aspect for him, it is all rose-hued;
and the joy of being able to communicate with others, and to be
understood and sympathized with by them, is almost too great for
him. Every glance, every movement shows that the mind within

Laura Redden
Searing, 1884

has at last been aroused, and is seeking to free itself from the fetters which have so long enthralled it. From the moment that the mute begins to *think*, we date a new era in his mental existence.[1]

Signs are the natural language of the mute. Writing may be used in his intercourse with others, but when conversing with those who are, like himself, deprived of hearing and speech, you will always find that he prefers signs to every other mode of intercourse; and every other established means of communicating his thoughts, no matter what facility he may have acquired in it, is no more nor less than what a foreign language is to those who hear

1. Like Laurent Clerc (see p. 10, n. 4), Searing dramatizes the effect of education on deaf people somewhat by suggesting that they do not truly think before coming to school.

and speak. It may be never so well learned, but still it is *foreign*.[2]
And this, I believe, is just as it should be. Pantomime is the language Nature has provided for the mute, and he should never be
discouraged in making signs. Teach him to articulate if you can,
make him a good writer if you will, but you will find, if he has
his choice, signs will always be the medium of his intercourse with
others. It is right. Do you not all love your mother tongue? Then
why should not the mute prefer his own language to any other?
The language of signs is not, as some may imagine, a confused
jargon. Signs, when used by one well versed in them, can be made
to convey the most subtle and abstract ideas. They are a language
built up like any other, and those who would acquire it perfectly
and thoroughly must make it a life-study.[3] Yet it is not to be denied, that as a means of intercourse with the world, it fails utterly;
but we use his own language to convey to the mute the knowledge of that which is foreign, and signs are the chief means of
instructing him in written language.

There are but few instances of the deaf and deaf-dumb having
attained literary eminence. It must be partly because the mind, in
most cases, does not rise above the common level; and partly because the language of signs, from its peculiar structure, disqualifies
them for expressing their thoughts in written language. How
could we expect an English poet to excel in writing French
rhymes? And thus a mute may be never so eloquent when expressing his thoughts in pantomime, but be utterly powerless to repro-

---

2. As we have seen, Clerc, Burnet, and Carlin make similar points
about the foreignness of English to congenitally deaf people. Cf. p. 14,
n. 9; p. 57, n. 10; and p. 104, n. 10.

3. Searing, like Burnet and other nineteenth-century deaf writers,
argues that ASL is a complex, fully developed human language. Yet this
fact continued to elude the popular consciousness until the early 1960s,
when William Stokoe published *Sign Language Structure* and the now-
classic *Dictionary of American Sign Language*. Those texts helped to galva-
nize a period of intense interest in and respect for signed languages.

duce the same on paper.[4] Massieu and Clerc are brilliant instances of what perseverance may accomplish.[5] But does any one doubt that if these men had been blessed with hearing and speech, their acquirements would have been much more extensive and varied? Dr. Kitto and Charlotte Elizabeth are noble examples of the triumph of intellect over all obstacles.[6] And here the light of genius burned brightly, in spite of disadvantages. But each of them became deaf after they had acquired speech, and distinct ideas of language. Semi-mutes have an immense advantage over those who are born deaf. A child endowed with hearing learns incidentally and without effort, things which it requires years of patient toil to teach the mute.

But yet, do not think that our lot is all dark; that because the many glad sounds of earth fall not upon our ears, and no words of affection or endearment pass our lips, all sources of happiness are

---

Today, scores of American colleges and universities accept ASL for their foreign language requirements, showing that society has come to embrace what Redden, Burnet, and others pointed out over a century ago.

4. For more discussion of this essential paradox, see the general introduction.

5. Jean Massieu (1772–1846) was an accomplished student and teacher in France. Born deaf, he had five deaf siblings. After he arrived at the National Institute for the Deaf in Paris, he quickly became Abbé Sicard's top student and main performer at public exhibitions. At age eighteen, Massieu became a teaching assistant, making him the first known deaf person to enter the teaching profession. He held the post for thirty-two years. Among other accomplishments, Massieu helped to teach French to the young Laurent Clerc and sign language to Thomas Hopkins Gallaudet.

6. Charlotte Elizabeth Tonna (1790–1846) was a British author and poet who became deaf at age ten. Her writings often address religion and social reform. In 1844, Harriet Beecher Stowe published a volume of Tonna's pieces, *The Works of Charlotte Elizabeth,* with which Searing was probably familiar. For information on Kitto, see p. 104, n. 11.

closed to us. Oh! no, no. Our God is a tender and merciful Father, and well has he provided for his "silent ones." We can read upon your faces the emotions of your minds as if they were written in a book.[7] All the world of nature is open to our eager gaze; and the eye almost supplies the deficiencies of the ear. Our life has much of sunshine; and our Father, in His all seeing wisdom, has blessed the greater part of us with buoyant spirits and quick sympathies. We are much more inclined to enjoy the present moment, than to repine for the past or doubt the future. And if sometimes a deep yearning for those blessings which we see you enjoying, but which are denied to us, dims for a moment the mirthful light of our eyes, it is soon swept away by the dear remembrance of our Father's promise, for we know "He doeth all things well." And when we reach our heavenly home, the deaf ear will be unsealed and the mute voice gush out in glorious melody, to be hushed no more through all eternity.[8] And this sweet hope, this dear assurance, gives me strength to say, with head bowed in meek submission, "Even so, Father, for so it seemed good in thy sight!"

Belle Missouri

Arise and join the patriot train,
    Belle Missouri! My Missouri!
They should not plead and plead in vain,
    Belle Missouri! My Missouri!
The precious blood of all thy slain
Arises from each reeking plain.
Wipe out this foul disloyal stain,
    Belle Missouri! My Missouri!

---

7. With the pronouns in this sentence, Searing makes explicit what has been implicit all along: she is writing specifically to hearing people in this essay.

8. Like Carlin at the end of "The Mute's Lament" and Jewel at the conclusion of the first part of her narrative, Searing looks forward to becoming hearing in heaven.

Recall the field of Lexington,[9]
    Belle Missouri! My Missouri!
How Springfield blushed beneath the sun,
    Belle Missouri! My Missouri!
And noble Lyon all undone,[10]
His race of glory but begun,
And all thy freedom yet unwon,
    Belle Missouri! My Missouri!

They called thee craven to thy trust,
    Belle Missouri! My Missouri!
They laid thy glory in the dust,
    Belle Missouri! My Missouri!
The helpless prey of treason's lust,
The helpless mark of treason's thrust,
Nor shall thy sword in scabbard rust!
    Belle Missouri! My Missouri!

She thrills! her blood begins to burn!
    Belle Missouri! My Missouri!
She's bruised and weak, but she can turn,
    Belle Missouri! My Missouri!

---

9. Lexington and Springfield are cities in Missouri that fell under Confederate control early in the Civil War.

10. General Nathaniel Lyon (1818–1861) commanded the Union forces in Missouri during 1861. A fiery, courageous leader, he won an early victory in Boonville that helped to establish Union control of Missouri and made him the North's first genuine war hero. Two months later, he found his forces greatly outnumbered. Instead of surrendering, he attacked. In the fighting, Lyon was slightly wounded twice and had his horse shot out from under him before he was killed, becoming the first general to die in battle during the Civil War. His death demoralized his soldiers, who had also almost run out of ammunition, and the Union troops retreated.

PART TWO

EVENTS AND ISSUES

8

1850 GRAND REUNION

On September 26, 1850, over two hundred alumni of the American Asylum for the Deaf assembled in Hartford, Connecticut. Together with the two hundred current students, it was the largest gathering of deaf people ever. They came from all over the country to pay tribute to Laurent Clerc and Thomas Hopkins Gallaudet, who had opened the institution thirty-three years before.

The event was the brainchild of Thomas Brown, an 1827 graduate of the school. Brown said his spirit could not rest until he had expressed his gratitude to Gallaudet and Clerc. He wrote letters suggesting the concept to other alumni scattered around the nation. They responded enthusiastically, contributing six hundred dollars. After some deliberation, organizers decided to use the funds to purchase silver pitchers and trays for Gallaudet and Clerc.

On the appointed day, the alumni gathered at the school. Luzerne Rae, a hearing teacher, later wrote:

> A more happy assemblage it was never our good fortune to behold. Former friends and fellow-pupils met again, after years of separation . . . to recall 'old times' and old scenes; to exchange fragments of personal history; and to brighten anew the chain

of friendship and gratitude that bound them to one another, and to the institution in which their true life began. And it was most pleasant to see the joy that beamed from all their faces, and gave new vigor and animation to their expressive language of signs.[1]

Rae added that the alumni had a "general appearance of intelligence and respectability. . . . To their old instructors, the whole spectacle was of the most gratifying character."

In the afternoon, a procession was formed that included alumni, students, teachers, the governor of Connecticut, principals and faculty from other deaf schools, citizens, and Clerc and Gallaudet. The group proceeded through Hartford to the Center Church. Lewis Weld, the principal of the American Asylum, welcomed the audience and a minister offered a prayer. After that, all of the presenters except Gallaudet were deaf. Brown signed a few opening remarks. He was followed by Fisher Ames Spofford, the orator of the day. A former student and teacher at the American Asylum, Spofford was known as the "mute Garrick" because of his exceptional signing ability. Finally, large silver pitchers, with accompanying trays, were presented to Gallaudet and Clerc. One side of the pitchers had an engraving depicting Gallaudet and Clerc leaving France; it showed the two men, ships and waves to represent their voyage, and the American Asylum beyond the sea in the distance. The other side featured a picture of the interior of the school, with teachers and pupils. Each pitcher had a long inscription indicating it was "a token of grateful respect" from "the deaf mutes of New England."

Gallaudet had taught for thirteen years, retiring in 1830. Clerc was still teaching at age sixty-five. In his acceptance speech, Gal-

---

1. Luzerne Rae, "Testimonial of the Deaf Mutes of New England to Messrs. Gallaudet and Clerc," in *Tribute to Gallaudet: A Discourse in Commemoration of the Life, Character, and Services, of the Rev. Thomas H. Gallaudet, with an Appendix,* 2nd ed. (New York: F. C. Brownell, 1859), 201, 203.

Detail of the silver pitcher presented to Laurent Clerc at the American Asylum in 1850.

laudet made it clear that the enterprise would not have succeeded without Clerc. "What should I have accomplished," he said, "if the same kind providence had not enabled me to bring back from France, his native land, one whom we still rejoice to see among us—himself a deaf mute, intelligent and accomplished. . . ."

The event demonstrated just how much deaf Americans had come together as a community and culture. The ceremony was in their language, the natural language of signs. It celebrated their common history and values. In Clerc and Gallaudet, they had tangible heroes responsible for bringing them together. The 1850 reunion was the first of many such assemblies and conventions organized by and for deaf people. It officially marked the emergence of deaf Americans' collective consciousness.

Thomas Brown's Remarks

After Weld had welcomed the assembly and a minister had offered a prayer, Brown addressed the gathering in sign language. His address was read in English by Weld for nonsigning members of the audience.

My deaf and dumb friends:

The object of our assembling here is chiefly to pay our grateful respects to our early benefactors—to those, to whose assiduous labors we owe our education, and the hopes and happiness it has afforded us.

Let me congratulate you on our happy meeting. How interesting to us all is the occasion, as one for the renewal of former friendships, and the expression of grateful acknowledgments to our best friends and benefactors. Let us ever remember them, and love the great and good institution with the sincere love of children.

Fisher Ames Spofford's Address

Fisher Ames Spofford, the orator of the day, then took the stand. Because Spofford had not prepared a written text, Thomas Gallaudet, the eldest son of Thomas Hopkins Gallaudet, interpreted Spofford's address into English as he signed it.[2]

Gentlemen and Ladies:

You have assembled here in this building, truly a large assemblage, for the purpose of witnessing an interesting ceremony. If the remarks I now shall make to you lack point, I trust I shall be excused from the peculiarity of the occasion. I feel a delicacy in expressing my ideas before so many to whom I am unknown, upon such an interesting topic.

We are assembled to express our love and gratitude to the

---

2. Because Spofford composed and delivered his address in ASL, the version here is technically not "written" by him, but rather a translation of his signs by a hearing person. In this respect, his address differs from the other orations in this collection, which deaf presenters wrote in English ahead of time.

founders of this institution, the first established in this country. There are present former pupils of the establishment, who left it ten, fifteen and even twenty years ago, from distant parts of the country. We once more warmly greet each other. We have experienced great pleasure in being allowed to assist in contributing for the object of this day, and thus testifying our gratitude to our instructors and to the founders of this institution. Their glorious example has been followed, and now, for the education of our fellow-sufferers, there are twelve or thirteen similar places of instruction, all arising from this institution. Thirty-three years ago, the deaf mutes in this country were in the darkness of the grossest ignorance. They knew not God. They knew nothing of the maker of heaven and of earth. They knew nothing of the mission of Jesus Christ into the world to pardon sin. They knew not that, after this life, God would reward the virtuous and punish the vicious. They knew no distinction between right and wrong. They were all in ignorance and poverty, with no means of conveying their ideas to others, waiting for instruction, as the sick for a physician to heal them.[3]

But their time of relief had come. In this city, a celebrated physician, Dr. Cogswell, had an interesting daughter who had been deprived of her hearing.[4] Though her father and her friends looked upon her with pity, yet her deprivation of hearing has proved to have been a blessing to the world. Had she not been left by God sitting in darkness and ignorance, the successful efforts

---

3. Like other writers, Spofford exaggerates the condition of deaf people before education. While many such individuals lived in ignorance, certainly not all did. For example, John Brewster, a deaf folk artist in colonial America, learned to read and write without formal schooling. Meanwhile, on Martha's Vineyard from the seventeenth to the nineteenth century, a high rate of hereditary deafness led to a community in which both deaf and hearing people used sign language. Such exceptions tend to be elided by Spofford and other commentators.

4. Mason Fitch Cogswell and his daughter, Alice.

that have since been made for our instruction might never have been attempted. Mr. Gallaudet was an intimate friend of the family, and devoted himself to contrive some means for her instruction. Dr. Cogswell's inquiries soon established the fact that there were many other persons in the same unfortunate condition, a number sufficient to form a school, if a system of instruction could be discovered. Some gentlemen of Hartford sent Mr. Gallaudet abroad for this benevolent purpose. He visited the London Institution, but circumstances prevented the acquisition of their plan of instruction. The same thing took place at Edinburgh. But at Paris, all the facilities that he needed were given him by the Abbé Sicard, the principal of their Institution. Here he spent some time, acquired the knowledge of their mode of instruction, became acquainted with Mr. Clerc, and with Abbé Sicard's leave, returned with him to this country. Mr. Clerc, at first, feared that he should be in a strange land without friends. But he soon found that by his amiable virtues and accomplished mind, he made friends here, among his pupils and in the best society of the city. Funds were immediately raised. Instructions were commenced in the building now called the City Hotel. The first class of pupils numbered seven. After a year, a building in Prospect street was taken, and then measures were adopted for the erection of spacious accommodations on Lord's Hill, the present building of the Asylum.

Thirty-three years ago, there were no educated deaf mutes sent out into the world—now, a large number. What a change does this fact present! Who have been the instruments of this change? Messrs. Gallaudet and Clerc, under the smiles of heaven. Our ignorance was like chaos, without light and hope. But, through the blessing of God, light has shone through the chaos and reduced it to order.[5] The deaf mutes have long wished to

---

5. Spofford draws on the imagery of Genesis to underscore the deprivation of deaf people before the advent of deaf education. Just as God created the world out of chaos and darkness, he says, so Gallaudet and

express their gratitude to these benefactors. Mr. Brown first conceived the idea, and addressed letters to all for their consent. All enthusiastically agreed. The idea flashed over the whole, like the fire on the prairie. The wishes which we then expressed, are now carried out in the offering before us, and the perfume of friendship which they convey to our old instructors, will be as fragrant as the offering of the spices in Persian temples to the sun.

Our thanks are likewise due to the founders of this institution, on which Heaven has smiled. Some may say that deaf mutes have no gratitude; that they receive favors as the swine do the acorns of the forest that are shaken down for them, but it is not so. We all feel the most ardent love to these gentlemen who founded this Asylum, and to these our earliest instructors. This gratitude will be a chain to bind all the future pupils together. Those who succeed us as pupils will be told of the debt of gratitude they owe to the founders of the American Asylum. Our ship, moored by this chain of remembered gratitude, will float safely hereafter, and never be wrecked on the rocks of pride and envy. I close with earnest prayers for the happiness of our instructors, both in this world and the next.

George H. Loring's Address to Gallaudet

The audience applauded Spofford's address for a long time. Next, George H. Loring, a former student and teacher at the American Asylum, presented the pitcher and the platter to Thomas Hopkins Gallaudet on behalf

---

Clerc, with God's blessing, helped to transform deaf Americans' lives. Deaf people often used biblical language to emphasize how the schools converted them from ignorance to knowledge, from isolation to community, from no language to ASL and English, and from heathenism to Christian redemption.

of all the school's alumni. He signed his address, which was then read to
the audience by Principal Weld.

Accept this plate which I offer to you in the name of the subscribers, former pupils of the American Asylum, as a token of their
profound gratitude and veneration.

Thirty-five years ago, there was no school for the education
of the deaf and dumb in this country. They had, for a long time,
been neglected, as their case was considered hopeless.

An interesting child, the daughter of a much esteemed physician in this city, was deprived of her hearing by severe sickness.[6] In
consequence of this misfortune, she was the object of the parents'
constant tenderness and solicitude. They used every means they
could contrive to teach her the simplest rudiments of written language, and, in the attempt, they partially succeeded. The physician
had read that there were schools in Europe in which the deaf and
dumb were successfully taught to write and read, and this fact he
communicated to you, and proposed to you to go to Europe to
acquaint yourself with the art of teaching the deaf and dumb, for
the benefit of your unfortunate countrymen. Moved by compassion for the deaf mutes in general, and sustained by several benevolent persons, you embarked for Europe, and after encountering
many difficulties, you accomplished the object of your mission in
France. In returning to America, you brought back an intelligent
and well educated deaf mute, for your coadjutor in your labors.
He demonstrated, by his intelligence and conversation, the truth
that deaf mutes are capable of being taught to write and read. The
public were induced to second, by their liberal contributions, your
efforts to establish a seminary for the education of the deaf and
dumb. On this occasion, a public demonstration of gratitude on

---

6. For a fuller version of the Alice Cogswell story, see the general
introduction.

the part of the educated deaf mutes is due to those benevolent persons who contributed by their benefactions, to the establishment of the American Asylum in this city. We lament some of them who have since died, and we will endeavor to show ourselves grateful on all occasions to those who survive.

It is fortunate and it was also by a kind dispensation of Divine Providence, that you adopted the best method of instruction of the deaf and dumb.[7] By this method we have been instructed in the principles of language, morality and religion, and this education has qualified us to be useful members of society. For these blessings of education, we have felt ourselves obliged to you; we have long wished to make you some permanent testimonial of our gratitude, and have happily succeeded in getting one prepared. In presenting it to you, we all offer our earnest prayers for your welfare in your declining years, and for your reward in the other world.

Loring's Address to Clerc

After Gallaudet accepted the gifts, Loring presented a pitcher and salver to Clerc.

Accept this plate, which I present to you in the name of the subscribers, former pupils of the American Asylum, as a testimonial of our heartfelt gratitude for the great benefits of education which you have bestowed upon us.

When Mr. Gallaudet had initiated himself in the art of teaching the deaf and dumb, under the illustrious Sicard, he proposed to you to come to America, to establish a school for deaf mutes;

---

7. The "best method" refers to education through sign language, as opposed to oralism, which was then dominant in Germany and common in some schools in England.

and you did not hesitate to leave your beautiful country. You accompanied Mr. Gallaudet in his travels to raise funds for the benefit of the deaf and dumb, and interested the public, by your intelligence and conversation, in favor of that unfortunate and neglected portion of this country. When the lamented Mr. Henry Hudson and yourself were in Washington, soliciting Congress to grant some bounty to the American Asylum, your intelligence and talents effectually pleaded in favor of that institution, so that Congress made that liberal grant of land which has since secured ample funds to the Asylum.

You alone have continued in your profession since the establishment of the Asylum. We are touched with a tender interest for you, when we see you growing old in your benevolent labors. We could not think of letting you make your exit, without offering you some substantial memorial of our high esteem and affectionate regard. May you spend the remainder of your life with comfort, and receive your reward in the other world.

Clerc's Address

Clerc responded in sign language, and Gallaudet read his address in English.

Dear Pupils and Friends:

This is the most pleasant day we have ever had: I do not speak of the state of the weather, but the day you have appointed to come and see us after so long a separation from each other; and glad indeed, are we to see you again. If we, your teachers, have done you any good, as you are pleased to say we have done, we are satisfied and ask nothing more: but you have chosen to present most valuable and valued gifts, both to Mr. Gallaudet and myself, in memory of our having been the first to teach the deaf and dumb in America, and as a testimony of your gratitude for the instruction you have received.

I thank you for my part of this beautiful present: I accept it, not that I think it due from you to me; but on account of the pleasure it affords me to see that our exertions to render you better, have not been made in vain. In fact, what were you before your instruction? Without communication with other men, and consequently without any means of learning from them any thing purely intellectual, never would you have been what you are now; nor would the existence of God, the spirituality of your souls, the certainty of another life, have been made known to you. The religion of Christ would have been for you a material religion, a religion of sense and not of faith. You would have been able to say no prayers; you would have attended church with your friends without deriving any benefit whatever either from prayer-book, or from sermons preached by clergymen. Strangers in mind and in heart to all the doctrines, to all the mysteries, to all the precepts of the gospel, you would have passed your whole lives in a kind of excommunication like that of the reprobate, shutting your eyes upon the continual miracles of divine mercy, and opening them only on justice.[8] Your unfortunate parents, deprived of the advantage of implanting in your souls what instruction has inculcated on your minds, would have lamented your birth. But instead of this, what a happy fate you have in exchange! And to whom are you indebted for it? Never, my dear friends, could we have thought of the deplorable destiny to which the misfortune of your deafness had condemned you, on your coming forth into being, without coming to join ourselves to those, who, in 1815, laid the foundation of the first school for the deaf and dumb in this country. And who were those benevolent persons who first thought of you? They were the citizens of Hartford in general, and the direc-

---

8. Like Spofford, Clerc paints a bleak picture of deaf people before education. Still, he points to the dramatic effects that the American Asylum had. His remarks carry special force because he directly addresses the alumni in attendance.

tors in particular, who were like fathers of yours.[9] Therefore, to them all, under God, is your gratitude due, and great indeed it must be. Most of the directors whom you have known, alas! are gone. The few who still remain, and the new ones who have been chosen to replace the departed, are still your friends and the friends of all the other deaf and dumb who are now with us, and who are to come hereafter. Some, if not all of those noble directors, are, I believe, among us in this church. If you please, we will rise and bow to them as a feeble mark of our gratitude toward them. Again, let us rise and bow to these ladies and gentlemen who also have been your earliest or latest friends.

Your gratitude is not the less due to the governors and legislatures of New England, who have supported, and still support you at the Asylum. If there be any of these benevolent individuals here present, and if I could point them out to you, I would also request you to rise and bow to them; but not being able to do so, let us give them three cheers by clapping our hands three times.

You have also another debt to pay: I mean that which you owe to certain citizens of the states of Massachusetts, Connecticut, New York, New Jersey and Pennsylvania, who, also, in the autumn of 1816, gave us handsome donations for your benefit. We have not yet done: there is still another debt due—it is that which you owe to the general government of the United States, for the grant of land it made us in 1819, '20, the proceeds of the sale of which enabled our kind directors to purchase the lot and erect the buildings where the American Asylum is now in operation. Three more cheers by three more claps of your hands, therefore.

---

9. Clerc's calling the hearing benefactors "fathers," together with Brown equating the deaf alumni with children earlier, could well strike modern readers as promoting paternalism. The parent–child rhetoric reflects how nineteenth-century deaf Americans, from Clerc on, were keenly aware that without hearing people's involvement, the schools probably would not have been founded.

I shall not speak of the gratitude you also owe your teachers, guardians and matrons; for I doubt not that you have already expressed it, either on leaving the Asylum or on seeing them again at a subsequent period.

I presume my dear friends, you would like to know how many deaf and dumb persons we have taught since the school commenced in the spring of 1817. Well, I will tell you. On examining our records a few days ago, I found the number to amount to 1,066 (one thousand and sixty-six) including those who are present at the institution, viz., 605 boys and 461 girls. The number is rather small in comparison with the number of the deaf and dumb in New England; but we have done as well as our means would allow. It is, however, gratifying to know that much has also been done elsewhere; for besides our own, there are now nine or ten other schools for these unfortunate beings in the United States, most of whose teachers have been qualified by us, and of course, employ the same method of teaching and system of signs; so that wherever you may chance to go, and whomsoever you may happen to meet, you will not be strangers to each other.

How many of your fellow-pupils have died since you departed, I cannot say exactly: I hope, nevertheless, the number is not great.

As far as I have been able to ascertain, upward of one hundred have married, the greatest part among themselves, and the remainder have wives or husbands who can hear and speak. Thanks be to God, with a few exceptions, they all are blessed with children enjoying all their faculties, which will be a great consolation to them in their old age. The fact that a few of them have deaf and dumb children like themselves, must not be wondered at: we are not more privileged than other men; for we also are condemned to undergo some of the chastisements which divine providence sees fit to inflict on us poor sinners.

You, young men, are all above twenty-one years old. You are freemen. You vote, and I know that many of you feel interested in political matters, and belong to one or the other of the two great parties which unfortunately divide our fellow-citizens. I do not pretend to dictate to you on this subject, as I am persuaded that you act according to the dictates of your conscience and best judgment; allow me, however, to recommend to you to vote only for good men, for honest men, for men who love their country, their whole country.[10]

But let me return to you, my dear friends, and repeat that I am very happy to see you once more. You are going to return to your homes soon. My best wishes for your health and temporal comforts accompany you, and my prayer is that when we must leave this world, we may all be tendered into another where our ears shall be unstopped and our mouths opened—where our happiness shall have no alloy, shall fear no change and know no end.

[*Editor's Note:* Following Clerc's address, the Reverend Job Turner of Virginia, an alumnus of the Asylum, offered a prayer in sign language and the event concluded.]

---

10. An allusion to the increasing tensions over slavery that divided the nation in 1850.

9

DEDICATION OF THE
GALLAUDET MONUMENT

(1854)

In September 1851, just one year after the grand reunion in Hartford, Thomas Hopkins Gallaudet died from a form of dysentery. His passing prompted an outpouring of tributes. The directors at the American Asylum called him "a central power in a movement destined to effect great good in the world."[1] Harvey Peet, the president of the New York school, praised Gallaudet's skill in pantomime, teaching, and especially religious instruction. *The Christian Examiner* pronounced him a "great man." But perhaps no tribute was as meaningful as that from deaf Americans themselves.

Shortly after Gallaudet's funeral, Thomas Brown called a meeting in Vermont to discuss the idea of a monument. An association was formed, with Laurent Clerc as its president. He appointed agents in various states to solicit contributions from deaf

---

1. This and the following quotes are from Edward Miner Gallaudet, *Life of Thomas Hopkins Gallaudet: Founder of Deaf-Mute Instruction in America* (New York: Henry Holt and Co., 1888), 329–31.

people. Albert Newsam, a deaf artist in Philadelphia, prepared the plans for the monument. John Carlin designed a prominent bas relief that showed Gallaudet teaching in a schoolroom, with three students around him. Another panel had the name "Gallaudet" in letters of the manual alphabet, represented by sculpted hands. The association raised the amount of money needed for construction of the monument in two years. A hearing man, James Batterson of Hartford, executed the work. It was a little more than twenty feet high, made of marble, and had a granite base.

On September 6, 1854, the monument was dedicated on the grounds of the American Asylum. Attendees included deaf people from all over the country and many citizens from the Hartford vicinity. Clerc gave a short address. Carlin was the orator of the day, giving one of his trademark speeches, filled with allusions and lofty rhetoric. Excerpts of both presentations follow.

The Gallaudet Monument

The effort to raise funds for the monument also led to the establishment of a permanent organization to honor Gallaudet, the New England Gallaudet Association of the Deaf. It was the first of many associations of deaf citizens in the United States, and marked another step in the coalescence of the American deaf community.

Clerc's Address

It is very gratifying to the graduates of the several Institutions for the Deaf and Dumb of the United States, to behold so many distinguished gentlemen and ladies here present, on the occasion of raising a monument to perpetuate the memory of the friend and teacher that mutes can never forget, the Rev. Dr. Gallaudet. It is a modest but elegant monument, at a cost of about two thousand five hundred dollars, wholly raised from the contributions of the deaf and dumb; for none who can hear and speak have been allowed to contribute one cent. . . .[2]

Mr. Gallaudet . . . was a good man. His physiognomy was the type of his goodness and mildness. In his manners and conduct there was nothing affected. He had the wisdom becoming a man of his age and profession. He was not ambitious, nor mercenary. He was content with what he received. His forte, however, was not the dexterous management of the perplexing business of so large an Institution; the school-room was the true arena for the display of his great abilities and greater affections. He made good scholars, many of whom we are happy to see here, expressing with tearful eyes their gratitude to him, who first brought them to *speak and hear*.[3] No bigot was he, although strict in his religious passions.

---

2. In their special tribute to Gallaudet and Clerc in 1850, and their insistence on erecting their own monument to Gallaudet, we can discern how deaf Americans increasingly viewed themselves as a distinct group.

3. Clerc writes metaphorically here. He implies that, by helping deaf people to learn both sign language and written English, Gallaudet enabled them to transcend their deafness.

He was not too denunciatory of others' faults; for so persuaded was he that genuine repentance can only come through the grace of God, that he loved to pray for sinners rather than reprove, when reproof only served to irritate. We therefore saw nothing in his piety but what ministered to our improvement and edification. His mind was well cultivated. His knowledge was extensive, and taste so correct, that in his usual conversation there appeared to be nothing but good taste and correct reasoning. When in discussion with others, he was deep as the sea, smooth as oil, and adroit as Talleyrand. Methinks, we are under vast obligations to such a man, who knew how to say thousands of fine things, but was always willing to say common ones, in order to accommodate himself to the capacity of those with whom he talked. No person knew better how to speak to others of what he himself knew, and of what he knew would please his listeners. He was a man of uprightness and equity. Neither greatness, nor favor, nor rank, could seduce or dazzle him. In a word, he was one of the best men who ever lived; benevolent, obliging, and kind to everybody. No wonder, therefore, that he was beloved by all the deaf and dumb.

Carlin's Oration

Ladies and Gentlemen:

This day—the sixth of September, a day to be remembered—has come, and we are on this occasion to witness the consummation of our work. We now behold there standing in graceful proportions the MONUMENT, reared to the memory of the First (next to our own illustrious Washington) in the hearts of the deaf mutes of America—Rev. Dr. Thomas H. Gallaudet. It is a substantial testimonial of our deep gratitude for his disinterested labors in promoting our mental and religious welfare, and of our high appreciation of his sterling worth.

As there is much reason to believe that this is the first monument in the world that has ever been erected by a community exclusively deaf and dumb, how exquisite is the satisfaction with which we look upon ourselves as its founders! What a source of gratification flowing through our veins while we contemplate this glorious result of our silent labors, commenced and accomplished within so short a time! Conscious as we may feel of its unassuming dimensions and moderate cost, let us congratulate ourselves upon our promptitude in raising up to the public gaze this symmetrical marble pile, to demonstrate the truth that our (the deaf mutes') warm hearts are not destitute of one of the brightest virtues of man—GRATITUDE! Oh, may the fact that it is our own work, devised and supervised by our minds—*once darkened, but now disenthralled from the horrible meshes of ignorance*—enhance the value of our Institutions in the eyes of the public!

Verily, my heart experiences sensations of pleasure from seeing so many mutes assembled here to enjoy the happy day, whose faces are stamped with such intelligence, and whose minds are endowed with such capacity of subjecting language to their wishes to represent their ideas. . . .

My mute friends. What deeds of the soul were perpetuated by Dr. Gallaudet so as to deserve this grateful tribute? Was he an eminent statesman, who our national senatorial floor, coped with the GREAT TRIO—Clay, Calhoun and Webster—flinging upon their heads his vivid thunderbolts of forensic eloquence?[4] No! He was too gentle in disposition, too modest to venture into that great political arena. Was he then a military genius, leading our little band of brave men victoriously from Palo Alto to Buena Vista, or from the impregnable castle of San Juan d'Ulloa, overlooking sullenly Vera Cruz, to the ancient halls of Montezuma?[5] Oh no! he

---

4. Henry Clay (1777–1852), John C. Calhoun (1782–1850), and Daniel Webster (1782–1852) were prominent congressmen during the first half of the nineteenth century. Together, they crafted the Missouri Compromise of 1820, which helped temporarily to resolve the slavery issue. All three had recently died.

5. Carlin alludes to battle sites of the Mexican War, which had concluded six years before with a United States victory. Palo Alto, Texas, was the location of the war's first major battle in 1846. Buena Vista, the

was too much of an evangelical messenger of God, blessed with a most fraternal heart, to relish the sight of human blood shed on the gory battleground. . . .

Nay, his achievements were of the pure benevolence, which, in a philosophical sense, were equal to those of Zachary Taylor and Winfield Scott in promoting the glory of our Republic.[6]

Before Dr. Gallaudet, whose soul was penetrated with the vital importance of the mission imposed upon his willing shoulders, embarked for Europe to acquaint himself with the mysteries of deaf-mute instruction, *all* the deaf mutes of this country were *ignorant heathen!*[7] Their minds were desolately blank! How vacantly their eyes wandered over the printed letters of the Holy Scriptures! In truth, they were absolutely isolated from society, even in the midst of civilization, where speaking men pursued their avocations in Arts, Sciences, Commerce, and Manufactures, besides their legislative, municipal, judiciary and ecclesiastical halls, and speaking women with their various female accomplishments moved in the elevated spheres allotted to them; and where schools, colleges and universities existed under such propitious auspices, with speaking students promising to grace their country by their brilliant talents and usefulness to the commonwealth.

---

site of another U.S. victory in 1847, was the single bloodiest conflict of the war. In March 1847, U. S. troops landed in Vera Cruz, the first step toward their ultimate goal of Mexico City. Montezuma's Castle, in Arizona, is a cliff ruin left by the prehistoric Sinagua Indians; it was actually abandoned almost a century before the Aztec emperor Montezuma (1466–1520) was born.

6. Generals Zachary Taylor (1784–1850) and Winfield Scott (1786–1866) commanded the American troops in the Mexican War. Taylor also was the president of the United States from 1849 to 1850.

7. For more on the use of "heathen" and the status of deaf people before education, see p. 37, n. 2; and p. 41, n. 2. Carlin's elevated rhetoric, like Spofford's at the 1850 Grand Reunion, suggests a mythologizing of the Gallaudet–Clerc story at work.

But when he, in his return home with the precious knowledge of the art in his keeping, landed on his native shores, Ignorance, who hitherto wielded her gross sway over the minds of the deaf and dumb, was startled at his unexpected arrival, and retreated scowling all the time before the steady approach of Enlightenment! The desponding parents wiped their tears, and looked with swelling gratitude for the blessed day their unfortunate children might be sent to his school! His landing here on the sixth of August, 1816, was the epoch, as glorious as it was memorable, of our deliverance from the degradation to which we were unavoidably consigned. Columbus landed on the newly discovered continent and secured the glory and wealth of his royal patrons, and ended his days—in disgrace, with his ungrateful sovereigns. Cortes and Pizarro sought their own aggrandizement in wealth by rapine, and in power by usurpation, in the auriferous regions of Mexico and Peru, and died, unwept, despised and cursed even by their own men who fought with them. But how different the scene was when Dr. Gallaudet landed here without any imposing array of followers, save one foreigner, and converted the mutes' heathendom into a grand field of benevolence, and he died, rich in faith in his Savior and in our love and gratitude.

Nevertheless, there were two serious obstacles in his way, namely, the want of money to commence his operations with, and his proverbial diffidence blended with modesty; yet, with the valuable services of that foreigner—a Frenchman whom he brought over from Abbé Sicard's school at Paris—his love for the deaf and dumb surmounted the latter obstacle by undergoing the exceedingly unpleasant ordeal of soliciting and collecting money from the benevolent in several of our principal cities; and with funds thus obtained he established an infant institution in this goodly city; though in a literal sense he was not its *founder*, for the late Dr. Cogswell of Hartford, who indeed fathered that grand idea, was fully entitled to the honor. And how gratifying it is to say that the result of that deed of Dr. Gallaudet's soul was thirteen

institutions, which sprung forth in full vigor and beauty in the
United States, and in which thousands of mute heathen have been
enlightened! Blessed be his name which he bequeathed to us to
be chiseled in our manual alphabet on this monument! Oh, let his
memory be cherished constantly in our hearts, and those of the
mutes of succeeding generations! May more institutions be produced with all possible dispatch, one or more in each state, according to the capacity of its legislature to maintain their
existence, and thousands of benighted souls be thereby enlightened brought to the footstool of Jesus Christ, whom Dr. Gallaudet
adored with the childlike simplicity and humility of a sincere
Christian. . . .

Whilst we move on in our pilgrimage toward the Valley of
Death, let us look back always to the day we have been here, and
contemplate with pleasing emotions the virtues and benevolence
of the American Abbé de l'Epée,[8] to whose memory our hearts
have been concentrated in this modest yet graceful Monument!

---

8. For more information on de l'Epée, see p. 41, n. 3.

10

DEBATE OVER A DEAF
COMMONWEALTH

In the late 1850s, deaf people had a remarkable discussion in the pages of the *American Annals of the Deaf and Dumb* about a proposal to create a separate deaf state in the West. The idea was not altogether new. Years before, when Congress gave land in Alabama to the American Asylum, Laurent Clerc had suggested selling part of it to cover the school's operating expenses and retaining the rest as a location where deaf people could settle. That did not occur. Similarly, in the 1830s, Edmund Booth and twelve other graduates of the American Asylum considered purchasing land out west so they might continue to live close to each other. However, members of the group found jobs in different states, and the project died.

Neither of these antecedents had the scope or ambition of the 1850s plan. The debate was ignited by John Jacobus Flournoy, a deaf man from Georgia. The son of a prosperous slaveowner, Flournoy briefly attended the University of Georgia, leaving when other students made him the target of ridicule. He also studied at the American Asylum, although he never actually enrolled. A rather eccentric person, Flournoy seldom cut his hair, wore a rain-

William
Chamberlain, 1897

coat in all weather, and assumed the appearance of poverty even though he was well off. At one point, he committed himself to a mental institution, but soon released himself when he decided he was not going insane. He supported polygamy; when his first wife became an invalid, he tried to marry a young teen. Despite such bizarre behavior, Flournoy was an important advocate for deaf people. He published dozens of pamphlets on deaf education and other topics at his own expense. He lobbied for the establishment of the Georgia School for the Deaf and, later, a national deaf college. Yet none of his activism gained as much attention as his call for a separate deaf commonwealth.

In 1855, Flournoy issued a circular suggesting that deaf people should petition Congress for land in the West. Those who desired could migrate there and establish their own state. All the citizens would be deaf. They would manage their own affairs, away from "rejections and consignments to inferior places" by hearing people.

Flournoy asked William W. Turner, then the principal of the American Asylum, for his opinion. Turner wrote that the plan was "beautiful in theory" but impractical. Deaf people would be unlikely to want to leave their friends and relatives, he said. Moreover, it would be difficult to keep the community deaf, since most children of deaf couples would be hearing. Finally, Turner denied that deaf people suffered from prejudice, saying instead that they had natural limitations. "You would not send a deaf and dumb man to Congress or to the Legislature of a State; not for the reason that he was deficient in intelligence and education, but because his want of hearing and speech unfits him for the place," he wrote.[1]

Flournoy responded with typical fervor, asserting (in the first letter below) that deaf people did commonly endure discrimination. He had experienced rejection firsthand. Driven by what his cousin called a "burning thirst for office," Flournoy ran for government positions several times without success.[2]

When the *Annals* published Turner's and Flournoy's letters, they struck a nerve with readers across the nation. Several deaf people sent in responses, which are excerpted here. Edmund Booth and John Carlin weighed in against Flournoy's proposal, arguing that it was in deaf people's interest to live scattered among the hearing. Others, such as William Chamberlain and P. H. Confer, expressed support, suggesting that some deaf people would be happier living among others who shared the same language and worldview.

---

1. William W. Turner, letter to J. J. Flournoy, reprinted in "Scheme for a Commonwealth of the Deaf and Dumb," *American Annals of the Deaf and Dumb* 8 (1856): 118, 119.

2. E. Merton Coulter, *John Jacobus Flournoy: Champion of the Common Man in the Antebellum South* (Savannah: Georgia Historical Society, 1942), 15.

In 1858, Laurent Clerc addressed the controversy at a meeting
of the New England Gallaudet Association of Deaf-Mutes. Clerc,
the most well-known deaf person in America, was seen by many
as the first person to have proposed the idea of a separate deaf
place. Now, however, Clerc spoke against Flournoy's idea, saying
it was too exclusive and impractical. He asked the deaf people
present if they felt themselves mistreated by hearing people. They
responded negatively. After that, the debate over Flournoy's plan
appears to have subsided.

Most deaf people who wrote about the proposal were against
it. Perhaps these writers did not experience the kind of estrange-
ment that Flournoy did. His odd behavior no doubt made him
more of a social outcast. Unlike other correspondents, he lived in
the antebellum South, which was often less progressive. In addition, most of the deaf people who responded were successful.
They did not have as much trouble with English as other deaf
Americans, and did not depend as much upon sign language. Uneducated deaf people, who made up a sizable portion of the deaf
population, did not really participate in the written debate. Perhaps many of them would have supported the plan.

Flournoy himself gave up pamphleteering by the time the
Civil War broke out. If in many ways he was a peculiar man writing incendiary prose, in others he was ahead of his time. His defi-
ant belief that deaf people could contribute much more to society,
and his refusal to accept limitations on their potential, anticipated
the more aggressive activism of deaf people in the twentieth century.

Flournoy's dream of a separate deaf place was by no means
unique. Not only did Clerc and Booth promulgate similar ideas
on a lesser scale earlier in the century, but also deaf people in
England and France debated separatist plans. In addition, during
the nineteenth century other minorities, such as African Americans, the Amish, and Mormons, occasionally sought to separate
themselves from mainstream society. Like these groups, deaf peo-

ple sometimes shared a utopian vision of having a place where they could escape prejudice and flourish on their own.

John J. Flournoy to William Turner

After William Turner, the principal of the American Asylum, gently rejected Flournoy's proposal for a deaf commonwealth, Flournoy sent him the following response. The letter was published in the American Annals of the Deaf and Dumb *in 1856.*

Rev. W. W. Turner:

Rev. and Dear Friend: I am in receipt of your kind favor of the 6th inst., replying to my inquiry of last summer, concerning the feasibility and propriety, in your view, of colonizing some small territory in our country with a population of mutes. Your objections I have duly considered and weighed: and although I accord to them that respect and that deference due from me to your sentiments, still I might confess my want of conviction as yet, unless you would do away with the force of the following observations, predicated as an answer to your remarks. . . .

You will observe that my appeal, circulated among my class of our people, and sent to Europe, did not have intention of persuading the migration of the *entire* deaf population of those regions— but only a portion of them! And it is presumable that there are among them a sufficient number who would agree to emigrate, provided the General Government would do what I clearly laid down, I believe, in those papers: *secure the government and offices of small territory or State, to the mute community!* Neither home, nor parents, nor friends, would or ought to deter a body of enterprising and resolute deaf men from moving to such a possession! We do not ask it as a grant, boon or charity from the government— the ruling powers and legislature have too much grudged us any pittance they have seen their predecessors give in its infancy to the

American Asylum at Hartford—but we will pay our pre-emptive right money for the acres, if only guaranteed the control of the commonwealth. That government will give us *such* a prerogative to a State about the size of Rhode Island or Connecticut, I confess I do not feel sanguine enough to hope! But there is nothing like trying. . . .

The old cry about the incapacity of men's minds from physical disabilities, I think it were time, now in this intelligent age, to *explode!* You asked, how could a deaf man legislate and govern among the hearing, any more than a blind man lead an army? (I use your ideas—not your language. The matter is just as I give it.) Did you ever believe lame men, and blind men, and deaf men, when usefulness was in view, were as useless as dumb beasts? Certainly not. Then where does your reasoning limit their capacity? You use a military figure: and I will dwell a little on one. Have you ever heard how Muley Molech had himself borne in a litter, when lamed by wounds, to the head of his legions, and how he vanquished the foe? So much for a *lame* man. Then, as for a *blind* one, such a one as the beggared Belisarius of declining Rome or Byzantium; was such a man of no military moment because sightless?[3] I would myself, if I were contemporary with himself, suggest to the Romans that he be provided with a military academy to teach the strategy of war—or be kept on a hill near a battle to direct emergencies, while the seeing faithfully inform him of events. Here then, literally meeting you with your own weapons, is a great blind general made consummate leader, if experienced. But the application of such views to the deaf is not legitimate. We

---

3. Belisarius (c. 505–565) was commander-in-chief of the Byzantine forces during the reign of Emperor Justinian. He led victorious campaigns in Africa, Sicily, and Italy. However, his achievements made him enemies. Implicated in a conspiracy against the emperor, his eyes were put out in 561. According to the historian Procopius, Belisarius lost all of his belongings and was reduced to begging in the streets of Byzantium.

do not claim *all* offices, nor to do *every* thing. But we do attest that we are capable of many of which the prejudice, and sometimes even malignance of our hearing brethren deprive us!![4] It were better that Congress had the presence of some blind philosophers to lead the way in legislation, than to have only seeing men without wisdom. The court of the Areopagus, at ancient Athens, blindfolded the judges to prevent prejudice against unprepossessing suitors. And so long as this was the custom, no judicial decision was so faultless as that of these people. So much for your simile in disparagement of the *blind*.

So of the deaf. Many of us have hearts, of an integrity superior to the *mad* hearing partisans that go to Congress and to legislatures, and fill presidential and gubernatorial seats; and when the fact is that some of us are sages, so far as rational views and Christian principles be taken into consideration;—you can not but observe that the loss is greatly the country's, in not being able to avail of our supervision, from the prejudices and disparagements of the world about a sense or two![5]

Advocating, therefore, a formation out West, of a deaf State, I wish to persevere in urging a measure by which alone our class of people can attain to the dignity and honor of Human Nature. Else our course is (under the idea that a deaf and dumb man is of little consequence) within the circle of diffident humility. *I* spurn this imputation of thousands of my hearing *inferiors*—who give the fatness of power and office to their own class—and keep me, like

---

4. This letter provides the strongest protest against oppression in this collection. It marks a counterpoint to the extensive gratitude to hearing people and occasional language of inferiority expressed elsewhere, such as at the Grand Reunion several years before.

5. Just as Clerc and Carlin argued earlier in this anthology that deaf education makes the United States a greater country, so Flournoy here contends that denying deaf people opportunities actually weakens the nation.

Lazarus, out at the gate of splendid and munificent patronage without sending me a solitary crumb from the table.[6]

Place *me* for an example in any Capitol with Legislative sanctity, and I will move for an *aid*, a hearer and amanuensis, to reveal to me what is said, what to be done, what to do, and to read my speeches. And by this way I can get along supremely well, as Legislator. The gist and gravamen being that my intelligence and judgment may prove better and superior to the hearing majority.[7] So your object about deaf incapacity is answered. . . .

Can I then concede that hearing men "are the ones and wisdom shall die with them?" No sir—No. I am to lead—and can only lead where deaf capacity be widely acknowledged. I am not in your estimation, I hope, descending to "fanaticism," or to "peculiarity." *Evasions like these will not do!* Men must think. They must investigate before they feel warranted to traduce sterling persons who are not made to sit down and acquiesce in perfidy to self and to mankind.

That deaf men have not my feelings and ambition, is no reason that they should not find a habitation of their own.

If only in such a State forty deaf men, or even twelve, were found, the constitution guarantying power to them alone, they may rule all the hearing collected in that small corner. Let not the audacity and avarice of the hearing owning continents, encroach on the deaf there. If our children hear, let them go to other States. *This Government is to be sacred to the Deaf alone.* In hearing communities how many children stay with their parents? Do brothers and sisters continue together? How then expect deaf-mutes to be such

---

6. In John 16, Jesus tells the parable of a rich man who feasted sumptuously every day while a diseased beggar named Lazarus lay starving at his gate.

7. Flournoy foreshadows modern activists and the Americans with Disabilities Act of 1990 by asserting that, if given proper access and support, he could contribute much to society.

perpetual children as to claim and assert nothing appertaining to the dignity and grandeur of humanity, but to stick to home.[8]

The idea, therefore, of acquiring a commonwealth for themselves ought not to be abandoned.

You say that deaf persons have privileges among the hearing and can amass wealth. But how tardily, where competition by the auricular is such that no isolated deaf person is able to break through a single web of its massive Free Masonry? The auricular are not satisfied with hearing, nor with the usual mutual sympathies of their own class, but are banded and combined together in associations, open, and societies, secret, until they form a compact moral mechanism, that fairly by their majority, puts us in the shade. I know not how at this day the people of your section comport towards the deaf. But when I was at Hartford, I saw that a tailor (A. S. B.) *disdainfully* repelled away a mute applicant for the post of *foreman* (D. A. S.). Even if it be better for our class *now* in New England, it is far from one-ninety-ninth so, in Georgia, whose Legislature, after my prayer in 1834, granting a deaf education to the mutes here, a few years thereafter, became chagrined at having *honored me*, and though they dared not revoke their education, still they made a law to *"make deaf and dumb persons idiots in law and to provide them guardians."** Thus in the South we are contemned, spurned, degraded and abhorred, and I see no redemption but in forming a powerful oligarchy of our own to control a State at the West—a Deaf-mute Republic.

We constitutionally allow no foreigner to be President—nationally. We would in that small State allow no hearing man to

---

8. By arguing against deaf people being "such perpetual children," Flournoy effectively challenges the rhetoric at the 1850 grand reunion, where Thomas Brown and Laurent Clerc compared deaf alumni to children and their hearing supporters to parents (see p. 150, n. 9).

*I have not, however, permitted any one to insult me with the application of such a law. [Flournoy's note.]

have any lucrative office.[9] This is all I care about. Its Legislature, Judiciary, &c., all mutes.

A deaf community, once established, to whom only offices are open to Congress and at home, as none others should be eligible—would easily draw mute recipients for the bounty from all sections. Once fixed, I see nothing deterrent.

I fear my letter is quite annoyingly lengthy, and will now close. I have said all I believe necessary to convince you of the propriety of our plan, which will only fail because the deaf and dumb are not worthy of a better destiny, or are as unlike as possible,

Your affectionate and obliged humble servant,
John J. Flournoy

Edmund Booth to Flournoy

Edmund Booth wrote this response to Flournoy. Although it was not intended for publication, Booth agreed to allow the Annals *to publish it in January 1858, along with a number of other letters on the subject of a deaf commonwealth.*

Dear Sir,

In regard to a community of deaf-mutes in the West, or any where—supposing you mean a community exclusively or mainly of mutes—let me say candidly that I hold it to be an impossibility, save in the commencement, and that on a very small scale. Just consider a moment. A community of this class would be a mixture of a few well and many half-educated; and among them must be

---

9. While previous deaf authors call English a foreign language to deaf Americans, Flournoy takes things further, suggesting that hearing people themselves are foreigners to the deaf experience.

many non-readers and frivolous.[10] And then the general equality claimed with all by the latter, would operate to keep the more sensible from joining such community; for we all know that gossip, scandal, backbiting and other diabolisms are as common among mutes as among hearing persons.

Again: They will need to work at a variety of trades, and a commonwealth of mutes could never exceed 10,000, supposing all in the U.S. were brought in. A sparsely settled state would make nobody rich, and would satisfy few; and no law could be made effectual to prevent their selling their lands, buildings, &c., to hearing persons. Thus the distinct nature of the community would soon be lost. And it would so happen in any event, for their children being mostly of the hearing order, it would become a hearing community faster than the fathers and mothers died out.[11]

I think the wiser course is to let the mutes remain as they are—scattered and in one sense lost—among their hearing associates. In such situations they are compelled to read and write, and thus keep their minds under the educational process through life.[12]

In reply to your other questions: the country *will* suit them. But in Iowa there is no land unsold or in market, save the railroad lands, which are withdrawn, and they are narrow strips and cannot be obtained save at $2.50 per acre or more, and that at cash down

---

10. An example of the occasional condescension that authors express toward uneducated deaf people in these pages. Compare Carlin, Burnet, and others calling uneducated deaf people "savage," "heathen," and so forth. Especially in this debate, we can see how the American deaf community was far from homogeneous and, like most groups, sometimes quite factional.

11. Approximately 90 percent of deaf people have hearing children.

12. Booth makes English literacy an issue in the debate over a deaf state. In arguing that deaf people should remain scattered so they will be forced to read and write English, he reveals how he, like Carlin and others, privileges competency in English over ASL and deaf culture.

the moment they are brought into market. Speculators have drained Iowa completely of her government lands, with the exceptions as above. Government lands can be obtained in Minnesota, where they are not yet in market, especially in the western part of that territory; but it is too far north and too cold to suit my ideas of a residence. The cold in the West is less than in the same latitude East. For a community of mutes, Nebraska is almost out of the question. It is mostly a barren country. I speak from observation, having traveled through it from the Missouri River to the South Pass. Iowa is a prairie country. Perhaps one-tenth of it timber. One-twentieth would be nearer the truth. The guide books say one-third or one-fourth. My own observations say one-tenth.

I see no country that would suit your ideas so well as Kansas. But to me the whole scheme looks much like those of other communities formed on the exclusive system, like those of Mons. Cabet, Rapp, &c.[13] They had the incentive of religion and friendship and community of goods, labor and profit. With us it would be otherwise; and we should break through before we had made half a trial.

Yours truly,
E. Booth

Flournoy to Turner

Flournoy's response appeared with Booth's letter in the same issue of the Annals.

---

13. George Rapp (1757–1847) founded the Harmony Society, a utopian religious and social community. They established a village called Harmony in Pennsylvania in 1805. The group prospered, but died out because of a rule of celibacy. Etienne Cabet (1788–1856) began the Icarian movement based on principles of pacifism and communism. In 1849 he founded a community in Illinois. Other villages were established in Missouri, Iowa, and California, but all were abandoned by the end of the century.

Rev. Mr. Turner:

My Dear Friend—This being a free country, where every "smart" man, and his name is legion, has his opinion whether crude and vulgar, or refined and intellectual, the American community are very unquiet and debatable, subject to a thousand though not very learned or profound sentiments, political and social. The deaf and dumb have taken a color of character from this disputatious habit, a specimen of which is evinced in the enclosed letter from Edmund Booth, Esq. Instead of meeting my project with a philosophical view, I am met by objections, some of which, like yours and Mr. Booth's, are truly formidable! It would seem then, that without intending to be the great leader and original mind, I am the chief in this cause, and that if I carry it not forward, the idea of a deaf community may prove abortive as to any practical result.

There is always some objection to every project under the sun, and often very cogent ones. What is a man then to do? Abandon every scheme because impeded by natural and conventional obstacles? Certainly not. Many of the greatest nations have been founded in time by defiance of the untoward predictions of impracticable visionaries. Many a costly experiment has been forsaken on no better hypothesis. The invention of the daguerreotype—the photogenic art—was not accidental, but by a design; and persistent, philosophical chemists began and followed out the plan, until Daguerre, in the final series of the successive experimenters, perfected the science by which our features are in exact copies transmitted to posterity.[14] Resolution and perseverance will accomplish wonders. And I pray God that the deaf and dumb may prove worthy of the name of men.[15]

---

14. Louis-Jacques-Mandé Daguerre (1789–1851), a French painter, invented the daguerreotype, an early process for producing photographs on a silver or a silver-covered copper plate.

15. In making his case for a deaf state, Flournoy repeatedly appeals to readers' manhood, independence, and pride. To be true men (and not

Mr. Booth thinks the West will not suit the mutes. From his description of the North-west I agree with him in that opinion. His other views have been answered before in the *Annals* and elsewhere.

I do not know what kind of a constitution the mutes may superstruct, whether to make real estate inherent only in the deaf, by that organic law all have to respect and defer to; or in case of default, to escheat to the estate. This, however, is certain, that the *control* of our community over the commonwealth would be strict and universal. This is what we want and for what we may emigrate. *The government of a piece of Territory.* Nothing more or less.

Mr. Booth believes we can do better, and will read more, scattered as we are and "lost" among the hearing. I challenge him to show me twenty deaf-mutes in a hundred, that are constant readers, adequate to comprehending either literature or science, as they now are dispersed among hearing people, who do not read any or much themselves, and who have a sense (auricular) by which they gather in their knowledge, a privilege debarred the deaf, who therefore are the more ignorant *for being thus scattered.* Whereas if convened in a land peculiarly their own, the concentration of reading intellects would set a beneficial example; and preaching and lectures in the sign language, and libraries of suitable books, may improve their minds and hearts, beyond what is attainable in their scattered condition. For this, as a principal cause and source of improvement, this colony is a desideratum.

But the difficulty that meets me on all sides is, how can you keep up the mute population? The children of deaf parents are mostly hearing. These will inherit property and the community will not endure. This reasoning seems to take it that our society is

---

children or second-class citizens), he contends, deaf Americans should emigrate to a place of their own.

to be organized like that of the hearing, and to be modeled upon the same principles. Now there is no such thing. I acknowledge that the hearing children of deaf parents may not inherit land in that anomalous and contracted community—neither power nor patronage. But the other States are so near, and their parents may supply them with the means to buy real estate in them. When they have a good location, the mutes would come in from all parts of the world. An Asylum for their education may be founded there, as well as other Institutions, so that there will be no lacking of the deaf *materiel*. What then of this visionary difficulty! We will allow such hearing persons as come for trade or residence, to vote with us. *We would give woman that right.*[16] Hence we may always possess sufficient population to be a State. But even if this be futile, we can remain a Territory of the Federal Government and enjoy its powerful protection under Omnipotence; the General Government guaranteeing to us the peculiar Constitution we may devise: "Republican in form."

If mutes *cannot* do this they are justly held as inferior and *useless* in the world. For they ought not to pretend to be "any body" among hearing men, who do what deaf *"dogs"* shrink from achieving *alone*. But we are men, and have under God only to try, and the thing is a finished work!

After this argument, which if published I hope may satisfy the overscrupulous, I would approach the great point that is before us. I think we can acquire territory enough from the Cherokees or other red men, West of Arkansas, and *very cheaply*, on which to make our experiment, or else from the State of Maine. Perhaps some one of the New England, Northern or Middle States may grant space enough for this purpose. I myself prefer the Indian Territory, if the U. S. government would sanction and aid a cession. Hence, no fear about trade and business. Capital will accu-

---

16. Since women were not allowed to vote in the United States during the nineteenth century, Flournoy takes a progressive stance here.

mulate in our hands when our skill and industry are concentrated, and our ruling prerogative unimpeachable. Whereas now, in their scattered condition, especially in the Middle and Southern States, few deaf men have employment of respectability, and their ignorance is "stereotyped," as I have shown, by their unfortunate and dispersed situation, without preaching or any instruction whatsoever. When combined, competition and a sense of high duty and responsibility will cause them to study books, documents, and men and things, and like other communities we shall produce men of intellectual predominance.

Even should the contemplated colony fail, as Mr. Booth predicts, one great utility to ourselves will have been derived from a practical experience. We shall have proved to the other nations and our own, that deaf and dumb people are capable of many things; and to our successors in misfortune, offices and employment may be opened. They may be treated as men and women of *some use* to society and to the country, and respected accordingly. And this will to us be no inconsiderable triumph; and the victory sure, as the deaf now continues to prove his competency and fidelity in lands and other trusts. And this, we, as accountable beings, who may not bury our talent in a napkin, owe to the long and harmless line of the "pantomimic generations" that are to come after us!

I have now fully, I hope, in attempting something like a reply to Mr. Booth, given what refutation I am able, to the many objects that are ever starting up to confound this project. I hope the *Annals* will embrace both Mr. Booth's letter and mine. I presume that invaluable periodical will devote some space to this discussion, as relating so closely to the welfare and interests of the community, to whose benefit it is so inseparately devoted.

I am, dear sir, truly and respectfully,
your most obliged, obedient, humble servant,
J. J. Flournoy

Mr. Flournoy's Project

The Annals *published this additional response from Booth in April.*

In the January number of the *Annals*, is a reply to my letter of Sept. 6th to Mr. J. J. Flournoy of Georgia. My letter being a brief answer to a previous letter of his desiring my views on the subject of a community of deaf-mutes, I necessarily took a practical view of the case; and Mr. Flournoy, in his reply of Oct. 3d, characterizes it as "a specimen" of the "disputatious habit" which prevails in the American community, and from which he says the deaf and dumb have "taken a color." Well, I am in a most unfortunate position, being put on the defensive.

Let me say to Mr. Flournoy that the idea of a community of deaf-mutes is to me nothing new. In the year 1831, William Willard and five or six others, including myself, formed ourselves into an association with a view of purchasing land in some favorable spot in the west, and so arranging that we might, through life, live in close neighborhood and continue to enjoy the friendships we had formed in Hartford. At that time, we were pupils of the Asylum, and all, except myself, were to leave in a few weeks or months. By election we added a sufficient number of past pupils to make our whole number thirteen. It was a sort of secret society, as we preferred to put it into practical execution rather than have the project dissipate in mere talk. Time went on, and we all found ourselves compelled to attend to the stern realities of life—procuring a self-support—before we could attend to carrying out what Mr. Willard afterwards, in one of his letters to me, called our Don Quixotic scheme. Mr. Willard became a teacher in the Ohio Institution, I in Hartford; the rest of us were scattered over New England, and the project gradually died away.

One of our objects had been to form a nucleus around and within which others of our class might, in process of time, gather.

But Mr. Flournoy's idea of electing ourselves to the presidency of the United States, to Congress, to legislative and judicial positions, had no place in our heads, much less our deliberations. Mr. Flournoy's idea of distinction in the world appears to be political elevation alone. Make a man, no matter how insignificant his amount of brains, president, judge of the Supreme Court, member of Congress; or send him on a foreign mission, and, forthwith, he is a *great* man! Socrates, the greatest man that Greece produced, and whom the populace and judges condemned to drink hemlock, should hide his head! We have in our own country, men— reformers—who would laugh to scorn the offer of a seat in Congress or on the bench, and who would not accept the presidency if the condition was that they should be bound by party ties. These are glorious men, who, like all such in all ages, are misunderstood and underrated, but whom the future will understand and appreciate. They work not merely for their own day, but for all coming times, and they can well afford to wait.

Mr. Flournoy says that I did not take a philosophical view of his project. I certainly did not view it as we do the abstractions of commercial conventions. Looking merely to the practical, and my letter being brief, I answered accordingly. But let us examine the philosophy of the thing. And here Mr. Flournoy admits difficulties "truly formidable," but he does not notice, and, perhaps, he does not see, all. He speaks first of the organic law—the constitution— which the mutes may construct; and, in another part of his letter, he would allow hearing persons who come among us for trade or residence, to vote. Nor could we, under the constitution of the United States, prevent them, unless we were to be forever a territory and under a government like that of the Cherokees. Allow, then, hearing persons to vote, and they, far outnumbering us, would change the organic law to suit themselves. He would *allow women to vote. Bravo!* I agree with him there.

Mr. F. challenges me to show him "twenty mutes in a hundred

that are constant readers, adequate to comprehending either literature or science, as they are now dispersed among hearing people,
who do not read much themselves, etc." The challenge is too
comprehensive. Literature, as read in the United States, is generally wishy-washy; and of science, the elements alone are commonly studied or read. The time has not come when the masses
are to be highly educated, but it will come; and the future will
look back on the present as we do on the past—as a semi-barbar-
ian era.

The masses—in the North at least—are almost universally
readers, and the educated deaf-mutes, as a general rule, are not
behind them in that respect. True, the deaf-mutes, taking them as
a class, do not so well nor so readily understand all the words and
technicalities of written language, but they obtain a pretty correct
idea, and, for the present, that is much. Let ten or twenty years
more pass by, and in all the schools for the deaf and dumb the
period of instruction will be extended to ten and fifteen years—
that is, from the earliest age to twenty-one.[17] The justice of such a
course will be clear to all men who are capable of thinking. Mr.
Flournoy's error in regard to *"scattered and lost,"* arises from judg-
ing from the Southern aspect of society. There, except among the
few wealthy, education is almost unknown and books and newspapers rarely seen. Among such a population, an educated deaf-
mute must necessarily be almost literally "lost." The remedy is to
educate the hearing masses; and if Mr. Flournoy, instead of fretting
away his life in complaints, would endeavor to remedy the evil,
he will have lived to some purpose. I hope he will not deem me
as speaking harshly, for such is not the case.

There is another "formidable" difficulty in Mr. Flournoy's
plan—the descent of estates to hearing children. He says the parents may supply means to buy real estate in contiguous states. It

---

17. Booth is right that the period of education for deaf students
would lengthen, but it did not happen as quickly as he anticipated.

happens, unfortunately, that in our country not more than one man in twenty is wealthy. Of course, few such parents could buy real estate in other states; but there is a still more "formidable" difficulty. How parents and children would consent or could be brought to consent to a separation for so utopian a whim, as I must call it, with all deference to Mr. Flournoy, as that of keeping up a separate organization of deaf mutes in order that they—the deaf-mutes—may be indulged in the desire of exercising the functions of government, and of sending some restless politician to represent them in Congress? I do not know whether Mr. Flournoy has a family. It would appear not, from the way he talks of sundering the ties of parent and child; and, besides, parent and child thus separated, the former, left alone in his old age, would most certainly be ready at any moment to join in any general effort for changing the organic law and bringing it more into consonance with the laws of nature. If the child must go, the parent must go with him. The rule is instinctive in the human heart and is universal. All or nearly all then go, and what is left of your community of deaf-mutes? Only the young and the middle aged, and they looking to self-banishment as their children grow up. Such a prospect is not the most pleasant for a man or woman to contemplate; and still less so when the chief motive advanced is only the glory of governing ourselves in our own way, and especially the glory of sending some ambitious aspirant—Mr. Flournoy for example— begging his pardon for so using his name—to the National Halls at Washington. We have already the full enjoyment of the rights, common to all, of voting at elections. We enter into such contests with the same zest and heartiness, and enjoy victory and defeat as fully; and if we are not ourselves elected, we are no worse off than the eighty or ninety odd thousand to every member, and who never set foot within the walls of the national capitol. I hold it to be a poor ambition which desires merely to figure on the stage of life without benefiting one's fellows. Any baboon can do that, and human baboons do it every day and have done it since the creation.

Mr. Flournoy suggests, as an alternative, in case of failure on the subject of real estate, etc., which I have been considering, that we "can remain a Territory of the Federal Government, and enjoy its powerful protection under Omnipotence." Mr. F. does not appear to be aware that, while powerful as regards foreign nations, because when it represents public sentiment it is backed up by the public, or, in common parlance, by the people, it is exceedingly weak as regards its power over that people. Theoretically speaking, there is no government except the government of the people. As a Territory, instead of governing ourselves, we should be largely under a foreign government. Our governor, secretary and judges must come from Washington. We should send only a delegate who would have no right to vote. We should elect that delegate, our own legislature and minor officers; and our politicians, desiring to be senators, etc., and to wield more power, would soon be clamoring for a State government. But, aside from all this, a Territorial condition is not agreeable to man's self-respect, nor the best suited to his development. It is holding the relation of child to parent, and the child full grown, energetic and lusty.[18] Heaven keep us from the "powerful protection" of the Federal, or any government other than our own! "We the people" of the States, scarcely know, save by its caprices, that such a thing as the Federal Government has an existence. In a Territory, we should feel its iron hand—sometimes light, sometimes heavy, and should at all times be reminded that we are more subjects than sovereigns.

Mr. Flournoy takes too disconsolate a view of the condition of educated deaf-mutes. Out of the three or four thousand who are educated, I am acquainted with at least one thousand and I have not perceived that they are much more unhappy than, or

---

18. Here we again encounter parent–child rhetoric. While Flournoy presents a deaf commonwealth as the adult choice, Booth contends that living in a territory would make adults feel like children because they would be ruled by the federal government.

held inferior to, the masses around them. It is true they can not, save in rare cases, hold office, but this is exceptional and consequent on their deafness. It is true, likewise, that they do not enjoy life in its fullness as do their hearing associates.[19] This too, results from the same cause; and, as regards the kind of happiness, must always continue so in a greater or less degree. The same may be said of the blind, the lame, etc. It is a part of the punishment inflicted for violation of nature's laws, which violation—whether it comes from carelessness, design or ignorance—results in deafness, blindness, lameness, etc., and will so result until man has so far improved, mentally, morally, and physically, that diseases and accidents of a severe nature will be unknown.[20]

Again, looking at the condition of the educated deaf-mutes in the Northern states, every year adds to their sources of enjoyment. They reside among a dense population, and that an educated population. Every year sends from the various institutions of the land, better educated mutes, for these institutions are compelled to keep pace with the progress around; and the time allowed their pupils, formerly four years, is already nearly doubled, and must, ere long, be extended further. Then, rail roads are covering the North and West as with a net-work, thus rendering conventions and individual meetings of educated deaf-mutes easy and frequent. The South is more slow in these matters, and it will probably require one or more generations to bring about the same state of things there. Mr. Flournoy need not despair. He is one of the wealthy slave-holders of the South, and, as such, is entitled to hold and utter his

---

19. The debate is circling around four major issues: deaf Americans' happiness and self-worth, their opportunities in mainstream society, their literacy, and the feasibility of creating a separate deaf commonwealth.

20. Booth addresses a question raised by Laurent Clerc in 1818: "Why are we deaf?" While Clerc, Carlin, and others view the answer as a divine mystery, Booth gives a more precise response: deafness is punishment for breaking "nature's laws." His comment contains tinges of the medieval view of deafness as a curse from God.

own opinions.[21] Instead then of confining his reading and con-
templations to the barbarian glories of Greece and Rome, where
were three or four white slaves to every freeman, let him discard
the ancients and their rude ignorance and vague surmisings, and
turn his attention to the writings of the philosophers who have
lived and written since the French Revolution of 1789. Let him
read the writings of Combe[22] and other philosophers of the progressive school, and the bold, vigorous essays of such periodicals
as the *Atlantic Monthly*, and become hopeful as regards man's destiny; and, thereby, he will be enabled to cast off what appears to
be a gloomy misanthropy; and, by so doing, he will increase his
own happiness. He is not the only one who has suffered mentally
from being endowed with greater capabilities than his fellows.
What he most needs is a more complete understanding of men,
and the hopeful and more cheerful spirit founded thereon.

I desire here to correct an error into which I fell in my letter
of Sept. 6th, to Mr. Flournoy. I stated that there were no government lands unsold in Iowa, except railroad lands. There is a large
amount in the western and north-western part of Iowa not yet
disposed of. My error arose from the fact that none were for sale
at the time. There is a plan on foot in Wisconsin, among some
Hartford and New York graduates—deaf-mutes—for going to one
of these northwestern counties and settling in one neighborhood.[23] This is carrying out the old plan formed by myself, Mr.

---

21. Flournoy did have some slaves. Somewhat paradoxically for a
person who railed against prejudice, Flournoy saw African Americans as
evil and wanted to send all black people to Africa. Since Booth was a
strong abolitionist, and this exchange took place only a few years before
the outbreak of the Civil War, we can perhaps understand why the tone
between Booth and Flournoy is often bitingly sarcastic, even hostile.

22. This reference may be to William Combe (1742–1823), British
writer and humorist.

23. Even as this debate waged, deaf Americans were already coming
together and forming small communities in various places around the
country.

Willard and others, over a quarter of a century ago, and free from
the deformities of exclusiveness and of begging land of Congress.
We are already, to some extent, carrying out the idea here in the
place of my residence. We are already three families of deaf-mutes
and expect as many more this spring; but I do not hold it wise for
many of the same mechanical occupation to crowd into one town,
unless such town is large. A city like New York can easily furnish
occupation for a hundred in ordinary times. Less than a tenth of
that number would be sufficient for a country village. . . .

Flournoy Elaborates on His Proposal

Further explanations from Flournoy also appeared in the April Annals.

Samuel Porter, Esq.:[24]

Dear Sir: The more I reflect upon the subject the greater is
my conviction of the practicability and utility of the scheme of a
Deaf Commonwealth. I am not the originator of it—though
without being aware of his early promulgation of the same, I had
suggested the views of my venerable friend, Laurent Clerc, to the
deaf-mutes of America. He is the real father of the idea.[25] To his
wisdom and originality belong the project. "Honor to whom
honor is due." For my own humble part it is sufficient if I be
deemed worthy, and receive a call from the deaf and dumb to the
post of leader, that I devote myself in the inception and germ of
the scheme to its virtual fulfillment. Difficulties, at first appalling,
seem to vanish as we grapple with them, and the establishment of
a sovereignty for our class, which are without tests of their capacity, tacitly rejected all election and preferment, appears to our an-
ticipation a matter of easy accomplishment.

---

24. Samuel Porter was the editor of the *Annals* at the time this
debate took place.

25. Flournoy makes this claim based on the fact that, in 1820, Clerc
had suggested using part of Congress's land grant to the American Asylum as a place where deaf people could settle.

The location of our *Empire* may be in Oregon. Its winters are mild—situated as it is on an ocean, over which sweep and are tempered, the wintry blasts. It need not be marine, or on the sea shore, for we can not hear in the dark, and in tempests, so as to act as mariners—have therefore little to do with shipping and with sailing. Founded interior, a space of country forty miles square may fully answer our purpose. But should this far off province appear too distant to the deaf, we may look to some of the old Atlantic, gulf, lake, or conterminous states for the gift. But if a general negative meets us at all points, we can, with the permission and security of the Federal Government, negotiate with the Indian tribes that exist west of Arkansas, and purchase a tract sufficient for the intention. The government itself might purchase this small territory and sell it to each of our men on the principle of pre-emption;—the only benefit we ask from it being the securement to us of a constitution guaranteeing no controlling agency except by deaf and dumb men. Our design is to exhibit our competency for public and other affairs, and hence the peremptory necessity of this guaranty.

That the government will do this for us, remains to be tested by a memorial which may be written and signed soon after the adjournment of the next convention of the deaf mutes of New England, at Worcester, next September, when as I am credibly informed, the subject of this migration and colony will be fully debated by the members.[26]

I would, beforehand, warn the intelligent mutes not to expect or anticipate that the government, or the Congress and executive constituting it, would receive, with a good grace, any proposal from us which may look to a *grant of land* to our people. *Congress will certainly give us no land.* It has grudged all former such dispensations. Members of Congress have stigmatized such donations as those to the first deaf-mute Asylum founded in America, as *"un-*

---

26. The proceedings of the relevant part of this meeting appear at the end of the chapter.

constitutional'' and to be repressed, and characterized the precedents which anticipate gifts to the insane and other poor people,
as perilous encroachments on the compact of our Union, which
may finally lead to unwarranted and colossal appropriations. Indeed, it is known that President Pierce,[27] when he vetoed (though
unwillingly, as he said) the appropriation of two hundred thousand
dollars to the construction and endowment of an Asylum for the
Insane in our country, instanced the grant of money and land to
the Deaf and Dumb Asylum at Hartford, in or about 1816, as a
precedent which should not be approved into a pattern for further
legislation. We are by this, therefore, admonished of the futility of
any application for a grant of land in personal *fee simple*, to our
class of the inhabitants of the country. . . . None, aside from such
and collateral services, have ever been granted for the last thirty
years. If any were, I know of none.

Our course, then, is to petition the Congress so soon as the
deaf and dumb have had the matter laid before them generally,
and have arrived at any conclusion, to lay out a small territory, to
be reserved for the purchase, settlement, and government of the
mutes, to whom only the pre-emption will hold valid. Nothing
more need be sought or asked. I believe there are mutes in pleni-
tude, who have enough money to take out bodies of land, and
thus to create a society and political organization. There will, if
untoward events deter emigration, be no lack of a sufficient number to be the governors of the country, or if that happen, there
may exist an *interregnum*, in which the auricular may be substi-
tuted, by the constitution, to hold the state strictly in trust, until
some deaf person approaches. Thus we can perceive that the commonwealth may be perpetuated indefinitely for our special use.

This is the plan, and it should be kept scrupulously in view.

---

27. Franklin Pierce (1804–1869) served as U.S. president from
1853 to 1857. The grant of land was made to the American Asylum in
1820.

The difficulty of the whole vanishes as we approach to touch the thing, like the mists of morning before the rays of the sun. Mr. Booth, in his letter to me, published in the last *Annals*, believed it impracticable and an impossibility, if the state is to be entirely composed of deaf-mutes. I have shown that this was not the feature intended, and I suppose his objections may vanish. His answer, however, I await with cool anxiety. . . .

We deaf-mutes have a sort of abiding melancholy at our unfortunate deprivation, although our sanguine hope in a common and Almighty Father, who as He has led others to establish growing communities, will lead us also, and protect, uphold and prosper those who call on His name with a sincere and relying spirit, induces us to be gay and contented. It is the quiet of deference to our hearing brethren, and of dependence on Providence. We assume no arrogance in devising this benefiting project; pretend to no superiority, nor do we cogitate a mastery. We indeed do, as I have in my opening circular, sent to my class of the people, complain of rejections and consignments to inferior places or to none, without tests of capacity; but we do not arrogate to dictate, or to accomplish any policy, or to confirm any principle without the guidance or co-operation of our hearing friends, to whom, in some measure, by the order of Providence, we are in a state of pupilage. We feel duly grateful to them for what we know, which is due to their instructions; we are sensible of and grateful for their sympathy, and alike for them and ourselves, commiserate the circumstances of the whole human family upon the earth. But here we all have to live, and here must work and thrive and suffer, until the hour of withdrawal by death; and we ask only for some place, in which, without interfering with their business, we may quietly evince some competency that may tend to the welfare of coming generations of our unfortunate class.

Yours, etc.,
J. J. Flournoy

William Chamberlain on Flournoy's Project

Other deaf people also had their opinions published in the April Annals. *William Chamberlain, a deaf journalist in Massachusetts, became the first deaf person to give support (although limited) to Flournoy's plan.*

Samuel Porter, Esq.:

Dear Sir: The articles by Messrs. Booth and Flournoy, in the January number of the *Annals*, on a "deaf-mute commonwealth," have interested me, and I am induced to send you some rough ideas of my own. Like Mr. Booth, I have some objections to Mr. Flournoy's plan, although they may not prove so "truly formidable" as those of that gentleman and Mr. Turner; yet I can not agree with Mr. Booth in some of his ideas. He thinks a community composed exclusively or mainly of *deaf-mutes* "an impossibility;" I think that one *exclusively* of deaf-mutes could not long remain so, but I believe that if a company of deaf-mutes, say two or three-hundred, more or less, with such of their hearing friends and relations as choose to join them, should go west, settle in some place where there was room enough, and form themselves into a community, governed by suitable laws, and headed by able leaders, such an institution would be both *permanent* and *beneficial*.

As far as my experience goes, I have always found deaf-mutes to be greater readers, better informed and more intelligent, where there are a number of them in the same place, than when *scattered*, as many, if not most of them are, among the hearing. I therefore can not agree with Mr. Booth that "the wisest course is to let them remain *'lost'* among the hearing." It is true, as Mr. Booth says, that deaf-mutes are compelled to read and write while in this *"lost"* condition, but it is for want of any better mode of communication with those with whom they live. It does not prove them to be better informed or more intelligent than they would be if placed in a body by themselves. A deaf-mute, generally speaking, is not apt to *understand* what he reads, by himself, so well as when he has access to some individuals of the same class.

What one does not understand another can explain, and thus they promote each other's improvement.

Mr. Booth says that "scandal, backbiting and other diabolisms" are as common with deaf-mutes as with hearing persons; I do not doubt it, but if he intends it as an objection against the formation of a community, it is a weak argument, for every one knows that other communities flourish in spite of such things.

I do not pretend that a community of deaf-mutes would be without disadvantages, yet when all things are considered, I think the benefits to be derived from one, if well regulated, are enough to render such a community desirable.

Mr. Flournoy wants Congress to grant us the *government* of a "piece of territory" large enough for a *state*; we, of course, to pay government prices for the land: it is not the land that he asks as a gift, but the *government* of the land. He seems to think that the *land* without the *government* would be undesirable. The extent of territory proposed "about the size of Rhode Island or Connecticut," is an objection; all the deaf-mutes in the country could not settle it to advantage.[28]

The government of a "state" would be a very undesirable and inconvenient responsibility. There are ability, energy and talent enough among the deaf-mutes of this country to govern a state with credit to themselves and all concerned; but, as I believe that "politics and government, so far from being the 'chief end of man,' are a necessary evil, of which the less we have the better," I propose to try the experiment on a smaller scale. I believe that an application to Congress would be a *failure*, and I do not intend to encourage a movement in that direction. It would be a waste of time, and in case of its failure, discouragements would arise. Our *first* movement must succeed, or many who would otherwise go

---

28. In his most recent letter, Flournoy had scaled down his proposal, suggesting an area of land "forty miles square" for the commonwealth.

with us will not come up to the aid of another and different plan. It becomes us to be prudent, and consider well, which of *all* the plans offered is most likely to succeed.

Mr. Booth would have us remain in our original *"oblivion."* Mr. Flournoy would scatter us over a tract of territory where we should be like angel's visits, "few and far between."

I suggest that when a sufficient number of mutes, with their friends, are found, as I have no doubt there might be, they emigrate to some previously selected spot in the west, and buy up a piece of land six miles square. This would make a township of 23,040 acres, which, bought with land-warrants at present prices, would cost not far from $20,000. Let them settle it, choose leaders, and make laws to govern themselves, the laws always to be framed in accordance with the territorial laws and the Federal constitution.

There are enough in the States, willing and able to do this, and all they need is a call from some of their more influential unfortunates. Aside from the benefits to be derived from association with each other, there would be no need of applying to Congress, and the *government* of the township would be as much as they would care to be troubled with. They could regulate their own affairs, build and plant, and would no doubt grow to be a respectable colony. They could have their own Sunday schools and churches, where the gospel would be preached in the silent but expressive language of signs, understood by all and felt by not a few. If a mute wishes to sell out, let him do so, and to whom he pleases; let the colony be truly republican in spirit. Of course, advantages would arise from the mutes being in the majority. They could not be kept so by hereditary descent, but let it begin well and be conducted wisely, and deaf-mute emigration will keep up the required number. The motives which govern those who go should be a desire for personal and mutual benefit. Let brotherly love prevail among them, and let them not go because they thirst for power and wealth. These will accrue to the colony in years to come; no one expects to find them in the wilderness without toil and patience.

I may have more to say in future numbers of the *Annals*. In

the mean time, if any of my fellow mutes should have any ideas
to communicate, I should be glad to hear from them.

Yours, &c.,
Wm. Martin Chamberlain

P. H. Confer Supports the Commonwealth Plan

*A deaf man in Indiana, known to us only as P. H. Confer, was the first
in print wholeheartedly to embrace Flournoy's proposal. He gives poignant
testimony of the prejudice encountered by some deaf Americans and their
loneliness living among hearing people.*

Mr. Samuel Porter:

I saw in the *American Annals* for January 1858, letters from E.
Booth and J. J. Flournoy, speaking of forming a colony of deaf-
mutes, and to that I would say that it would make me happy, as
well as many more of my class of people, if such a thing could be
brought about—for a great many reasons. The deaf-mutes would
all be happy, as they can not now be, because they have nobody
that can or will converse with them, and many people look on a
deaf-mute as if he were a fool, because he can not talk, and because to them deaf-mutes look so foolish, just because they can
not understand them. If they were by themselves, they could be
happy; but as they are separated, they are in many cases despised
by hearing men. That I have found out myself, because the hearing man says to the mute, You are a fool and crazy imposter.
Therefore, I say, I am for a place where all my deaf-mute brethren
could live and be happy; and I would say to J. J. Flournoy, that I
like his enterprise, and if it should come so far as to buy the land,
I would say, that I would give $5,000 to it in cash, and if all would
help, the thing could be done. I am an orphan. I became deaf by
sickness. I was then ten years old, and could never since enjoy
myself, with all my father left me, a good farm of two hundred

and fifty acres, worth $18,000. I am all alone. My father and mother, brother and sister, are all dead, and left me the farm and $2,000 in cash, which I loan out at ten per cent. But with all that, I am not happy, with the present condition of the deaf and dumb. I am twenty-four years old and am not married.

This is what I think of the case, and I would like to see it carried out as soon as possible. Please give me a place in the *Annals*.

P. H. Confer

John Carlin to Laurent Clerc

Carlin wrote the following opinion in a personal letter to Clerc. Though not composed for the public, he agreed to let the Annals publish it.

I read in the *Annals*, the January number, the letters of Messrs. Flournoy and Booth, in reference to the "Commonwealth of Deaf Mutes," in some territory, for which I would most respectfully suggest the name of DEAF-MUTIA. Or, for euphony's, sake, GESTURIA. They both are ably written, do much credit to their heads and to their Alma Mater. As to the merits of Mr. Flournoy's theory, all that I can say is, that nothing is more pleasurable to our sensations, as we loll in our armchairs by the fireside, than the building of castles in the air. Without manual labor, we can rear up in the vacuum, structures surpassing Solomon's temple in magnificence and costliness of materials, kingdoms of vast magnitude and power, or ladders of eminence to ascend to the summit of fame. But in practice, to ensure success, it requires dollars, eagles and dimes in countless bags, to commence the work with, besides perseverance, patience and industry to keep the work steady; we all would have to lend our shoulders to the wheel, and not to stand looking on or gesturing all the long day.

As regards the founding of a deaf-mute commonwealth any where, the obstacles to its ultimate success are truly formidable. It must be borne in mind that nine-tenths of the whole deaf-mute community in this country can not raise up the wind so as to swell the flapping sails of Mr. Flournoy's scheme; besides, it is a well known fact that the majority of them show little decision of purpose in any enterprise whatever. For my own part, failing to perceive the practicability of the scheme, to which Mr. Flournoy clings with a constancy worthy of a better cause, I am content with my being "lost among the hearing persons," whose superior knowledge of the English language benefits my mind far more than would the perpetual gestures of the thousands of the *bona fide* residents in Gesturia. Drive to the neighboring states our hearing children whom we love so well! I reckon Mr. Flournoy has no little prattlers of his own to cheer the solitude of his plantation.

John R. Burnet Weighs In

Burnet also sent in a rather flippant treatment of the proposal.

I wish to offer the tribute of my admiration for the magnificent views put forth by Mr. Flournoy. I hope he will go on and prosper. The government of a territory is the object to which he at present modestly limits himself. I think I foresee his views will soar higher yet, till he and the deaf-mutes of America will be content with nothing less than the control of an independent republic. Will not *President* Flournoy sound better than *Governor* Flournoy?[29] For myself, having a turn for foreign travel, I would rather

___

29. The editor of the *Annals* included the following note: "It is proper for us . . . to advise Mr. Burnet, that Mr. Flournoy would tell him he has hit wide of the mark in one of his points. Mr. Flournoy writes, to Mr. Chamberlain, that he should not feel at liberty even to join the colony in person. 'I have long been attempting,' he says, 'to play a sort of moral reformer in Georgia, to induce the deportation of the slaves to Liberia, and I fear, if I should go west now, I should be

be an attaché to the embassy in London or Paris (for which post I hope my application may have precedence on file), than a member of the state government; not intending, however, to decline any office in which it may be judged that I may be useful to my country that is to be; provided the acceptance does not oblige me to neglect my own family.

Speaking of family, I would suggest a way of getting over the difficulty raised by Mr. Booth. Let it be provided that the estates of deaf-mutes may pass to their daughters who hear and speak, *provided these daughters marry only deaf husbands.* And if there be no daughters, I would so far respect the paternal feelings of worthy deaf-mute citizens that I would let their hearing sons inherit, provided they would consent, like Ulysses on the coast of the Syrens, to stop their ears with wax. They would then have no advantage over deaf-mutes in public meetings and conversation at least, which is all that can be reasonably required.

I would further suggest, to make the scheme more practicable, that we need not insist on permanent residence in voters. Let all deaf-mutes come, pay tax, and vote, and then *vamos, a la Kansas.*[30] Many would do that, who might not find it for their interest to pitch their stakes in the new promised land.

Flournoy's Final Reply

Flournoy's final comments on the subject appeared in the July Annals.

The April No. of the *Annals* contains the remarks of Mr. Booth, Mr. Chamberlain, Mr. Carlin, Mr. Confer and Mr. Burnet;

---

abandoning a sacred duty. . . .' " Apparently Flournoy realized that even if deaf people did decide to emigrate west, they would be unlikely to elect him their leader.

30. Burnet probably is referring to the recent struggles over the Kansas–Nebraska Act of 1854, which left the question of whether Kansas would be a free or slave state up to its inhabitants. Both proslavery and

all excepting those of Messrs. Chamberlain and Confer, repudiating my scheme. I do not look upon Mr. Chamberlain's suggestion as adverse, it is a substitute, by a diminution. But he should have viewed the project with a more enlarged survey, and observed that as our Commonwealth is to be founded for all coming time, numerous, *eventually*, may be the emigrations of deaf-mutes from all parts of the civilized world; and hence, a six miles square would prove insufficient for them; and this is the *contingency* for which we should sagaciously provide, by the selection of a forty miles square territory. The deaf residing in its contiguous towns and settlements will never be materially scattered. Still, should the effort to induce this exodus of the deaf be practicable, some such plan as Mr. Chamberlain's may be *tried*, on the principle and policy, "better a little than none."

Mr. Carlin says he does not fancy a confinement among deaf-mutes, listening to their signs, as improving. Mr. Chamberlain has already refuted some of these objections, as to the facility for intelligence by such unions. But I would respectfully say to Mr. Carlin, that any amount of learning we deaf fellows can amass from conversational intercourse with the hearing, is greatly less than what we could derive from a conjunction of, and intercourse with, our own class of people. There is not a hearing man, that, except for occasional novelty and to while away a *tedium*, would *like* to hold written converse with any of us. It is too irksome. I always endeavor to make it a point never to put my neighbors to such *trouble*. They often have complained of the *burden* of conversing *thus* with me. And such hearing people as know the sign language, or alphabet of our class, never make it a point to convey to us one ninety-ninth of the information they constantly impart to each other by oral converse. Our last resource, then, is to have a unity; to read and to mutually impart our knowledge.

---

antislavery settlers went to Kansas in an effort to affect the vote, resulting in the tragedy of "bleeding" Kansas and moving the nation closer to Civil War.

The subject of the Editorial remark on the disposition of Messrs. Flournoy and Confer, to consider the mutes as "despised" by the hearing, has two aspects.[31] It is too obvious for denial, that, while by some we are not estimated of any importance at all to society, and encounter insurmountable prejudice where we would assert an equality, by others, we are only regarded *patronizingly*. It is true indeed, that by some few, and these the more philosophical and Christian portion of the hearing community, who also are intimate with some of us, we have respectful or affectionate consideration. But how few are these among the mass! The Editor therefore erred, in supposing Mr. Confer's declaration groundless or unmerited by the world.

This communication must indispensably be long, but inasmuch as it is the *last* that I regard as requisite on this matter for me to put forth, I hope the indulgence of the Editor of the *Annals*. After this article the argument on my part is exhausted, and the project submitted to the choice of the deaf and dumb. Mr. Booth may reply as a finality, but I have with this concluded my lucubrations.

Mr. Booth sets out with calling his reply to my letter a practical one. It is its *impracticability* to which I object. He goes on to say, that himself, Mr. Willard, and others, had "formed an association with a view of purchasing land" at the West, which was abandoned by their appointment as teachers. Now I do not suppose this plan analogous with mine. It had none of the main features of the Commonwealth System, and any mention of it at all as cogent reasoning against what is now contemplated, is unnecessary and irrelevant. I say to Mr. Booth again, that if the ideal of going West embraced nothing more than a settlement under the auspices and supervision of the hearing, we might as well and better, remain in

---

31. The editor of the *Annals* included a curious note with Confer's letter disputing his claim that deaf people were sometimes despised by hearing individuals. Such feelings, the (hearing) editor wrote, had "no foundation . . . in fact."

our present positions. I wish to be comprehended. It is a political independence, a STATE SOVEREIGNTY, at which I aim, for the benefit of an unfortunate *downtrodden* class, for they are downtrodden enough, when the human soul is denied its right because of our bodily imperfection. How else, but by acting with such an establishment, can we evince our intelligence, capacity and usefulness? Shall our energies be forever dormant, that is, the mass of us be made little better than slaves, with ability of course to vote for others, but to have none to vote for us; and without such commercial and agricultural facilities as our Union can engender, because Edmund Booth is satisfied with that summit of his ambition, a newspaper, and because George Homer and perhaps some few others, have a *clerk's* place in the customs?[32] Certainly, such contented deaf-mutes as they can stay where they are. My call is to those who have no emolument or hope beyond the incomes of their humble *daily* labor, which hearing competition abridges, and whom hearing arrogance effectually shoves aside. Until our hearing brethren will embrace us as co-equal *spirits*, we shall ever talk of them *thus*.

My object is not so much political honors for the mute, as the exhibition of our dormant qualifications. My plan is to make a HOME for the mutes, for mutual intercourse and improvement; and to show the world our abilities, which may induce governments and opulence to employ our brother-mutes in many posts for a living.

The prevailing idea of rulers and of people is that mutes are not capable of *any* political accomplishment; that, while hearing men are at hand, such unnecessary expletives may well be forever dis-

---

32. George Homer, a member of a distinguished Boston family, had gradually started losing his hearing at age ten. Although he attended the American Asylum and was one of the founders of the Boston Deaf-Mute Christian Association, he opposed the idea of deaf people congregating together.

carded. No deaf-mute therefore has any money by performing political services; besides, no one having an extensive manufacturing
or other establishment, would *prefer* or *allow* him to have the
profitable post of manager or overseer. All he can get is that of day
laborer or mechanic. Such positions do not elevate him into
wealth, while the hearing get rich by having the best employments.

Now, could we exhibit in some State, where all office and
business is free to us, our competency, the prosperity of our Society will convince the world that we could do many things; and
hence, office and lucrative appointments may be open to us in
other lands. Does Mr. Booth now comprehend? Such of us as
have devoted a life-time to politics, can give satisfaction if employed as ministers plenipotentiary, since in diplomacy all intercourse is carried on by writing. Many of us also could act as
governors and legislators, all that is needed is some new arrangement in the order of representation. We could also very well be
head-men or managers in some lucrative establishment, and in
banks, and *no mute will be a defaulter*.

Mr. Booth goes on to allude to ambition as my governing
motive. . . . In this matter I had no *personal* ambition. From a sick
bed I sent out a call to my fellow-citizens who are isolated from
all preferment by government, and patronage, by opulence as
overseers and managers, directing their attention to meditations
for the common good. I was to stay where I am and still to contend for the buried truth. The deaf-mutes I considered capable, if
my advice be adopted, of acting without my personal agency.
How, in this, can Mr. Booth, or any man, see ambition as the
propelling passion?

If I become an inhabitant of our State, that may be, to be
called GALLAUDET, and have election to Congress, I shall not have
gone there without benefiting the people that sent me, by attending to *their interests*. It is mockery and disparagement of themselves
and a depreciation of their intrinsic capacities, to see deaf persons
talking about ambition as the motive of the would-be benefactors

of their class. A slave could not utter a more significant idea of negro degradation, than when one tells another whose master grants him extra privileges, that he wishes to strut about like a white man! It is time for us, poor deaf men, to drop all such *caricaturing,* and to gravely and solemnly address ourselves to the plan of ameliorating our condition, without doing injury to our hearing brethren, and perhaps benefiting them by our devout and consistent examples.

The next objection of my friend, Mr. Booth, is on the score of the separation of parents and children. He supposes, with another correspondent, that I have no family. I have only a daughter, married, and removed to Wisconsin—and she left against my wishes. Children we see will not always abide at home, or near their parents. I do not see how this scheme would separate families before the adult age; but adults will disperse of themselves. The deaf and dumb appear to dwell on this subject. The affections of their parents for them in particular, is such as to stand no separation. Mothers and fathers are fond of deaf, more than of any other children. So wrote a deaf-mute of Columbus, Ohio, name unrecollected— Chase, I believe. Now the true philosophy of such a view is that parents can follow such adult children to the State of Gallaudet. But on what is this extraordinary attachment, forbidding all improvement of the condition of such favorites, founded? Be it founded not on rational affection, but rather on that favoritism that makes a child a perpetual *pet*, very much as some old woman in single blessedness loves a monkey, a cat, or a poodle dog—such enfeebling and frustrating attachment to a deaf child *in particular,* does not very much recognize it as an intelligence, and can not be tolerated, against the manifest destiny of its useful citizenship. But I will meet Mr. Booth's philosophy on its very face. He had said that it would not be right (I use his ideas, not words) to part families. Again, he in the next postulate has a flattering picture of the fact that deaf schools may retain scholars fifteen years, "from infancy to twenty-one." And here is a virtual separation of parent and child at the tenderest age of the *pet*. To what then amounts his reasoning, when he infers that after such academical absence, the educated mute, long weaned from such *lap-dog* attachment, is to be retained by the family as a living automaton, a perpetual "darling"—doing nothing but some mechanical endearment all day long!

I respect the affection and sacredness of the family circle, and would forever consecrate such associations. But can not they be perfected equally in the community we wish to form? Nor when an emergency demands, can the energies of rational minds be contracted into everlasting childhood.

I have observed in my intercourse with the world, that if a first sight of me induce a deference of demeanor in the spectator, when he hears that I am deaf, he is at once familiar, even by speech and look; and though this would appear as a friendly disposition, it soon wears off, and attention and respect is given to others, while I am treated with neglect, or only occasional notice. Attention to us is thus exhibited as based upon inferior considerations. When we would claim equality, it offends. Viewing the case this way, I doubt if the estimation of parents for deaf children is as deep and abiding, all things considered, as that for the others. It is but cruelty to them, if adults, thus to contract their resources to the domestic hearth.

Mr. Booth had in his first letter asserted that by remaining "scattered and even lost" amid the hearing, deaf-mutes are induced to be a reading class. I demanded proof of one in a hundred, thus scattered, being a reader of many books. He replied, not by producing the proof to sustain his first position, but by disclaiming that in our age many of even the hearing are literary and scientific! In this as he fails to sustain his argument, his objection falls to the ground.

In his next attack, he observed that I "complain" and take a "wrong view of men," and make myself unhappy by what he calls a "gloomy misanthropy"—after advising me to read other than Roman and Greek works, and those of the progressive philosophers of the present times! Such misanthropy, as he calls it, has nothing to do with any effort to institute a deaf society. It was a movement of philanthropy. If he make out my proposal to be a complaint of a gloomy spirit, in what light would he conceive to have been the temper and feelings of those great master-spirits that in all epochs have ameliorated the condition of men? What authority had he for restricting a deaf-mute from using, though in a humble attitude, the weapons of Luther, of Columbus, or of Washington? Was Patrick Henry a "complaining, gloomy misanthrope," because he was for independence? Was Washington no better, for contending against such a colossal power as Britain? The case of every reformer or ameliorator is analogous. If he could regard me as an unhappy, complaining misanthrope, he must so consider Luther and Washington, and the founders of the American Colonization Society, and those of the Domestic, Foreign and every other Mission—for they are all based on principles identical with mine—as aiming to correct the imperfection of actual circumstances. But here Mr. Booth finds himself placed *hors de combat*. He is himself the complainer—the "unhappy misanthrope"—for he opposes the improvement of the resources of his class of people, and arrogantly and patronizingly calls upon us all to do like himself, and diminish our prospects into a settlement out west of some village, where in one generation we shall have vanished away, without the trace of history or tradition! . . .

I know that if I could have induced Georgia early to adopt my plans (and they are not a single one), that she would have stood morally sublime, and the example of all the republic. I know too that if the deaf and dumb would cease to carp and cark, and to find objections, and to theorize, and move to the adoption of my emigration suggestion, that they would build up a commonwealth, governed solely by themselves, that would astonish the hearing by the magnitude of faculties they had hitherto conceived as impossible. So Mr. Booth need no longer oppose the manifest destiny of our people. God hath "turned our captivity," and we are no longer the useless objects that the world has not yet ceased to consider us. We will have a small republic of our own, under our sovereignty, and independent of all hearing interference. We will also inhabit all parts of the country; and to such of us as remain in the old homesteads, the proof of our competency exhibited in the Deaf Commonwealth would be a material benefit. Whenever our hearing brethren acknowledge our use and equality, and conceding the privilege of office and preferment, so reorganize structures as to admit our participation in business and duties, national, state, and secular, and even religious, then will be the appropriate time for hearing such arguments as Mr. Booth and Mr. Carlin have given. Till then "our work is great," and we can not attend to any of the Sanballats of society.[33]

The objection to the commonwealth, on the score of inability to buy land for the hearing children in the contiguous states, not thirty miles away, any way, from the center, may be refuted by the supposition that, should the deaf not live in fashion and luxury like the French and English and wealthy Americans, every man would have money enough to give to his children as they attain age. The mutes are proverbially a temperate people. We would have no drunkards or grog-shops among us. None need, therefore, be too poor to help his children to settle just less than twenty-five miles off. Again, as Mr. Booth held it, if the children must leave, the parents will; and there may be no mute population sufficient to keep up the state; and that it is poor inducement to remain there only to send *me* to Congress. But how many of our children may be engaged in mercantile employments, how many in mechanical? Such as will have real estate can rent it, or have it a little distance off. By this means a sufficient number will remain to people the state and its cities, and to carry on the government. Mr. Booth has given only one side, and that the darker one of the

---

33. In Nehemia 4, the governor of the province of Samaria, Sanballat, tries to prevent Nehemia from rebuilding Jerusalem's walls.

picture; whereas there are more favorable lights in the same compass; and should there be but forty deaf mutes in the country, they, with the government, will preserve the association, and exhibit what mutes can do; while experience will come in to correct mistakes and defects.

It is presumable that the Convention at Worcester will, if the idea be seriously entertained to found *Gallaudet*, thoroughly examine into the several aspects of the state. They would thus arrive at some definite shape in which the economy of these matters may be comprehended—our qualification for office, the order in which landed property may be owned and bequeathed, or the tenure by which it is to be held. It is true that nature has not separated the deaf and the hearing by any wide and imprescriptible margin, and no organization can be fixed that can have any precedent in former ages or former plans. It would be a quite novel experiment, which is alone for ends that we wish to attain; and *some sacrifices must be made for the general welfare.* We, as the right to the soil is in deaf mutes, may hold the territory subject to future legislation; we may ordain it that our hearing progeny shall live on, and work free of cost, our lands, on the principle of usufructuary rent, to be entailed upon the next deaf child that is born in the family, on the English plan of primogeniture; and that money be given to the hearing children, equal to the proportional value of the land. Our good management would make this easily possible at all times.

How can Mr. Booth think that such an organization would be of no benefit to the mute community? Why does he not look upon them as scattered among the hearing, all the world over, and denied all office and all lucrative employment, and the only affluent ones among the nations being so by inheritance alone? It is impossible to see how a mute, with his present facilities and under prevailing prejudices, can, like the hearing man, with all his advantages, and privileges and prerogatives, become wealthy himself from original poverty. The transition, then, to this community, can not by any means injure the emigrants. It *must* be a benefit. It would advance the interest of the masses, whose situation is certainly worthy our consideration, instead of that of Mr. Booth and some others of the more favored of our class. The maxim, "the greatest good of the greatest number, and for the longest possible time," is to be our controlling axiom; and no dogma that is satisfied with the gains of a *few*, exercises a predominating influence over deliberations which look to the future by the lights of the present, and rely on the same Divine Benignity that will qualify all innocent systems to the happiness of His creatures. . . .

We are not beasts, for all our deafness! We are MEN! The Era of de l'Epée has been the epocha of our birth of mind. After a long night of wandering, our planet has at length attained an orbit round a central luminary. Let us go manfully to the work. I welcome brothers Chamberlain and Confer, as spirits that stand forth in this early light of our history.

Mr. Chamberlain abjures political affairs, as constructed into government, as an evil with which we should have little or nothing to do. This sentiment is exceedingly unphilosophical. Our friend should recollect that he is *under* some government, and that he might as well be under *his own*, as that of others, who, more unwise than himself, might mold his destinies as they please. *We can not avoid having to do with government!* . . . We think, as deaf-mutes, that we can superstruct a more perfect model for our own benefit, than the one under which we now exist, which discards us from all honorable and lucrative posts; while to hearing men, often our inferiors in every thing but hearing, it gives large rewards for services and distinction. . . .

What do Messrs. Chamberlain and Booth want? A small township of deaf-mutes, like the Shakers at Lebanon, New York, in which even our social organization and habits must conform to rules, in which, from the nature of things, we can have no agency? Our few votes, in our scattered aggregate, have not a jot of influence in the deliberations of capitals. Every law and legal rule is made independent of the wishes of mutes. Often our peculiar necessities and such arrangements as may be indispensable to our welfare, are not known or provided for. In our trade and inter-course, in our multifarious concerns, some new regulation is nec-essary; and if the thing could be re-arranged, many of us could sit on juries, and consequently be impartial, and hold offices of emolument.

I had forgotten to notice the observations of Mr. Booth re-garding the incongruities of a territorial state of government with our object as mutes. This, however, may be obviated by an early admission on the Kansas policy, when the population is less than the required number. For my own part I can not intend it to be a slave territory, or even to admit free Negroes.[34] Our object is peace and happiness; and we wish to have, if possible, as seques-trated people, nothing to do with what is an ever threatening and pregnant bane to mar the harmony of our country, and to periodi-cally menace the Union—that casket of liberty—the very *sine qua non* of it. Like the independency of Frankfort, or Hamburg, or the small Italian territory of San Marino, always exempt from wars and desolation, and as the inhabitants of ancient Delos, in Greece, we would be a province, in which, on approaching our soil, mar-tial arms are hushed into silent repose. So far from imitating the fashions, dress, luxuries and customs of other men, we must orga-nize a state of society in which brotherly and sisterly love shall continue without invidious distinction. Thus we shall endeavor to form a model in ourselves of what a Christian community *can* be, and Providence our guard and guide, shall enter the stream of life for Eternity.

Last Remarks by Booth

The July Annals *also contained Booth's closing words.*

The April No. of the *Annals* gives us the views of some of the representative members of the deaf-mute community on Mr.

---

34. We can infer that Flournoy would exclude deaf African Ameri-cans from the commonwealth.

Flournoy's project. Messrs. Burnet and Carlin speak of it with philosophical good humor, and manifest a disposition to be quizzical at Mr. Flournoy's expense. Mr. Confer, like other wealthy men, has more money than he knows how to enjoy, and wishes somebody to help him enjoy it. He, like Mr. Flournoy, has formed too low an estimate of the standing of persons who are deprived of one of the faculties common to mankind at large. It is evident that he is a ready reader; and if he is not able to enjoy life surrounded by books and newspapers, the best thing he can do is to seek associates such as he desires. Mr. Flournoy gives us another letter explanatory of his scheme, and in this I will touch on only one or two points.

In politics, in religion, in medicine, and in all other callings, we have a class of men who are fond of tracing out castles in the air, and who pass their lives in calling on the nation or the surrounding community to build the airy structures, with airy or un-airy materials. They possess an unbounded confidence in possibilities, and usually an equally unbounded enthusiasm, and are often useful men in their way. They, on many occasions, show how much better the world can be made, by the pictures which they draw of a better and more elevated life than is the present; and thus man's hopes, aspirations and energies are increased in activity, and so strengthened that his progress onward and upward is far greater than it otherwise would have been. Mr. Flournoy belongs to this class of dreamers; and, like many of them, he, while tracing out his castle in the air, gives but superficial attention to the nature of the materials with which it is to be built, or the foundation on which it is to be laid.

For instance, after casting about for some time for unoccupied territory wherein to place his commonwealth, he says, "The location of our *Empire* may be in Oregon." Is not this capping the climax of absurdity, and the capstone of sufficient weight to crush the whole imaginary structure of a deaf-mute commonwealth to atoms? The proposal to locate in so distant a place as Oregon, with so little regard to the difficulties and cost of reaching that region, gives his whole project the air of a joke contrived for his own amusement. The government will do nothing toward building a Pacific railroad for years to come; and nothing short of a blind religious faith worked into fanaticism, would suffice to induce any number of deaf-mutes to encounter the expense of a sea-voyage, or the dangers and watchings of a land journey through a thousand miles of sandy desert, in order to obtain that which they have already—the right to self-government.

One other point in Mr. Flournoy's "Further Explanations," and I have done with it. He says . . . "We, deaf-mutes, have a sort of abiding melancholy at our unfortunate deprivation." It may be, and doubtless is so with him. There is an abiding melancholy, or something like it to be found in certain persons among all classes of men and women, both mute and hearing. It is not so much owing to any particular misfortune or deprivation, as such persons generally imagine, as to the want of activity in the moral and intellectual life of those persons. A monk in a cell, wrapped up in his egotism, with his *pater-nosters* and his beads, is a type of that class. Their views do not extend beyond their own petty selves, which they surround with imaginary woes. Mr. Flournoy's assertion no more applies to deaf-mutes as a class than to hearing persons as such; and as applied to myself, I scout it altogether.

Having said so much in the negative on Mr. Flournoy's project, I ought to say something in the affirmative, and the more so as I am for progress in all things that tend to good, and this brings me to Mr. Chamberlain's letter in the *Annals*. Mr. C. proposes to buy up a township of land six miles square, or 23,040 acres, and he says, "the government of the township is as much as they [the deaf-mutes] would care to be troubled with." This plan is far more reasonable than Mr. Flournoy's, and if Mr. Chamberlain can induce a sufficient number to enter into his project, it is far more practical. I imagine, however, that after a year's experience, the deaf-mutes would care very little about the government part of the matter. I will give him an idea how it is managed. Here in Iowa, each township elects annually three trustees—generally staid, elderly or middle aged men—a township clerk, two justices of the peace, and two constables; also a president and directors of the township schools. Mr. C. will see that these offices are not such as make a man famous, or that in themselves they are particularly desirable.[35] Hence, the government motive for an emigration is, after a short experience, blown to the winds for lack of weight.

I would not take up so much time on this subject were it not to come before the convention next autumn. Instead of voting, in convention, to migrate to the West, to Oregon, to the South Sea Islands, or to the moon, I would suggest that they discuss the subject—for thereby information may be diffused, reflection excited, and good done—and then lay it on the table, or lay it over till the next convention. In the two intervening years, a correspondence may be kept up between those now in the West, or who may come into the West, and those who remain in the East. The best plan, after all, is for deaf-mutes to follow the general current, and settle, a few in each neighborhood, and work at whatever mechanical occupation they may have learned while in school. Those who are not chambered with families might do well to push into western and north-western Iowa, or other thinly settled districts, where they can purchase land at a dollar, or two or three dollars, per acre. They will grow with the country, and can give information and advice to their friends in the East, who, if so disposed can follow them. After living nearly twenty years in the West, I am satisfied this plan is far better than any other yet proposed in the *Annals*.

Views of a Deaf Teacher

In addition, the July Annals *featured the following letter from P. A. Emery, a deaf instructor at the Indiana Institution.*

---

35. Booth writes from experience, since he served in various minor government positions in Iowa.

Mr. W. Martin Chamberlain,

Dear Sir: I have been much interested in the scheme called the "Deaf-Mute Commonwealth," which has been set afloat upon the public wave through the *American Annals*. As to who is the originator of the plan I care nothing about, nor their motive. If the plan proves of service to the mute community, and not to their own aggrandizement, then I say with Mr. J. J. Flournoy, "Honor to whom honor is due." I do not wish to be understood as discussing the subject, but merely to state my own views.

I am in favor of something, no matter what, so it renders more of the mutes happier than I have found many of them to be in their lost and lonely condition. Let the purpose be to find them plenty to do, where they can enjoy themselves best, and prevent them from falling into that melancholy state peculiar to deaf-mutes, and give them a place where they can have the gospel preached in their silent yet expressive language. If there are not enough of them at the first settling to support a minister, and to build a church, they can have a Bible Class until their numbers and means become greater.

I have thought some about the matter, but have not come to any settled conclusion, as I always make it my motto to "Look before I jump." As to Mr. Flournoy's plan, I, as one, have my objections; nor do I agree with Mr. Booth in considering it an impossibility. I believe in a practical life and not one of dreams. Your plan as set forth in the April number of the *Annals* is good, and in my humble opinion is the best. I think the best course to pursue, is, for those in favor of Mr. Flournoy's, and those of yours, to form themselves into separate bands, and set their respective policies in operation; and which ever succeeds the best, we will set down as No. 1. . . .

Discussion at the Convention of the New England Gallaudet Association

Members of the New England Gallaudet Association of Deaf-Mutes discussed the idea of a deaf commonwealth at their third convention, which took place in September 1858 in Worcester, Massachusetts. The Annals *published the proceedings of the meeting the following month. Excerpted here are the portions dealing with Flournoy's proposal.*

Prof. L. Clerc then mounted the platform, and his appearance was greeted with hearty cheers.

He expressed his pleasure at seeing so many present; he had derived much pleasure from such gatherings in former years, and hoped for many more such social reunions; he held that we (the mutes) were not, as a general thing, inferior to our hearing brethren, and he did not believe that we were so considered by them. Hard times and distance probably had kept many of us at home who would otherwise have been present. He referred to the discussion which had been carried on, in the *American Annals*, for some months past, in relation to a commonwealth of deaf-mutes, the main features of which, according to Mr. Flournoy, of Georgia, the propagator of the scheme, were, the obtaining of a grant of land from Congress, and the *exclusive* right of *deaf-mutes* to the *occupation* and *government* thereof. He remarked that Mr. Flournoy had said in one of his letters, published in the *Annals*, that the credit of originating the Enterprise belonged to him (Mr. Clerc), and he would endeavor to explain his position in regard to the matter. It was well known that, in the early days of the American Asylum, Congress donated a tract of land in Alabama, for the benefit of the funds of that Institution. He had once said something about the plan of selling such part of the land as was necessary for the Asylum, and then having the rest as *headquarters* for the deaf and dumb, to which they could emigrate after being educated. Mr. Flournoy getting hold of the idea, published it, with such additional embellishments as he deemed expedient.

Mr. Clerc said that a mature deliberation on the whole matter had made it appear an impracticable plan; it could not be kept up without *exclusiveness*, and that was a very undesirable condition, for as most of his auditors would agree, it was very convenient to have some hearing persons within call in many cases, as for instance, sickness and fire. Besides all this, as the Commonwealth, if established at all, must be placed in some out of the way position, there was great probability that the inhabitants would have aggressions and encroachments to contend with, against which the laws of the land would be of little avail. He gave it as his opinion that the project was, in its main features, the offspring of a disordered imagination; to take it as a whole, if Mr. Flournoy had counted on the influence of Mr. Clerc in favor of his plan, he had reckoned without his host. The general opinion of the mutes seemed to be that they had better stay at home. Some curiosity had been expressed as to the absence of Mr. Flournoy's name on the list of pupils of the American Asylum, it being well known that he was educated there, Mr. Flournoy was not, properly speaking, a pupil. Mr. Clerc taught him French and Mr. Turner, English.

[*Editor's note:* Several hearing people also addressed the assembly about the commonwealth plan. The Rev. W. W. Turner, the principal of the American Asylum, denounced Flournoy's suggestion that deaf people were despised and excluded, pointing to parents' affection and concern, the legislatures that had allocated thousands of dollars to deaf education, the teachers who worked for the benefit of deaf people, and so forth. Turner concluded that "Mr. F's objections and assertions rested on no foundation whatever." The Reverend Thomas Gallaudet of New York, the eldest son of Thomas Hopkins Gallaudet, told the convention that "he regarded the plan of Mr. Flournoy as a result of a morbid state of feeling, a dislike to the society of hearing men."]

Mr. Clerc asked the Convention whether the members were despised or maltreated at home. Receiving a general *no!* for answer, he asked, then why emigrate? He also asked them whether they would prefer to form a community of deaf and dumb, and the general answer was, that they had rather live mixed with those who hear and speak.

11

INAUGURATION OF THE NATIONAL DEAF-MUTE COLLEGE

(1864)

In 1864, during the Civil War, Laurent Clerc traveled to Washington, D.C., to take part in the official opening of the National Deaf-Mute College. For the seventy-eight-year-old Clerc, it must have been a gratifying event to witness. When he had arrived in the United States almost a half-century before, the nation had no deaf education at all. Now, in 1864, there were not only twenty-six residential schools for the deaf, but also a new college, the first of its kind in the world. The college confirmed everything Clerc had worked for during his long career. Authorized by Congress and President Abraham Lincoln, it demonstrated that many Americans had come to share his belief in the intellectual potential of deaf people.

Clerc himself did not lead the drive for a college; others took up that task. The first public call for more advanced deaf education came in 1851, when Jacob Van Nostrand, a hearing teacher at the New York school, published an article in the *Annals*. He wrote that "something must be done" to help the deaf student "take his place among the scholars and sages of the world."[1] At the time, deaf schools provided only an elementary education and vocational training in such fields as carpentry, shoemaking, printing, and sewing. Although he supported the schools, Van Nostrand said that deaf students did not have enough opportunities. He argued that schools should offer one or two years of additional course work to students who showed promise.

However, Van Nostrand did not advocate a college. Responding to Van Nostrand in the next issue of the *Annals,* John Carlin agreed that deaf education was too limited but said Van Nostrand did not go far enough. A few years later, in 1854, Carlin published an essay giving a full argument for a college (see p. 100).

If Carlin provided the vision of higher education for deaf people, Edward Miner Gallaudet was chiefly responsible for making it a reality. Born in 1837, Gallaudet was the youngest child of Thomas Hopkins Gallaudet and Sophia Fowler. He grew up signing, since his mother was deaf and the family involved in the deaf community. His father died when he was just fourteen. In 1855, shortly before he graduated from college, Gallaudet accepted a teaching position at the American Asylum in Hartford, which his father had cofounded with Clerc thirty-eight years before. Gallaudet became intrigued with the idea of a college, discussing the concept with a fellow teacher; however, they did not see a way to establish such an institution unless a millionaire could be found to endow it. Ambitious and restless, Gallaudet considered becoming a missionary to deaf people in China, but gave up that idea due to lack of funds. In 1857 he accepted a well-paid position at a Chicago bank. He was preparing to leave when he received an unexpected letter from Amos Kendall, a prominent civic leader in Washington, D.C.

---

1. Jacob Van Nostrand, "Necessity of a Higher Standard of Education for the Deaf and Dumb," *American Annals of the Deaf and Dumb* 3 (July 1851): 196–97.

Kendall had had a distinguished career. A former journalist and postmaster general of the United States, he had made a fortune through investments in the telegraph. Now an elderly man, he had become involved with deaf education in 1856, when a person named P. F. Skinner appeared with five deaf children and asked for Kendall's assistance in opening a school. Kendall gave Skinner a house and two acres of land for the school and helped him to set up a board of directors. He also persuaded Congress to incorporate the new Columbia Institution for the Deaf and Dumb and the Blind and to provide $150 per year for each student. Yet despite such generous backing, Skinner badly neglected the children. When Kendall discovered the situation, he sued for custody of the five deaf orphans and began to search for a new superintendent. Harvey P. Peet, the head of the New York school, suggested Edward Miner Gallaudet for the post. Since Gallaudet was just twenty years old, Peet recommended that Gallaudet's mother accompany him and act as matron of the school. Kendall agreed and wrote to Gallaudet to offer him the position.

Gallaudet saw the perfect opportunity to establish a college. He shared his dream with Kendall, who promised to help him to achieve it. In June of 1857 Gallaudet moved to Washington, D.C., with his mother, Sophia Fowler Gallaudet. At first, Gallaudet focused on the residential school, adding more students and securing additional funding. Then, in 1862, his annual report to Congress contained a recommendation that a college be established. The proposal came during the Civil War; the capital was filled with wounded soldiers and the school itself surrounded by a military encampment. Still, Congress passed the legislation in 1864 and President Lincoln signed it into law.

On June 28, 1864, people assembled for the inauguration of the new institution. Representatives of several other colleges, including the president of the University of Pennsylvania, were present. Both Clerc and Carlin signed speeches, which are included here. Clerc talked of the joy the college would bring to deaf people, while Carlin noted that the institution marked a "bright epoch in deaf-mute history," a time of increased opportunity and possibility. The college was such a dramatic step forward that even Clerc and Carlin expressed some uncertainty about what deaf people would accomplish. Clerc, in his old age, struck a cautionary note: "On account of their misfortune," he signed, "they cannot become masters of music, and perhaps can never be entitled to receive the degree of Doctor in Divinity, in Physic, or in Law." The younger Carlin was more optimistic: "Is it likely that college for deaf-mutes will ever produce mute statesmen, lawyers, and ministers of religion, orators, poets, and authors?" he asked. "The answer is: They will, in numbers . . . few and far between."

Carlin received the first degree awarded by the college, an honorary Master of Arts. The school was renamed Gallaudet College in 1894 in honor of Thomas Hopkins Gallaudet. In 1986 it became Gallaudet University.

Address by Laurent Clerc

My dear friends: The President elect of your Institution, Edward M. Gallaudet, has invited me to come and attend the inauguration of a "National College for the Deaf and Dumb" in Washington, the Capital of the United States, to take place on Tuesday, June 28, 1864.

I have accepted the invitation with much pleasure, and here I stand before you to say that I feel a just pride in seeing that the American Asylum at Hartford, Conn., has been the means of doing so much good and has produced so many evidences of intelligence and learning. Our school at Hartford was the first of its kind ever established in America, not only through the exertions of the late Rev. Dr. Thomas H. Gallaudet, and your humble speaker, but also by the generous subscriptions and contributions of both ladies and gentlemen in Hartford and other towns of New England. It has broken that barrier which had separated for several

Laurent Clerc (ca.
1850) in a portrait
by John Carlin

centuries the deaf and dumb from those who hear and speak. It
has repaired the wrongs of nature in enabling them to replace
hearing by writing, and speech by signs. It has also enabled many
among you to become the teachers of your unfortunate fellow-
beings. It has qualified your kind Principal and many gentlemen
and ladies who hear and speak, to teach deaf and dumb persons in
this and other schools which have since sprung up in several other
portions of the United States.

Now, my dear friends, let me ask what is the object of the
foundation of a college? It is for the purpose of receiving such
graduates of the other institutions as wish to acquire more knowledge in Natural Science, Astronomy, Mathematics, Geography,
History, Mental and Moral Philosophy, and Belles-Lettres.

Science is a most useful thing for us all. It is one of the first ornaments of man. There is no dress which embellishes the body more than science does the mind. Every decent man and every real gentleman in particular ought to apply himself above all things to the study of his native language, so as to express his ideas with ease and gracefulness.[2] Let a man be never so learned, he will not give a high idea of himself or of his science if he speaks or writes in a loose vulgar language. The Romans, once the masters of the world, called the other nations, who did not know the language of Rome, barbarians; so, now that there are so many schools for the deaf and dumb in the United States, I will call *barbarians* those grown up deaf-mutes who do not know how to read, write, and cipher.

Finally, a well educated man, a gentleman by example, ought to add to the knowledge of one or two languages, that of Ancient and Modern History and Geography. The knowledge of History is extremely useful. It lays before our eyes the great picture of the generations that have preceded us, and in relating the events which passed in their time, we are taught to follow what is good and to avoid what is bad in our own time. It lays before us the precepts of the wise men of all ages, and acquaints us with their maxims. The crimes of the wicked are of no less use to us. Seldom does Divine Justice let them remain unpunished. The fatal consequences that always attend them preserve us from the seduction of bad example, and we endeavor to become good as much through interest as inclination, because there is everything to lose in being wicked and everything to gain in being good.

The degree of Master of Arts can be conferred on the deaf and dumb when they merit it; but, on account of their misfortune, they cannot become masters of music, and perhaps can never be entitled to receive the degree of Doctor in Divinity, in Physic [i.e., medicine], or in Law.

---

2. Clerc's calling English a "native language" here is somewhat ironic, since he and other writers had argued that English is a foreign language to those born deaf.

In closing, let me express to you my dear young friend, Mr. E. M. Gallaudet, President elect of this Institution, the earnest hope that in the great work which is before you, you will be blessed and prospered, and receive for your efforts, in behalf of the deaf and dumb, such proofs of its benefits as will reward you for the glorious undertaking.

John Carlin's Oration

Mr. President, ladies and gentlemen: On this day, the 28th of June, 1864, a college for deaf-mutes is brought into existence. It is a bright epoch in deaf-mute history. The birth of this infant college, the first of its kind in the world, will bring joy to the mute community. True, our new Alma Mater has drawn its first breath in the midst of strife here and abroad; but as the storm now raging over our heads is purifying our political atmosphere, the air which it has inhaled is sweet and invigorating—how favorably this circumstance augurs its future success!

I thank God for this privilege of witnessing the consummation of my wishes—the establishment of a college for deaf-mutes—a subject which has for past years occupied my mind. Not that the object of my wishes was to enter its precincts with the purpose of poring once again over classic lore, but it was to see it receive and instruct those who, by their youth and newness of mind, are justly entitled to the privilege.

To begin its history, I find it a very pleasant task to introduce here its founders. Yale College had its Elihu Yale, through whose munificence it has lived long and prosperously, enjoying a position high in our esteem; Harvard and Brown Universities had their John Harvard and Nicholas Brown, whose memories are embalmed with perpetual fragrance in the hearts of their students. The founders, if I may so express myself, of this college are—allow me, I pray you, to carry your memory to the Federal halls of legislation. You remember it was several weeks ago; a month wherein you saw thousands and thousands of patriots passing through your streets on their way to the horrid Moloch of War; our good President, ably assisted by his Secretaries of War and Navy, labored most incessantly to ensure Grant's success . . . and the members of both the Houses were busily occupied in what their country expected to see, the salvation of Columbia.[3] Was it to continue the sanguinary strife? Yes; to save our Union. Sacrifice thousands of lives and millions of dollars in order to save the Union? Yes; to preserve our liberty and religion. In the midst of their arduous labors of patriotism they paused awhile to listen to a few humble petitioners; they considered the memorial; they probably remembered the unenviable condition of their unfortunate brothers, sisters, daughters, sons, and friends, and, notwithstanding the rapidly increasing debt, they did not hesitate even for a moment to grant the boon embodied in the memorial.

Such are the founders, so far as dollars and cents are regarded; for, without their co-operation in this laudable act of philanthropy; the labors, however great, of their private fellow-founders would have come to naught. In behalf of the mutes I beg leave to tender to them my most hearty thanks. . . .

Is it likely that colleges for deaf-mutes will ever produce mute statesmen, lawyers, and ministers of religion, orators, poets, and authors? The answer is: They will, in numbers, like angels' visits, few and far between. No doubt this assertion strikes you as unsound in logic as it is contrary to the laws of physiology, since, in your opinion, their want of hearing incapacitates them for exercising the functions of speech in the forum, bar, and pulpit, and therefore the assumption that mutes, no matter if they are learned,

---

3. At the time, Ulysses S. Grant (1822–1885), the commanding general of the Union Army, was attempting to break through the Confederate forces and go to Richmond. However, although he had numerical superiority over southern troops, in a series of bloody battles he had failed to make much headway.

will ever appear as legislators, lawyers, and preachers, is untenable. Be this as it may, I shall have only to remark that they, such as may appear with extraordinary talents, will be able to speak to audiences exactly in the manner my address is now read to you. At all events, as to the appearance of mute Clays and Websters, remembering the fact that every graduate of Dartmouth College, which produced a Daniel Webster, is not a Webster in colossal intellect, you will have too much sense to hurry yourselves to Mount Vesuvius this summer to witness its next eruption which may perchance take place on your arrival there. It may occur in ten years or later instead of this year.

Well, my friends, with regard to mute literati, Dr. Kitto, the great Bible commentator, himself a mute, rather semi-mute, for he lost his hearing in childhood; James Nack, of New York, and Professor Pelissier, of Paris, both semi-mutes of high repute, and Professor Berthier of Paris, a born mute author, fully demonstrate the possibility of mute poets and authors, with minds maturely cultured at college.[4]

The avenues of science, too, are now about to be opened to the mute in this college, and as these are not interfered with by the necessity of speech, its scholars will be enabled to expand their minds as far as their mental capacities can allow. Thus we may safely expect to see among the graduates a distinguished astronomer, scanning the starry field, tracing the singular yet beautiful courses of Ursa Major and Ursa Minor—measuring mathematically the exact, if possible, distance of the Nebulae—ever and anon exploring the solar spots, and making deductions from his researches and demonstrations as to whether the moon is really a huge, rugged mass of white metal, utterly devoid of water, vegetation, and breathing creation; a chemist, in his smoky laboratory, analyzing unknown substances, ascertaining the exact qualities of

---

4. For information on Kitto, Pelissier, and Berthier, see p. 104, n. 11.

ingredients embodied in each, and with the industry and learning of a Leibig or a Faraday, setting forth works on his discoveries; a geologist roaming, hammer in hand, the rocky fields, diving into the fossiliferous strata for a stray Ichthyosaurus or a Megatherium, or perhaps, a fossil man, in order to sound the correctness of the Lamarckian (development) Hypothesis.[5]

Though, by no means impossibilities, these and mute poets are rarities. So you will please remember Mount Vesuvius. But mute authors of respectable ability and clerks of acknowledged efficiency will be found here in a number quite as satisfactory as may be wished.

These observations being duly and candidly considered as correct, you cannot but feel the indispensability of this pioneer college to the advancement of intelligent mutes to the point from whence they will be able to employ their minds in still higher pursuits of intellect, or in attending their professions with credit. Such are its advantages which cannot be afforded by our existing institutions, excellent establishments as they are for the initiated. Nowhere but in this college the field of knowledge, replete with aesthetic flowers of literature, can be roamed over with a full appreciation of the pleasure so freely given by its benefactors.

However flattering the prospect of its success, it must be borne in mind that, by reason of the peculiar character of the deaf-mute's mind, of which I shall by and by treat, and of the popular *modus operandi* of instruction, now pursued at our institutions, which, it must candidly be admitted, is as yet far from being the *ne plus ultra* of perfection, he—now a college-boy—cannot be expected to

---

5. Carlin refers here to Justus von Liebig (1803–1873), German chemist; Michael Faraday (1791–1867), English chemist and physicist; an Ichthyosaur, an extinct marine reptile; and a Megatherium, an extinct gigantic sloth. The Lamarckian Hypothesis held that environmental changes caused structural changes in animals and plants, which were then passed on to offspring.

compete with the hearing college-boy in the extent of literary acquirements and in the accuracy and fluency of language. . . .

The mute's sensorium, in consequence of his deafness, is all blank—speaking of oral impressions. True, it receives impressions of all objects which he has seen, felt, smelt, or tasted. It continues so until he goes to the deaf-mute school-room at the age of twelve years; perhaps older than that. What a sad spectacle this poor child presents! Looking into the depths of his mind, whether he has any distinct idea of Deity, you are shocked to find him an absolute heathen. A heathen in your very midst! At home his brightness of expression that seems to imply high yet dormant intellect, all affection which his kin can possibly lavish on him, and the Christian influence of religious persons with whom he uses to come in contact, cannot deliver him from the thraldom of abject heathenism. Nothing useful or ornamental can ever emerge from his dark mind. Where no schools exist for the benefit of mutes, the unfortunates move in a most pitiful condition, and in certain places are believed to be possessed with devils; in India and elsewhere mute infants are murdered lest they should grow up dead weights on their kin; and even in civilized nations where deaf-mute schools flourish, uneducated mutes are often regarded hardly above beasts of burden, and therefore are employed in the drudgeries of life. In short, an uneducated mute—an innocent outcast, with a mind semblant to a gold nugget still embedded in the earth, yet to be brought up and refined in the crucible—drags a miserable existence.

He enters school—remember, as a general rule, young mutes are admitted to schools at not less than twelve years of age. It may be worthwhile to say that the New York Institution, much to her credit, took last fall the courage to receive them four years younger than that. So much the better. It is much to be hoped that this example will be extensively imitated. Our youth's mind begins to develop its faculties—the seeds of knowledge one after another take root—they now germinate in a manner warranting the success of a mode of instruction altogether different from that of the hearing. See here what a triumph of art! Whoever be its inventor, let him be blessed now and forever! Thomas H. Gallaudet and Laurent Clerc are none the less entitled to our gratitude for their introduction of the art into our midst. Shall I expatiate here on their noble disinterestedness—their patient labors in the school-room—their devotedness to their welfare and the affection and veneration of the mutes for them? This is hardly necessary, for you all know them. Dr. Gallaudet is now asleep in Christ. Ere he departed this life, he, like Elijah of old, flung his ample mantle upon his two sons, Thomas and Edward.[6] This mantle is the love for deaf-mutes. When it alighted on those sons, it divided itself into two, and pleasing to say, each of the two portions is equal to the original mantle in the extent and depth of the sentiment. And Mr. Clerc, the venerable father of American instruction is still in the land of the living. He is shortly to be an octogenarian. O, may he enjoy many more golden days of peace and happiness in the midst of his loving friends.

To return to the youth. In a month or two he ceases to be a heathen, though by no means familiar with the Scriptures, and through his term—seven years—he acquires sufficient for his general business of life. Owing to the brevity of his term and the fact that knowledge does not reach him through one main avenue, his knowledge is exceedingly crude, his grammar wanting in accuracy, and his language not quite as fluent as that of a hearing youth of twelve. Should he, if he be a bright scholar, enter the high class

---

6. In 2 Kings, chapter 2, the prophet Elijah ascends to heaven in a fiery chariot, leaving only his mantel behind for his disciple, Elisha, who then uses the garment to perform a miracle. The Rev. Thomas Gallaudet (1822–1902), Thomas Hopkins Gallaudet's eldest son, served as rector of St. Ann's Episcopal Church, which he and Carlin helped to found for deaf people in New York. He also advocated sign language services for deaf people in churches across the nation.

(there are but two of this kind in our country, one at the New York Institution and the other in the American Asylum at Hartford), he would certainly, with ambition stimulating his mind to make efforts, acquire as much literary treasure as his short term could afford. Still his language is found to have come short of perfection, and his intellectual appetite is, therefore, not satisfied. Like Oliver Twist, he is still asking for more.[7] In other words, he wants to go to this College. He knocks at her gates for admittance.

Alma Mater—young and comely, and breathing with the most healthy vigor of life under the aegis of Columbia—behold this youth! See how he thirsts after knowledge! Open your gates wide, that he may joyously cross your threshold! Oh, stimulate his heart to the pursuit of the coveted prize—ripe scholarship! Unfold to his eager mind the hidden beauties of classic literature! Like Aristotle, instructing his scholars while rambling under the azure arch, you will lead him through the walks of sacred lore under the soul-delighting canopy of Heaven, formed of angels and cherubims, with their wings spread out, watching the world and counting every pilgrim that seeks to be admitted to the Celestial Abode. And in time, send him forth into society, a *man,* to whom the world will give the respect due to him, a *gentleman,* whom all will delight in making acquaintance with, and a *student,* still enlarging his store of knowledge at home, always remembering you and your Congressional patrons, to use Massieu's words, with the memory of the heart—Gratitude![8]

---

7. In chapter two of Charles Dickens' novel, *Oliver Twist* (1838), the children in the Poor House are given very little gruel to eat. Oliver famously says, "Please, sir, I want some more," and is immediately placed in confinement for daring to doubt the adequacy of the dietary provisions.

8. At one of Sicard's public exhibitions, Jean Massieu (see p. 133, n. 5) was asked to define gratitude. He wrote, "Gratitude is the memory of the heart."

SOURCES

CHAPTER 1. LAURENT CLERC

The Diary of Laurent Clerc's Voyage from France to America in 1816 (Hartford, Conn.: American School for the Deaf, 1952), 5–12, 18, 22. Laurent Clerc Papers no. 68, Manuscripts and Archives, Yale University Library.

"Laurent Clerc," in *Tribute to Gallaudet: A Discourse in Commemoration of the Life, Character, and Services, of the Rev. Thomas H. Gallaudet, with an Appendix,* 2nd ed. (New York: F. C. Brownell, 1859), 107–8.

Laurent Clerc Papers no. 69, transcription by Clerc from the *Albany Daily Advertiser,* Nov. 12, 1816, and from the *Philadelphia Gazette and Daily Advertiser,* Dec. 11, 1816. Manuscripts and Archives, Yale University Library.

An Address Written by Mr. Clerc: And Read by His Request at a Public Examination of the Pupils in the Connecticut Asylum, before the Governour and Both Houses of the Legislature, 28th May, 1818 (Hartford, Conn.: Hudson and Co., printers, 1818).

Letter to Frederick A. P. Barnard, 1835, Laurent Clerc Papers no. 38, Manuscripts and Archives, Yale University Library.

"Laurent Clerc," in *Tribute to Gallaudet: A Discourse in Commemoration of the Life, Character, and Services, of the Rev. Thomas H. Gallaudet, with an Appendix,* 2nd ed. (New York: F. C. Brownell, 1859), 102–12.

CHAPTER 2. JAMES NACK

"The Minstrel Boy," in *The Legend of the Rocks, and Other Poems* (New York: E. Conrad, 1827), 58–61.

CHAPTER 3. JOHN BURNET

"What the Deaf and Dumb are before Instruction," in *Tales of the Deaf and Dumb, with Miscellaneous Poems* (Newark, N.J.: Benjamin Olds, 1935), 47–50.

"On the Early Domestic Education of Children Born Deaf, or Who Have Lost Their Hearing by Sickness or Accident," in *Tales of the Deaf and Dumb,* 7–28, 35–39, 42–44, 46.

"The Orphan Mute," in *Tales of the Deaf and Dumb,* 152–81.

"Emma," in *Tales of the Deaf and Dumb,* 196–97.

CHAPTER 4. JOHN CARLIN

"The Mute's Lament," *American Annals of the Deaf and Dumb* 1 (1847): 15–16.

"Advantages and Disadvantages of the Use of Signs," *American Annals of the Deaf and Dumb* 4 (1852): 49–57.

"The National College for Mutes," *American Annals of the Deaf and Dumb* 6 (1854): 175–83.

CHAPTER 5. EDMUND BOOTH

Letter to Mary Booth, Jan. 21, 1852, reprinted in *Edmund Booth, Forty-Niner: The Life Story of a Deaf Pioneer* (Stockton, Calif.: San Joaquin Pioneer and Historical Society, 1953), 50–52.

"On Emigration to the West by Deaf Mutes," *American Annals of the Deaf and Dumb* 10 (1858): 46–51.

CHAPTER 6. ADELE M. JEWEL

A Brief Narrative of the Life of Mrs. Adele M. Jewel (Being Deaf and Dumb) (Jackson, Mich.: Daily Citizen Steam Printing House, c. 1860).

CHAPTER 7. LAURA REDDEN SEARING

"A Few Words about the Deaf and Dumb," *American Annals of the Deaf and Dumb* 10 (1858): 177–81.

"Belle Missouri," reprinted in Jack Gannon, *Deaf Heritage: A Narrative History of Deaf America* (Silver Spring, Md.: National Association of the Deaf, 1981), 7.

CHAPTER 8. 1850 GRAND REUNION

"Testimonial of the Deaf Mutes of New England to Messrs. Gallaudet and Clerc," in *Tribute to Gallaudet: A Discourse in Commemoration of the Life, Character, and Services, of the Rev. Thomas H. Gallaudet, with an Appendix,* 2nd ed. (New York: F. C. Brownell, 1859), 189–203.

CHAPTER 9. DEDICATION OF THE GALLAUDET MONUMENT

"Ceremonies at the Completion of the Gallaudet Monument," *American Annals for the Deaf and Dumb* 7 (1854): 23–26, 31–44.

CHAPTER 10. DEBATE OVER A DEAF COMMONWEALTH

John J. Flournoy, Edmund Booth, et al., "Scheme for a Commonwealth of the Deaf and Dumb," *American Annals of the Deaf and Dumb* 8 (1856): 120–125; 10 (1858): 40–45, 72–90, 140–56, 212–15.

Laurent Clerc, cited in "Proceedings of the Third Convention of the New England Gallaudet Association of Deaf-Mutes," *American Annals of the Deaf and Dumb* 10 (October 1858): 212–15.

CHAPTER 11. INAUGURATION OF THE NATIONAL DEAF-MUTE COLLEGE

Laurent Clerc, "Address by Laurent Clerc, A.M.," in *Inauguration of the College for the Deaf and Dumb, at Washington, District of Columbia* (Washington, D.C.: Gideon and Pearson, 1864), 41–43.

John Carlin, "Oration: A College for the Deaf and Dumb," in *Inauguration,* 45–55.

INDEX

abolition, 109

"Advantages and Disadvantages of the Use of Signs" (Carlin), 94–100

African Americans, viii–ix
Booth and, viii, 183 n
Flournoy and, viii, 182–83, 183 n, 205, 205 n
Jewel and, viii, 118, 126, 126 n, 127 n
slavery and, 152 n, 157 n, 182–83, 183 n, 193 n, 205, 205 n

After a Long Cruise (Carlin), 92

Alexander I, czar of Russia, 27 n

American Annals of Education, viii, xx

American Annals of the Deaf and Dumb, 39, 90, 109, 129
calls for National Deaf-Mute College in, 100–106, 212–13
deaf commonwealth debate in, 161–211

American Asylum for the Deaf, xii, xvi–xix, xxx, 3, 64 n, 113, 211, 213, 224
Clerc and, 4, 215
1850 grand reunion and, 139–52
Gallaudet monument and, 153–60
land grant to, 4, 31, 150, 161, 165–66, 184 n, 185–86, 210

American Colonization Society, 201

American Notes (Dickens), 96 n

American Sign Language (ASL), xi, xvii–xviii, 142 n
Burnet on, 51, 51 n, 55 n, 69 n
deaf authors and, xxiii–xxiv, xxvii–xviii
fingerspelling and, 97, 97 n, 100, 100 n
intelligence and, xix–xx
Jewel and, 118, 119
privileging of English over, 98 n, 171 n
public perception of, xix, 132 n, 133 n
universality and, 12 n, 51 n
See also sign language

Americans with Disabilities Act of 1990, 168 n

Anamosa Eureka (newspaper), 107, 109

Anthon, Charles, 101, 101 n

Aristotle, xix, 224

articulation, 24, 24 n, 60–63, 132

Asten, Abraham, 32

Atlantic Monthly, 130, 183

Backus, Levi, xxi

Bakhtin, Mikhail, xxviii

Barnard, Frederick A. P., vii, xix–xx, xxv, 20 n
Clerc letter to, 20–22

Barnes, William, 104, 104n

Batterson, James, 154

Baynton, Douglas, xxxii, 12n

Belisarius, 166, 166n

Bell, Alexander Graham, 130

"Belle Missouri" (Searing), 129–30, 134–35

Berthier, Jean-Ferdinand, 104, 105n, 220

Bible, xxv, 17, 76
  Carlin on, 102, 158, 220, 223
  Spofford and, 143–44, 144n–45n
  See also Elijah; Jesus Christ; Lazarus; Sanballat

blindness, 40–41, 107, 124–25, 126–27, 166, 166n, 167. *See also* deaf-blind people

"Blue-Eyed Maid, The" (Nack), 32

Boardman, Eliza. *See* Clerc, Eliza Boardman

Bolling, William, xxix

Booth, Edmund, viii, xii, xxi
  abolitionism and, 109, 183n
  background of, 107–8
  California gold rush and, 108–9, 110–12
  Chamberlain on, 188–91
  Confer on, 191
  on deaf commonwealth proposal, 163, 170–72, 177–84, 205–8
  Emery on, 209
  Flournoy's reactions to, 172–76, 187, 194–205
  letter to Mary Ann Booth, 110–12
  "On Emigration to the West by Deaf Mutes," 112–17
  public affairs and, 109–10

Booth, Frank, 108

Booth, Mary Ann Walworth, ix, 108–12

Booth, Thomas, 111, 111n

Boston Deaf-Mute Christian Association, 197n

Brace, Julia, 63n–64n

Braidwood, John, xxix

Brewster, John, 143n

Bridgman, Laura Dewey, 64n, 95–96, 96n, 97

Brief Narrative of the Life of Mrs. Adele M. Jewel (Being Deaf and Dumb), A (Jewel), 118–28

Brown, Nicholas, 218

Brown, Thomas, 139, 140, 145, 150n, 153
  1850 grand reunion remarks of, 141–42

Bryant, William Cullen, 90, 104, 104n

Burnet, John R., vii–viii, xii, xxiii, xxv, xxvi, 104
  background of, 38–40
  on deaf commonwealth proposal, 193–94
  "Emma," xxvii, 40, 86–88
  Nack and, 34
  "On the Early Domestic Education of Children Born Deaf," 44–64
  "Orphan Mute, The," 40, 64–86
  "What the Deaf and Dumb Are before Instruction," 40–44

Burnet, Phebe Osborn, 39

Burnet, Rachel, 39

Cabet, Etienne, 172, 172n

Calhoun, John C., 157, 157n

Candy, Elizabeth. *See* Clerc, Elizabeth Candy

Carlin, Andrew, 89

Carlin, John, viii, xii, xxiv, xxv, 34
  address at dedication of Gallaudet monument, 154, 156–60
  address at inauguration of National Deaf-Mute College, 92, 214–15, 218–24
  "Advantages and Disadvantages of the Use of Signs," 94–100

art and, 90, 92, 154, 216
background of, 89–90
on deaf commonwealth proposal, 192–93
Flournoy's response to, 195, 202
lobbying for National Deaf-Mute College, xxvii, 92, 100–106, 213, 218
"Mute's Lament, The," xxv–xxvi, 90, 92–94
"National College for Mutes, The," 100–106
public affairs of, 91–92
Carlin, Mary Wayland, 90
Catlin, George, vii
Chamberlain, William, 188
Booth's response to, 207–8
on deaf commonwealth proposal, 163, 188–91
Emery's reaction to, 209
Flournoy's response to, 193n–94n, 194–95, 204
Chase, Mestapher, xx
Christian Examiner, 153
Christianity, 17–18, 45, 167, 222
deaf parishioners and, 91, 223n
Civil War, viii, 109, 164, 183n, 212, 214, 219n
Searing and, 129–30, 134–35
Clay, Henry, 4, 30, 30n, 157, 157n
Clerc, Elizabeth Candy, 23
Clerc, Eliza Boardman, xx, 4, 7, 20, 20n
Clerc, Francis Joseph, 4
Clerc, Joseph Francis, 23
Clerc, Laurent, viii, xii, xvii, xxiv, xxv, xxvi, xxviii, 1–5
address to Connecticut legislature, 13–20
address at dedication of Gallaudet monument, 154, 155–56
address at 1850 grand reunion, 148–52

address at inauguration of National Deaf-Mute College, 212, 214–18
autobiographical sketch, 22–31
background of, 1–2, 23–24
as Booth's teacher, 108
Carlin and, 90, 104, 192, 216
deaf American creation story and, xiii–xvi
deaf commonwealth proposal and, 161, 164, 184, 192, 210–11
on deaf people's capabilities, 15, 15n, 215, 217
first American speech of, 9–11
first impressions of America, 12, 28–29
on Gallaudet, 5–6, 7–8, 9, 24–26, 28, 31, 155–56
journal during voyage to America, 2, 5–9
land grant and, 4, 31, 150, 161, 184, 184n, 210
letter to Barnard, 20–22
on marriage, xxviii, 6–7, 7n
Monroe and, xx, 30–31, 30n
responses to audience questions, 11–13
revered as benefactor, xvi, 1, 4–5, 139–41, 147–48
Sicard and, xiv–xv, xxv, 2, 10, 24, 24n, 26–27
on sign language, 12, 12n, 13, 20–22, 24n, 25, 28, 216
visit to Congress, 4, 30
on writing, xxi, 21, 21n
Clough, 108
Cogswell, Alice, xiii–xvi, 143, 143n, 146, 146n
Clerc's first impression of, 29–30
Sigourney on, 29n
Cogswell, Mason, xiv, 9, 29, 29n, 143, 159

Columbia Institution for the Deaf and
    Dumb and the Blind, 214
Combe, William, 183n
communal bonding, xvii–xix, 141,
    155, 155n
Confer, P. H., 163, 191–92, 196n
    Booth's response to, 206
    Flournoy's response to, 196, 204
Congress, 114
    American Asylum, land grant to, 4,
        31, 150, 161, 184n, 185–86, 210
    Clerc's visit to, 4, 30
    deaf commonwealth debate and,
        162, 167, 178, 180, 189, 198,
        202, 210
    Searing and, 129
    support of National Deaf-Mute
        College, xi, 212, 214, 218–19
Connecticut Asylum, For the Educa-
    tion and Instruction of Deaf and
    Dumb Persons, xxix–xxx, 3. See
    also American Asylum for the
    Deaf
Connecticut Legislature, xv, 13
    Clerc's address to, 13–20
Cooper, James Fenimore, 40
Coulter, E. Merton, 163n
Critic (journal), 33
Crystal Palace, 95, 95n

dactylological images, 96, 99
Daguerre, Louis-Jacques-Mandé, 173,
    173n
Davis, Jefferson, 90
Day, George E., 94, 94n
DEAF (ASL sign), xxvii
"deaf" (English word), xxiv
    deaf writers changing meaning of,
        xxvi–xxviii
deaf-blind people, 63, 63n–64n, 96,
    96n
deaf commonwealth proposal, xviii,
    xxviii, 161–65

    Booth's disagreement with, 170–
        72, 177–84, 205–8
    Burnet on, 193–94
    Carlin on, 192–93
    Chamberlain on, 188–91
    Clerc's disapproval of, 164, 210–11
    Confer on, 191–92
    Emery on, 208–9
    Flournoy's argument for, 165–70,
        172–76, 184–87, 194–205
    Turner's reaction to, 163, 211
    Worcester convention and, 210–11
Deaf Mute, The, xxi
Deaf-Mutes' Friend, The, ix
deafness
    after learning speech, 63
    as advantage, 16, 17
    as divine mystery, 17, 106, 134
    partial, 62
    as punishment, 182, 182n
    social construction of, 41n
    writing and, xxii–xxix
deaf people
    African American, viii–ix, 126,
        126n–27n, 205, 205n
    children, 38, 44–64
    deaf American creation story and,
        xiii–xvi
    despising of, 191, 196, 196n, 211
    double-consciousness of, xxii,
        xxviii
    education and, xvi–xxii (see also ed-
        ucation)
    1830 census and, 44
    emigration and, 112–17, 162
    as family, xviii, 124
    happiness of, xix, xxvii, 181–82,
        182n
    intelligence of, xix–xxi, 12n
    isolation of, 17n, 171, 188, 191
    potential of, xii, xxvii, 92, 101n,
        164

sign language and, xix–xx, xxiii–
    xxiv (*see also* sign language)
women, ix–x, 175, 175n, 178
writing and, xii–xv, xxi–xxix, 12,
    12n, 56–60, 104, 104n, 131
Delaroche, Paul, 90
Dickens, Charles, 96n, 224n
Dictionary of American Sign Language
    (Stokoe), 132n
double-consciousness, xxii, xxviii
double-voiced words, xxviii
Du Bois, W. E. B., xxii
Dwight, Timothy, 29, 29n

ear, 47–48
education, xvi–xxi, 124, 130–33, 179
    Carlin on, 94–106, 218–24
    Clerc on, 10, 10n, 14–15, 23–24,
        215–18
    condescension and, 170–71, 171n
    deaf American creation story and,
        xiii–xvi
    early domestic, 44–64
    National Deaf-Mute College and,
        100–106, 212–24
    oral, xvi, 24, 61, 94n, 108, 147n
        (*see also* oralism)
    sign language and, xvi, 21, 49–50,
        94–100, 131–32, 147, 147n (*see
        also* sign language)
    Spofford on, 143–44, 143n
    writing and, xxii–xxix, 57 (*see also*
        literacy)
Elijah, 223, 223n
Emery, P. A., 208–9
emigration, 112–17, 162. *See also* deaf
    commonwealth debate
"Emma" (Burnet), xxvii, 40, 86–88
Empire State Association of Deaf-
    Mutes, xi
empowerment, xxi–xxii
English, xiii, xxi–xxiv, xxvii–xxviii,
    164

Clerc learning, xv, 5–9, 21, 28
educational method and, 14–15,
    56–60, 91, 95–100
foreignness of, to deaf people, 14,
    14n, 57, 57n, 104, 104n, 132,
    132n
hearing people's superiority in, 95,
    193
privileging over ASL, 98, 171n,
    193
Epée, Charles-Michel de l', 41n, 95,
    204
Everett, Edward, 92
eyes, 77, 88
    as deaf people's ears, 48–49, 56, 63

Fairbairn, Elsie, 124
Faraday, Michael, 221, 221n
"Few Words about the Deaf and
    Dumb, A" (Searing), 130–34
fingerspelling, 91, 97, 97n, 100,
    100n. *See also* manual alphabet
Florida School for the Deaf and Blind,
    xxix
Flournoy, John Jacobus, viii, xxviii
    argument for deaf commonwealth,
        162–64, 165–70, 172–76, 184–
        87, 194–205
    background of, 161–62
    Booth's reactions to, 170–72, 177–
        84, 205–8
    Burnet on, 193–94
    Carlin on, 192–93
    Chamberlain on, 188–91
    Clerc's response to, 164, 210–11
    Confer on, 191–92
    Emery on, 208–9
    slavery and, 182–83, 183n, 193n,
        205, 205n
    Turner's reaction to, 163, 211
    as visionary, 164

foreignness, of deaf experience to
    hearing people, 169–70, 170n
foreignness, of English to deaf people,
    xxii–xxiii
  Burnet on, 57, 57n
  Carlin on, 104, 104n
  Clerc on, 14, 14n
  Searing on, 132, 132n
Fowler, Sophia. See Gallaudet, Sophia
    Fowler
French Sign Language, xvii

Gallaudet, Edward Miner, 153n, 213,
    223
  National Deaf-Mute College and,
    213–14, 215, 218
Gallaudet, Sophia Fowler, 213–14
Gallaudet, Thomas Hopkins, xxvii–
    xxviii, 1, 2–3, 38, 133n, 213
  as Booth's teacher, 108
  Carlin's homages to, 156–60, 223,
    223n
  Clerc on, 5–6, 7–8, 9, 24–26, 28,
    31, 155–56
  in deaf American creation story,
    xiii–xvi
  death of, 153
  dedication of monument in mem-
    ory of, 153–60
  1850 tribute to, 139–42, 144–47
  naming deaf commonwealth after,
    198
  National Deaf-Mute College re-
    named after, 215
  resignation of, 31, 31n
  on sign language, xix
  use of "heathen," xxv, 37n
Gallaudet, Thomas (son), 142, 211,
    223, 223n
Gallaudet Home for Aged and Infirm
    Deaf, 92
Gallaudet monument, dedication of,
    xii, 153–60

  Carlin's address, 91, 156–60
  Clerc's address, 155–56
Gallaudet University, 100n, 215. See
    also National Deaf-Mute College
Gannon, Jack, xxix, xxx
George, Adele M. See Jewel, Adele
    M.
Georgia School for the Deaf, 162
Glyndon, Howard. See Searing, Laura
    Redden
God, 134, 147, 182n
  Burnet on, 42, 74, 76
  Carlin on, 106, 218, 222
  Clerc on, 10, 16–18, 150
  Flournoy on, 201, 204
  Jewel on, 121, 123, 125, 126
  Spofford on, 143, 144, 144n–45n
government, 181, 189, 190, 194
  Flournoy on, 165–66, 168, 174,
    185, 204
grand reunion of 1850, xii, 139–52
  Brown's remarks, 141–42
  Clerc's address, 148–52
  grateful rhetoric of, 150n, 167n
  significance of, xi, 141
  Spofford's oration, 142–45
  tribute to Gallaudet and Clerc at,
    139–41, 145–48
Grant, Ulysses S., 129, 219, 219n
Greeley, Horace, 90
Groce, Nora Ellen, xxx

Harmony Society, 172n
Harper's, 130
Harvard, John, 218
heathenism, xxv, 34, 37, 37n, 41n,
    158, 158n, 171n, 222
Homer, George, 197, 197n
Howe, Samuel Gridley, 96n
Hudson, Henry, 4, 30
Humphries, Tom, xxxii

Icarian movement, 172n
iconic symbols, 53
Idylls of Battle (Searing), 130
Illinois School for the Deaf, 109
imitation, 50
Indiana Asylum, 127
Indians, 175, 185
intelligence, xix–xxi, 12, 98, 188
Iowa State School for the Deaf, 109
Irving, Washington, 40, 100, 101n
isolation, xvi, xxvi

Jauffret, Jean-Baptiste, 2
Jesus Christ, 10, 17, 37n, 143, 160,
    168n
Jewel, Adele M., viii, ix, xii
    background of, 118–20
    Brief Narrative of the Life of Mrs.
        Adele M. Jewel (Being Deaf and
        Dumb), A, 118–28
    education of, 124–25
    marriage of, 119–20, 128
    religion and, xxiv–xxv, 121, 123,
        125, 128
    on school for deaf and blind African
        Americans, 118, 126–27,
        126n–27n
    sign language and, 118, 119, 120,
        124
    writing and, 119, 122, 124, 125
Johnson, Alphonso, xi, xviii, xxvii

Kansas–Nebraska Act, 194n
Keller, Helen, 64n
Kendall, Amos, 213–14
Kentucky school for the deaf, xvii
Kitto, John, 104, 104n–105n, 133,
    220
Knight, Almena, 119, 124, 127

Lamarckian Hypothesis, 221, 221n

Lamartine, Alphonse-Marie-Louis de
    Prat de, 104, 104n
Lane, Harlan, xxxi, 27n, 108n
Lang, Harry G., 33n
Lazarus, 168, 168n
Legend of the Rocks and Other Poems,
    The (Nack), 33
Liebig, Justus von, 221, 221n
Lincoln, Abraham, 129–30, 212, 214
lipreading. *See* speechreading
literacy, xx–xxi, xxii–xxiii, xxxi, 96n
    Burnet on, 57, 74
    in deaf American creation story,
        xiii–xv
    in deaf commonwealth debate,
        171, 171n, 174, 178–79, 188–
        89, 200
    See also writing
Loring, George H., 145
    address to Clerc, 147–48
    address to Gallaudet, 145–47
Lucas, Ceil, xxx

Macaulay, Thomas Babington, 104,
    104n
Machwitz, Alexander de, 27
Manhattan Literary Association of the
    Deaf, 92
Mann, Edwin, xviii
manual alphabet, 58–59, 95, 97, 154
    British, 39, 97n
Martha's Vineyard, xvii, 143n
Massieu, Jean, xiv–xv, 133, 133n, 224
    Clerc and, 2, 24
Meath-Lang, Bonnie, 33n
meningitis, 107, 129
Mexican War, 157n–58n
mind, development of, 46, 100, 158,
    222–23
"Minstrel Boy, The" (Nack), 34–37,
    91
Missouri Compromise, 157n

Missouri School for the Deaf, 129
Monroe, Charlotte, 120
Monroe, James, xx, 4, 30–31, 30n, 52
mothers, 47–48, 49–50, 50n, 56. *See also* parents
Mott, Lucretia Coffin, 101, 101n
"Mute's Lament, The" (Carlin), xxv–xxvi, 90, 92–94
mutism, xxvi
mythologization, xvi, xxv, 10n, 143n, 158n

Nack, James, vii, xii, 104, 220
    background of, 32–33
    "Minstrel Boy, The" 34–37, 91
    poetic achievement of, 33–34
name signs, 53, 77, 77n, 98, 98n
Naryshkina, Marie Antonova, 27n
National Association of the Deaf, 110
National Deaf-Mute College, xi–xii, 40, 109–10, 130
    Carlin and, 92, 100–106, 213, 214–24
    Clerc and, 4, 212, 215–18
    E. M. Gallaudet and, 213–14, 215, 218
    inauguration of, 212–24
    See also Gallaudet University
National Institute for the Deaf (Paris), xiv, 24n, 41n, 53, 62
neglect of deaf children, xxvi, 46, 48
New England Gallaudet Association of Deaf-Mutes, 155
    deaf commonwealth proposal and, 164, 209–11
Newsam, Albert, 154
New York Institution, xvii, xx, 39, 40, 90, 102, 122
New York Times, 130
North American (magazine), 39
Notable Men in the House of Representatives (Searing), 129

Ohio Institution, xxii
Oliver Twist (Dickens), 224, 224n
"On Emigration to the West by Deaf Mutes" (Booth), 112–17
"On the Early Domestic Education of Children Born Deaf" (Burnet), 44–64
oppression
    deaf African Americans and, viii–ix
    deaf women and, ix
    Flournoy on, 166–69
oralism, 24n, 61–63, 108
    deaf American creation story and, xvi
    as inferior method, 94, 94n, 147n
    as valuable, 60, 63
    See also articulation; speechreading
"Orphan Mute, The" (Burnet), 64–86
Osborn, Phebe. *See* Burnet, Phebe Osborn
Osgood, Polly Ann, 121, 123

Padden, Carol, xxxii
pantomime, xxii, 30n, 97–98, 132, 153, 176
Paradise Lost, 90
parent-child rhetoric
    Booth and, 181, 181n
    Clerc and, 150, 150n
    Flournoy and, 169, 169n
parents, 38, 46
    deaf commonwealth debate and, 174–75, 179–80, 193, 199–200, 202
    early education of deaf children and, 47–50
partial deafness, 62
paternalism. *See* parent-child rhetoric
patriotism, appeals to, 10, 10n, 37, 134–35
    by Carlin, 105, 105n, 157–60
    See also Civil War

Paulmier, M., 53
Peet, Harvey P., 153, 214
Peet, Isaac L., 102
Pelissier, Pierre, 104, 105 n, 220
Pennsylvania Institution for the Deaf,
    xvii, 4, 90
People's Friend, The (newspaper), 39
Pierce, Franklin, 186, 186 n
Pilgrim's Progress, 90
poetry
    by Burnet, xxvii, 38, 40, 86–88
    by Carlin, xxvi, 90–91, 92–94
    by Nack, 32–37
    by Searing, 129–30, 134–35
Porter, Samuel, 184, 184 n, 188, 191
potential of deaf people, xii, xxvii, 92,
    101 n, 164
prejudice, 42, 196
Presbyterian, The (newspaper), 129
public exhibitions, xiv–xv, xxi–xxii,
    xxv
    Carlin on, 98–99
    by Clerc in America, 3, 9–20
public perception
    of American Sign Language,
    132 n–33 n
    of deaf people, xii, xviii–xxii, 15 n

Rae, Luzerne, 139–40
Rapp, George, 172, 172 n
Redden, Laura Catherine. *See* Sear-
    ing, Laura Redden
religion, xxviii, xxxii, 18 n, 76 n, 145
    Carlin and, 98–99, 160, 222, 223 n
    Clerc and, 149
    Searing and, 134
    Spofford and, 143–44
Rochester Method, 100 n
Roebling, John, 126 n
Rose, Mary, xx

St. Ann's Episcopal Church for the
    Deaf, 91, 223 n

St. Louis Republican (newspaper), 129
Sanballat, 202, 202 n
Sapir–Whorf hypothesis, xxiv, xxxi
schools
    Burnet on, 45, 61, 72–79, 86–88
    Carlin on, 100–106, 218–24
    Clerc on, 215–18
    deaf American creation story and,
        xiii–xvi
    impact of, xvi–xxii
    pupil's arrival at, 73, 76 n, 96–97,
        99, 108, 124, 130, 222
    See also education; National Deaf-
        Mute College; *individual schools*
Scott, Winfield, 158, 158 n
Scratchsides Family, The (Carlin), 92
Searing, Edward W., 130
Searing, Laura Redden, viii, xii, 91
    background of, 129–30
    "Belle Missouri," 129–30, 134–35
    "Few Words about the Deaf and
        Dumb, A" 130–34
    on foreignness of English to deaf
        people, xxiii, 132
    on sign language, 131–32, 132 n
Seixas, David, 90
Seward, William, 90
Sicard, Roch Ambroise, xiv–xv, xxv,
    xxviii, 24 n, 53, 95
    Clerc and, 2, 10, 24, 26–27, 144
sign language
    called "best method," 147, 147 n
    Carlin's reservations about, 91,
        94–100
    descriptions of, 51–56, 68–69, 69 n,
        77, 77 n
    development of, 53 n
    difficulty of learning, 51, 132
    early education and, 49–50
    as means to teach religion, 14, 88 n,
        223 n
    as natural language of deaf people,
        21, 131–32

sign language (*continued*)
  psychology and, 20–22, 97
  respect for, xix, 132n, 133n
  universality of, 12n, 51n
  See also American Sign Language;
    manual alphabet
Sign Language Structure (Stokoe), 132n
Sigourney, Lydia (Huntley), 29, 29n,
  88n
silence, 88n, 92–94
Skinner, Dr., 126
Skinner, P. F., 214
slavery
  Booth and, 182–83, 183n
  Clerc and, 152, 152n
  Flournoy and, 193n, 205, 205n
  Missouri Compromise and, 157n
social construction of deafness, 41n
sound, 12–13, 35, 62, 92–94
speechreading, 39, 60–62, 91, 130
Spofford, Fisher Ames, xvi, 140,
  142–45
Stokoe, William, 132n
Stone, Collins, xxii
Stowe, Harriet Beecher, 133
Strong, Nathan, 30, 30n
superstition, 15n

Tales of the Deaf and Dumb (Burnet),
  38–40
Taylor, Zachary, 158, 158n
Texas School for the Deaf, xxix
Tonna, Charlotte Elizabeth, 133,
  133n
Turner, Job, 152
Turner, William W., 163, 211
  Flournoy's letter to, 165–70

Valli, Clayton, xxx
Van Cleve, John Vickrey, xxix
Van Nostrand, Jacob, 212–13

Virginia School for the Deaf and
  Blind (Staunton), xxix

Walworth, Mary Ann. *See* Booth,
  Mary Ann Walworth
Wayland, Mary. *See* Carlin, Mary
  Wayland
Webster, Daniel, 100, 101n, 157,
  157n, 220
Webster, Noah, 100, 101n
Weld, Lewis, 94, 140–41, 146
"What the Deaf and Dumb Are before Instruction" (Burnet),
  40–44
Whorf, Benjamin Lee, xxiv, xxxi
Wilder, S. V. S., 27
Willard, William, 177
Woodward, James, xxx
women
  domestic role of, ix, 50n
  right to vote and, ix, 175, 175n,
    178
  writing and, ix–x
  See also specific deaf women
writing
  as bridge to hearing people, xx–xxi,
    79, 79n
  by deaf African Americans, viii–ix
  in deaf American creation story,
    xiii–xv
  by deaf women, ix, 118–37
  difficulty of conveying deaf experi-
    ence through, xxii–xxix, 131–32
  education and, xx–xi, 56–58
  emergence of deaf community and,
    xii–xiii
  as link for deaf people, xxi
  as proof of intelligence, xii, xiv, xv,
    xxi, 12, 12n, 33

Yale, Elihu, 218